3/22/88

p. punctuation

p. 244 - definition of
Cognitive Therapy

Voice Therapy

Voice Therapy

A Psychotherapeutic Approach to Self-Destructive Behavior

Robert W. Firestone, Ph.D.
The Glendon Association
Los Angeles, California

 **HUMAN SCIENCES PRESS, INC.**
72 FIFTH AVENUE
NEW YORK, N.Y. 10011-8004

Printed in the United States of America
987654321

Library of Congress Cataloging-in-Publication Data

Firestone, Robert.
  Voice therapy.

  "The Glendon Association."
  Bibliography: p.
  Includes index.
  1. Self-destructive behavior. 2. Self-respect.
3. Self-hate (Psychology) 4. Psychology, Pathological.
5. Psychotherapy. I. Glendon Association. II. Title.
[DNLM: 1. Behavior Therapy. 2. Voice. WM 425 F523v]
RC569.5.S45F57   1987   616.85'8206   86-27762
ISBN 0-89885-352-4

Contents

¹Clinical material appearing in this section is excerpted from videotaped
productions filmed by Geoff Parr for The Glendon Association 1984–86.

Dedication

To those men and women in the field of psychology who had the courage to challenge conventional beliefs both in the field and in society at large in their powerful search for the truth of human experience; whose ideas and works have contributed to my excitement and determination to understand psychopathology and its causes; and whose writings I have taken as implicit support for my own thinking: notably among them are R. D. Laing, Alice Miller, Arthur Janov, Otto Rank, Ernest Becker, Erich Fromm, Hellmuth Kaiser, John N. Rosen, and Sigmund Freud.

On a personal level, to those people closest to me: my wife, Tamsen Firestone, my friends, Barry Langberg, Frank Tobe, and Joyce Catlett, who have encouraged me to share my ideas with others in the same manner that these eminent professionals have shared their knowledge and insights with me.

Acknowledgments

The author would like to express his appreciation to Joyce Catlett, M.A., associate and collaborative writer, who worked closely with me at every stage in the production of this book and added greatly to its intellectual background. I would like to thank Dr. Richard Seiden for his insights in the field of suicidology and his collaboration on two theoretical papers quoted in this work. I am grateful also to Dr. Jerome Nathan, Susan Short, M.A., and Lisa Firestone, M.A., who researched relevant material in the literature; to Anne Baker, Catherine Cagan, Eileen Tobe, and JoEllyn Barrington for their help in producing the final draft; and to Geoff Parr, who helped prepare the documentary film material referenced in this work.

Lastly, but most importantly, I want to acknowledge the Glendon Association, a large group of friends, former patients, and associates, who have employed me for the past ten years, contributed their support to the continuing investigations, and financed the production of documentary films and the dissemination of the many books and articles stating my theoretical views.

I thank them for their devotion to learning in the field of psychology, their personal quest for self-development and individual identity, and their openness and honesty in revealing their personal truths. Of even greater significance, I am appreciative to them for their ongoing participation in the study and growing body of knowledge about the voice process, fantasy bond, and other important concepts. Together they have created a unique psychological laboratory to investigate the psychopathology of everyday life in a normal or relatively healthy population. They have encouraged me to communicate my ideas to the professional community at large and have been strongly motivated to share their insights with others so that they may benefit from their experiences.

The names, places, and other identifying facts contained herein have been fictionalized and no similarity to any persons, living or dead, is intended. In the filmed material, names were not fictionalized, as individuals specifically requested that their names remain unchanged, and first names were retained.

*   *   *

The author gratefully acknowledges permission to reprint the following:

from *Steppenwolf,* by Herman Hesse. English translation copyright 1919 by Holt, Rinehart and Winston, Inc. Reprinted by permission of Holt, Rinehart and Winston, Inc.

from "Dear Mom And Dad," by David Breskin, *Rolling Stone,* November 8, 1984. Copyright 1984 by David A. Breskin. Reprinted by permission of David A. Breskin.

from *Schizoid Phenomena Object-Relations and the Self,* by Harry Guntrip. Copyright by Harry Guntrip. Reprinted by permission of International Universities Press, Inc., Mrs. B. Guntrip, and The Hogarth Press.

from *The Divided Self: An Existential Study In Sanity And Madness,* by R. D. Laing. Copyright 1969 by R.D. Laing. Reprinted by permission of Tavistock Publications Ltd.

from *Will Therapy And Truth And Reality,* by Otto Rank. Copyright © 1936, 1964 by Alfred Knopf, Inc. All rights reserved. Reprinted by permission of the Author's Representative, Gunther Stuhlmann.

Of Sigmund Freud, Vol. 21, translated and edited by James Strachey. Copyright The Institute of Psycho-Analysis. Reprinted by permission of Sigmund Freud Copyrghts Ltd., The Institute of Psycho-Analysis, The Hogarth Press, and W. W. Norton, Inc.

from *The Discovery Of Being,* by Rollo May. Copyright 1983 by Rollo May. Reprinted by permission of W. W. Norton & Company, Inc.

from *EQUUS,* by Peter Shaffer. Copyright © 1973 by Peter Shaffer. Reprinted by permission of Atheneum Publishers.

* * *

Note to Readers

Because of the awkwardness inherent in constructing sentences so as to avoid sexist language, the author has chosen to use the generic "he" at those times when "one" or "they" would have been cumbersome.

Foreword

I am pleased to introduce this work, as I feel that it is an important contribution to understanding those forces in people that serve to restrict or deny personal experience and genuine dialogue as well as fostering self-destructive behavior patterns. In this book, Dr. Robert Firestone has further developed his concept of the "inner voice," and his method for dealing with the internalized criticisms and self-attacks embedded in the negative thought process. The person is thus enabled to move from despair to affirmation. The author ably and often dramatically describes the basis of these "voices" in destructive early experiences.

These ideas have proven very fruitful in my own work with unhappy, self-destructive, and suicidal persons and their families, who are trapped too by their "voices," and can also be guided to more positive and affirmative behaviors, thus halting the inculcation of negative and self-defeating self-attitudes. We are not dealing only with mental illness and severe psychopathology. Such a destructive introjection-projection process is probably characteristic of all people, not only with their children but with their spouses, siblings, friends, and even parents. The destructive inner voice can be multidirectional or omnidirectional.

This book teaches us that these inner voices can be exorcised, and tells us how to modify or eliminate them, so as to permit adequate self-esteem and self-actualization. Another very significant concept, the fantasy bond or illusion of connectedness, is also particularly valuable. Underlying this basically regressive process is a secret agenda of avoiding true adult intimacy in order to preserve the earlier attachments with the primary family figures. Firestone recognizes the strength of these bonds. They are real and tenacious, and he warns us that we are not to tamper lightly with such fundamental ties and life-styles. To encourage a vulnerable person to question or defy this inner voice can result in guilt feelings over the betrayal of the parent who has been internalized, and a resulting negative therapeutic reaction. The timing must be right.

The book is replete with interesting and informative clinical material through which the reader learns much about human nature, as well as human healing. Dr. Firestone points out that the "inner voice" we carry around applies not only to internalized criticisms or derogative statements, but to various directives, such as: "Be secretive and do not confide in others"; "Do not make friends"; "You have no one else but me." Fortunately, the destructive or harmful effects can be controlled, modified, eliminated, or transformed through the use of the techniques here described, and even more importantly, the care and commitment of a dedicated therapist.

Dr. Firestone, like his mentor John Rosen, along with Joseph Rheingold, Nancy Friday, and others, is sensitive to the destructive effects of the mother in the genesis of emotional illness and self-destructive behavior, but in this more comprehensive view of the family, he illustrates how negative experiences are imprinted on the psyche of the child and connect him in fantasy to his parents; the greater the rejection, the stronger this connection. Dr. Firestone recognizes that parents and children are alike victims of the demonic inner voice. To counteract this negative process, family therapy can enable family members to help each other towards a constructive life affirmation, as I have seen over and over.

Still another major contribution is Dr. Firestone's emphasis upon the role of separation anxiety in the development of destructive relationships and its association with death anxiety. The anxiety applies not only to one's own death but the deaths of significant others. The role of the fantasy bond is to maintain the sense of immortality, not only of one's self but of loved ones. The threat of dying supports the role of fantasy over seeking gratification in the real world, and fosters voices that are self-denying and self-limiting. Finally, the author emphasizes the need to face the fact of our finitude as a condition for personal growth.

By becoming conscious of the voice, the self-destructive person can grow and mature. He can then accept responsibility for himself instead of seeing himself as the helpless victim of destructive parental introjects internalized and then externalized in therapy as the inner voice. Finally, he will be able to transcend the negative and to respond to the positive qualities of his family and others, for to deny family experiences is perilous, but we can overcome and transform them.

Dr. Firestone recommends that Voice Therapy procedures be applied by therapists of various theoretical persuasions. I agree, and suggest that it can be applied even by those whose approach appears radically opposed to his. For example, nothing might seem further removed from Dr. Firestone's approach than theories that emphasize only positive regard and interpret all behavior positively, as is advocated by some writers. Yet even in this approach, the careful and sensitive communication of the inner voice by a suicidal person in a family therapy meeting can further open the channels of communication and lead to a dialogue, with positive results for all. Fortunately, overcoming the self-destructive inner voice can become a growth experience for the entire family. It is through the promise of this family interaction that I see the most important implications of Dr. Firestone's work: to help people move from the introjected inner voice to dialogue.

In conclusion, it is significant that Dr. Firestone arrived at his views through first working with schizophrenic patients, usually considered the most deeply disturbed; from there to the depressed and the suicidal; and then to the normal or neurotic. His work progressively brings out the common factors in all these conditions, and ultimately the universal humanity of us all. He points out that, as children, we all introjected inner voices representing the attitudes of our parents, who earlier had the same attitudes imposed on them by *their* parents. Dr. Firestone is among those laboring to break the chain of destructiveness and to substitute love, caring, and growth.

Joseph Richman, Ph.D.
Albert Einstein College of Medicine

1

Introduction

My life's work as a psychotherapist has focused on the problem of resistance. In my study of people's resistance to change, I have been deeply perplexed by a seemingly paradoxical phenomenon: the fact that most people consistently avoid or minimize experiences that are warm, successful, or constructive. I have observed that most of my patients tend to manipulate their environments in order to repeat painful past experiences and to avoid positive emotional interactions that would contradict their negative personal identity within the original family. I have been searching for an answer to the question of why most individuals, in spite of emotional catharsis, understanding, and intellectual insight, still hold on to familiar, destructive patterns of the past and refuse to change on a deep character level.

In our years of study, my colleagues and I observed clinical material that expanded our understanding of human self-destructiveness and its probable sources. Although I was not involved in the field of suicidology as a specific area of specialization, I could not help but apply this growing body of knowledge to the complex problem of suicide and suicide prevention. We were able to generalize from the myriad forms of partial or parasuicide to the extreme manifestations of suicidal individuals. As we addressed the problem of micro-suicidal symptomatology in our patients, we became increasingly involved in the mental or cognitive processes associated with self-destructive behavior.

All along, we were concerned with the stubborn resistance to changing a conception of self that was negative, self-critical, or self-accusatory. In our work with schizophrenia, it became increasingly clear that these seriously disturbed patients were involved in a process of idealizing their parents at their own expense. This tendency to preserve an image of the "good mother" together with an image of being the "bad child" was first elucidated by Arieti in one of his early works (1955). The child, who is so dependent on the mother for satisfaction of his needs and, indeed, for his very survival, must perceive her as being adequate and good. If not, the situation would be truly hopeless. The child then assumes that "if the parent is punitive and anxiety-arousing, it is not because she is malevolent but because he, the child, is bad" (p. 48). In that sense, the critical part of the adult patient's defense system is an attempt to hold on to the parent by accepting the blame and seeing himself as unlovable. We have come to understand this concept in a broader and enlarged perspective that plays a very significant role in our understanding of psychopathology.

To illustrate, a patient recalled that when she approached adolescence, her father began beating her at night. At frequent intervals, he would come into her bedroom, wake her up, and physically abuse her. She said that at the time, she "knew" he was right in punishing her, that she must have done something to make him angry. The next morning, in spite of her innocence, she would invariably apologize to him for causing trouble and being a problem child.

If the patient had *not* assumed the blame for the beatings and instead had seen her father as being in the wrong, then she would have felt the full brunt of being in the hands of a highly disturbed, irrational, or even potentially murderous person who was out of control. It was the lesser of two evils for her to make his actions appear of rational character.

Working in Direct Analysis under the auspices of Dr. John N. Rosen, my associates and I challenged the idealization of the parent with schizophrenic patients. We noted that there was considerable resistance to changing both the idealized image of the parent and the negative image of self, and that the two processes were interrelated. In fact, when this idealization process was challenged directly in sessions where the patient was instructed to express negative ideas and critical comments about the parent image, there was a significant reduction in bizarre symptoms and thought disturbance.

Later, in our work with children ages ten to fourteen and with neurotic adults in a feeling release therapy, we were impressed that they possessed a deep-seated conviction that they were "bad." When asked to make positive statements about themselves with feeling, strong primal emotions were induced, manifested by extreme sadness and sobbing. Statements such as "I'm not bad," when taken seriously by the patient in an accepting atmosphere, were accompanied by powerfully painful emotions. Other positive statements, i.e., "I'm good," or "I'm lovable," brought out similar outbursts when expression of affect was encouraged. We concluded that this core of negative feeling toward self was an important dynamic in neurotic symptomatology and inimical life-styles and was the basis of resistance to therapeutic change. Indeed, separation from the negative conception of self appeared to be related symbolically to a break in the bond with one's family and therefore tended to create separation anxiety. Even those individuals who were geographically separated or independent of parental ties were afraid, as though a basic change in self-concept would break important bonds or fantasies of connection with their parents.

Interestingly enough, when children are threatened with statements such as, "If you're bad, you won't get any presents," or "You won't be allowed to go with us," they frequently cry painfully as though the punishment were a foregone conclusion, as though they were powerless to change. Many neurotic adults exhibit the same characteristics.

In my early work with shizophrenic patients and later in my office practice, I was progressing in my understanding of the dimensions of the self-destructive process, but important aspects were missing. My associates and I were very excited when we came upon several new developments in the early 1970s.

At that time I focused on the emotional pain that patients experienced when they were confronted with certain types of verbal feedback or information about themselves. They would have strong negative responses to selective aspects of this information and feel bad for long periods of time. Initially, I considered the old adage, "It's the truth that hurts," but then I realized that evaluations from others, regardless of accuracy, that support or validate a person's distorted view of himself, tend to arouse an obsessive negative thought process.

From these observations, I discovered that most people judged and appraised themselves in ways that were extremely self-punishing and negative. Thus, their reactions to external criticism were usually out of proportion to content, severity, or manner of presentation. I thought it would be valuable for people to become aware of the areas and issues about which they were the most sensitive, so I began to study this phenomenon with my patients and associates. In 1973, we formed a therapy group, made up of a number of psychotherapists, to investigate this problem and pool our information. This group became the focal point for my ongoing study of the specific thought patterns associated with neurotic, repetitive behaviors and later with self-destructive actions and life-styles.

The participants focused on identifying the negative thoughts they had about themselves as well as discussing their reactions to feedback or criticism. Their observations corroborated my early hypotheses about a well-integrated pattern of negative thoughts, which I later termed the "voice." When the therapists verbalized their negative thoughts out loud, they began by describing what they were telling themselves about their personal qualities and the events in their lives, such as "My voice is telling me that I'm not really competent," or that "I'm a mean bastard," or that "I'm going to be rejected," or that "I'm no good." Later they found it useful to separate out their voice attacks in the second person, and they sounded like: "You're no good"; "You're a phony"; "You're incompetent." They discovered that when they expressed their negative thoughts in this manner, the self-attacks were most easily identified and had a greater emotional impact. Often, deep feelings of compassion and sadness were aroused when an especially sensitive area was explored for the first time.

In my office practice, similar material was being uncovered as patients began to articulate their self-critical thoughts in the second person. At times patients displayed an animosity toward themselves that became very intense. I was shocked at first by the viciousness of these self-attacks and by the derisive tone of voice as my subjects gave words to their negative view of self. I was pained to see how divided people were within themselves and how insidiously they sabotaged their efforts to adapt and cope with their everyday lives.

It became evident that the self-attacks isolated by these individuals from both populations were only the tip of an iceberg in terms of the underlying anger and hostility toward the self. Clues began to emerge that pointed to the depth and pervasiveness of this thought process. For example, when the participants attempted to trace the cause of an erratic mood change to a precipitating event, they were able to uncover the pervasive self-attacks that controlled their lives. When these strong self-attacks were then expressed in the "voice," or second person, there was generally a good deal of angry affect accompanying their expression. However, these dramatic emotional sessions were usually followed by an improvement in mood and a return of good feeling.

As various aspects of the voice were elicited in both populations, my thinking about the concept of the voice unfolded and evolved. In the process of searching for the probable sources of this antithetical voice process, my associates and I expanded our study of a variety of procedures that could be utilized to elicit the voice.

As we refined our techniques, and participants began to loosen their controls while vocalizing their inner thoughts, we learned that the expressions of intense anger against the self that had been noted in our earlier studies were not isolated occurrences. It became quite apparent that most people hated themselves with an intensity that surpassed by far anything they conciously *thought* they felt toward themselves.

As material of this nature accumulated, it became a logical

extension of our work to study this voice process in more depressed patients and in patients who had a history of suicidal thoughts and attempted suicides. We explored the self-destructive thought patterns that appeared to influence their life-threatening behaviors and life-styles. When my colleagues and I interviewed depressed and/or suicidal individuals, we found that they were able to expose and identify the contents of their hostile way of thinking about self. Even though they had no previous knowledge of the concept of the "voice," they generally related to the concept with ease and familiarity. We concluded that the thought process which we had observed in "normal" or neurotic individuals was essentially the same mechanism that leads to severe depressive states and self-destructive behavior.

This book is the outcome of several years of fruitful explorations into the dynamics of the "voice," which we consider to be an unnatural overlay on the personality. The voice appears to be an integrated, systematized, cognitive process, interwoven with varying degrees of negative affect, that is capable of influencing a person's behavior to the detriment of physical and mental health.

Our purpose in writing this book is to elucidate and demonstrate manifestations of the voice or alien point of view and thereby to advance our knowledge of suicide and other forms of human self-destructiveness. In proposing a correlation between the voice and self-destructive behavior, we will describe laboratory procedures (Voice Therapy) which have been used to elicit this hostile thought process, thereby bringing it more directly into consciousness.

In developing the concept of the voice, we have drawn upon findings of previous investigators to develop hypotheses which, on the one hand, are continuously and organically connected to prior formulations and, on the other hand, provide new insights. Our hypotheses are empirically based on experiences in a wide variety of settings, including hospitals, inpatient and outpatient clinics, individual and group psychotherapy, and population survey studies. Our population ranged from severely regressed schizophrenic patients to the average patient population encountered in private practice. It included colleagues and associates who participated in our preliminary investigations into manifestations of the "voice." In addition, we have excerpted from interviews with a number of individuals who, having made serious suicide attempts, wished to share their experiences in the hope that others might benefit. While the pilot studies that we have undertaken to examine and analyze this destructive point of view are still in the early stages, we believe that continuing research will further clarify the close relationship between the voice and the self-destructive process.

I

The Voice

2

The Concept of the Voice

[Paranoid] patients . . . complain that all their thoughts are known and their actions watched and supervised; they are informed of . . . this agency by voices which characteristically speak to them in the third person ('Now she's thinking of that again', 'now he's going out').

This complaint is justified; it describes the truth. *A power of this kind, watching, discovering and criticizing all our intentions, does really exist. Indeed, it exists in every one of us in normal life* [italics added].

Sigmund Freud (1914/1957, p. 95)

A man on vacation checks into a high-rise hotel, steps onto his balcony to look at the view and, noting the drop-off, thinks to himself: "What if you jump?" Feeling anxious, he unconsciously steps back from the ledge.

Mr. X, driving along the freeway, thinks: "Why don't you drive across the center divider or off the side of the road? Why don't you just close your eyes for a minute?" He pictures a tragic accident—images that torment him and make him uneasy.

A person prepares to give a speech and thinks: "You're

going to make a fool of yourself. What if you forget everything you were going to say or act stupid?''

A man calls an attractive woman for a date and hears: "Why should she go out with *you*? Look at you! She probably has lots of better offers."

During sex, Mr. Y thinks: "You're not going to be able to hold onto your erection," and actually begins to feel cut off from his sexual feelings.

An alcoholic tells himself: "What's the harm in having another drink? You deserve it—you've had a hard day." The next day, in the throes of a hangover, he thinks: "You let everyone down again. You're a despicable person."

In the last moments of life, a suicidal patient thinks: "Go ahead, end it all! Just pull the trigger and it'll all be over."

Thoughts such as these have always concerned me and aroused my curiosity. What were the common threads underlying the apparent attacks on self or self-destructive urges? Why, for example, did the motorist picture himself crashing into the center divider? Were his thoughts and mental images simply part of a self-protective process that was warning him of realistic dangers and potential harm? Were they just meaningless ruminations? Did these thoughts indicate a human propensity for self-hatred?

In studying the manifestations of this thought process, my associates and I have found that this type of thinking is widespread and that a person's actions and general approach to life are regulated or controlled by this manner of thinking. For example, the man in the hotel *did* step back from the edge, even though he disregarded the command to jump. And Mr. X ignored the urge to drive across the divider, but felt uneasy and depressed following these thoughts and images. Mr. Y *did* have difficulty sexually after running himself down as a man. We observed that even when disregarded or contradicted, this thought process had negative consequences. We discovered that the pattern of negative thoughts about the self predisposed self-destructive behavior and was at the core of suicidal and micro-suicidal actions.

Psychotherapists have long been aware that people tend to think destructively, that they have many misconceptions of self, or that they have a "shadow" side to their personality. Indeed, since biblical times, prophets, Eastern and Western philosophers, and psychoanalysts have made efforts to interpret man's dark side and to support ways of defeating it or effecting a resolution with it. Goldbrunner's (1964) analysis of Carl Jung's works noted that: "Man has to undergo the fateful experience of being conscious of the dark part of the soul. This is the positive quality in neurosis, that it can lead man to knowledge of his nature" (p. 113).

Brief suicidal impulses, distracting and frequently disturbing, are familiar to most people. Internal conflict, ambivalence, contradictions and division are reflected in the symptoms of our patients or clients. However, many of us have tended to *under*estimate the depth of this division within the personality, as well as the pervasiveness of man's tendency for self-destruction.

Our clinical experience has shown us that human beings possess two diametrically opposed views of themselves and of their personal and professional goals. All people suffer to some extent from conflict and a sense of alienation from themselves— dynamics that go far beyond such descriptive terms as ambivalence or dissonance. On the one hand, each person has a point of view that reflects his natural strivings, his aspirations, his desires for affiliation with his fellow beings, his drive to be sexual, to reproduce himself, and to be creative; while on the other hand, he has another point of view that reflects his tendencies for self-limitation, self-destruction, and hostility toward other persons. This alien view is made up of a series of thoughts, antithetical toward self and cynical toward others, which we refer to as the "voice."

THE VOICE

The voice, as we have defined it, is the language of the defensive process. It refers to a well-integrated pattern of negative thoughts that is the basis of an individual's maladaptive behavior. We conceptualize the voice as being an overlay on the personality that is *not* natural or harmonious, but learned or imposed from without. Although the voice may at times relate to one's value system or moral considerations, its statements against the self often occur *after* the fact and are generally harsh or judgmental. The voice process tends to increase one's self-hatred rather than motivating one to alter behavior in a constructive fashion. Indeed, our definition of the voice excludes those thought processes generally concerned with values or ideals, as well as those involved in creative thinking, constructive planning, and realistic self-appraisal. It does not refer to mental activity that is generally described as fantasy or daydreams.

The voice is not an actual hallucination but an identifiable system of thoughts. The negative statements referred to here occur more in the form of statements *toward* oneself than *about* oneself; therefore, they lend themselves to expression in the second person, e.g., "*You're* this or that," rather than "*I* am thus and so." In that sense, voice statements are distinguishable from statements a person is making about himself. They are experienced more as outside commentary, as in the form that another person would address him. When voice statements are expressed in the second person, they are frequently accompanied by strong affect and hostility toward the self.

Ideas originating *in* the self and *about* the self sound like: "I feel bad about losing my temper"; or, "I have a mean temper." These self-statements, or "I" statements, can be differentiated from voices or internal self-attacks, which sound more like: "*You're* so impatient." "*You* always fly off the handle." "*You* have no control."

In the usual thought process, the self is central and is harmonious or integrated, whereas the voice process is discordant and the self becomes an *object* of criticism and attack. It is akin to delusions of reference or persecution where the self is perceived as the object of concern or abuse from outside and is the passive victim of an external process.

Angry voice attacks in the form of punitive statements *toward* self are at the core of one's identity or self-concept. Incidentally, these attitudes are generally reflective of one's identity within the nuclear family. When these voice attacks are accepted as a part of one's identity, they tend to be acted out in a manner that is self-confirming and therefore logic tight. In that sense, they perpetuate the continuity within the family bond.

In order to fit our criteria of the voice, the patient's thoughts must be identified as an external attack on the self. Through eliciting and identifying these specific forms of self-attack with laboratory procedures, the therapist gains access to that part of the personality that is opposed to the self and that is causing the patient the major part of his unnecessary suffering.

DIMENSIONS OF THE VOICE

Voice attacks are sometimes experienced consciously, but more often than not, they are only partially conscious or may even be totally unconscious. In general, the average person is largely *un*aware of his self-attacks and of the fact that much of his behavior is influenced and even controlled by the voice. Indeed, "listening" to the voice predisposes an individual toward self-limiting behavior and negative consequences. In other words, people make their behavior correspond to their self-attacks.

For example, one patient, a college student with low self-esteem, was referred by his counselor because of failing grades, procrastination, and inability to concentrate. The patient attempted first to determine the negative thoughts that lay behind his habitual pattern of procrastinating. In verbalizing the thoughts that occurred to him while he was studying, he discovered that he had been torturing himself for days prior to each exam with an internal dialogue that went as follows:

You're never going to be able to pass this exam. You should have dropped this course. You'll never catch up. Why bother studying? You're going to fail anyway.

In a later session, the patient, with considerable angry affect, verbalized a more powerful self-attack:

You don't belong in college anyway. Who do you think you are? You're a stupid clod! Your brother is the smart one in the family, not you!

Note that the patient did not verbalize the thoughts that

preoccupied him as "I" statements: "*I* should have dropped this course"; "*I'm* stupid"; "*I'm* going to fail anyway." Instead, he was talking to himself as an object, one step removed from himself. In verbalizing his punitive style of attacking himself in this way, he was better able to separate out the attacking part of this thought process and develop a deeper understanding of his problem.

In our investigations, it was evident that some people were more in touch with manifestations of the voice process than others. Many patients reported that they experienced the voice as a continuous stream of negative thoughts or a running commentary that was belittling or sarcastic in tone. To illustrate, a patient diagnosed as suffering from an anxiety neurosis also exhibited a number of compulsive behaviors. A devoutly religious woman, she reported that she frequently became self-conscious and intensely anxious during church services, to a degree approaching a panic state. She said she had thoughts that instructed her to humiliate herself:

> What would happen if you yelled out loud right now? Why don't you scream out something vulgar? Better be careful. Just sit very still or you're going to do something terrible.

These thoughts raised the patient's level of anxiety and sometimes culminated in a full-fledged anxiety attack. Further, she felt very ashamed of having impulses that seemed completely foreign to her own point of view.

As our patients became more familiar with verbalizing their self-attacks out loud to the therapist, they were able to make connections between undesirable intrusive behavior and negative thought patterns. It became clear that voice attacks not only affected people at times of stress, but could cause them discomfort in a variety of circumstances. Predictions of personal rejection, worries about competency, negative comparisons of themselves with rivals, and guilty self-recriminations for failures and mistakes were common "voices" reported by our subjects as they became acquainted with the concept.

There was a good deal of commonality of thought content among individuals with a common cultural heritage. For example, older patients tended to tell themselves: "You're too old to change. You've always been this way. What makes you think you can change now?"

Young people, beginning to establish relationships with members of the opposite sex, had thoughts that increased their feelings of self-consciousness and undermined their self-confidence, such as:

> You don't know what to do on a date. You won't be able to think of anything to say. She'll find out you don't really know how to kiss.

Comparisons with rivals were almost universal. Men reported painful attitudes in relation to competitors, such thoughts as:

> He's smarter, better-looking, more sophisticated than you. Or: You're stupid. You don't have a good job. You're phony. She'll reject you when she really gets to know you

Female patients or subjects depreciated themselves and their attributes in comparing themselves negatively with other women. They told themselves:

> She's much prettier than you. What makes you think men will notice you when she's around? Look at you, how plain you are. You're a fool to try to compete with her.

During sex, men reported telling themselves:

> You're not going to be able to satisfy her, to make her feel good. You don't know how to touch her. Look at your hands—they're sweating. You're clumsy, inept. Your penis is too small.

Many women reported similar self-attacks:

> You're not feeling enough. You're not going to be able to have an orgasm. He doesn't really like you; your breasts are too small; your hips are too big.

It was found that both partners, more often than not,

"heard" internal negative comments about their performance and about their bodies while making love. These thoughts aroused anxiety, inhibiting their pleasure to a considerable degree. Many forms of sexual dysfunction and problems of sexual desire appear to be related to the ascendancy of the voice process during lovemaking.

People of various minority groups reported that they often perceived themselves in an inferior, derogatory light that corresponded to prejudicial views and social biases. They revealed that they told themselves they didn't belong, they were different, out of place in society, or even out of step with their own people. For example, a black patient identified a voice that told him:

> What are you doing here, talking to this white doctor? Who do you think you are? Why do you think you're different from your family? Why can't you be like the rest of us—normal?

Patients using drugs or alcohol to excess were observed to be strongly influenced by thoughts that urged them to indulge their habit and subsequently punished them for yielding to temptation. They were able to identify specific thoughts they used to rationalize habitual, self-destructive substance abuse. Individuals who were obese and those who were attempting to control their weight had a similar pattern that first supported the ego-syntonic nature of their addiction and later attacked them for their weakness.

The negative thoughts and attitudes reported by these patients were typically accompanied by agitation, irritability, or depression. It is important to note, however, that the critical thoughts cited above were merely isolated fragments of a more complete underlying system.

The author contends that the "voice" process is an important factor in every psychological disorder, yet it is of particular concern in cases of paranoia, acute and chronic depressive episodes, and schizophrenia. In the following pages we will (1) examine the types of events that precipitate self-attacks; (2) discuss the relationship between the voice process in neurosis and its manifestations in the psychoses; and (3) distinguish the voice from a system of values.

EVENTS THAT PRECIPITATE SELF-ATTACKS

When people are energetically pursuing personal or vocational goals, they may be relatively free of voice attacks for a period of time. However, when they become self-conscious about their progress or positive changes, they tend to interpret events and circumstances in a manner that disrupts the ongoing movement. The more they are conscious of expanding life experiences, the more they are susceptible to self-critical thoughts, warnings, and admonitions. In that sense, important transitions and changes in one's circumstances will typically activate the voice process. Indeed, any event or experience that can act to cause separation anxiety will precipitate voice attacks.

Moving geographically, changing jobs, getting married, starting a family—all present unfamiliar situations that increase anxiety and feelings of self-consciousness. Becoming a parent for the first time represents a significant step in the transition from symbolically being a child to becoming an adult. This step frequently triggers strong voice attacks in both men and women. One woman who wanted to have a baby had many doubts about her ability to be a good mother. Her uncertainty took the form of self-critical thoughts that increased her ambivalence and fear:

> You're so foolish to think you can have a baby. You don't know anything about how to handle a baby. You're going to hurt that baby. If you don't hurt it physically, you'll hurt it mentally.

Similarly, a man who recently became a father could not accept his new identity. He told himself:

> So you had a baby. So what? That doesn't make you a man. It was an accident, a mistake. You're still a kid. You can't handle the responsibility of having a baby. You don't make enough money to support a family, etc.

Negative Events That Arouse Self-Attacks

Illness, financial setbacks, academic failure, rejection by a loved one, loss through the death of someone close, are all stressful events that can activate thoughts of self-recrimination and associated feelings of self-hatred.

Failure. Academic and vocational failures are often precipitating factors in self-attacks. Patients who had experienced business failures or setbacks in their professional careers reported telling themselves:

> You're a total failure! You'll never get anywhere in life. You always mess up. Everybody hates you—you might just as well give up.

Over an extended period of time, this kind of thought process can lead to serious states of depression and ultimately to suicidal behavior. It appears that individuals who are perfectionistic and are driven to maintain high levels of performance are exceptionally susceptible to this form of self-attack. For example, among college students, it is more often the academically superior student who kills himself, usually following a sharp decline in his grades. The rash of suicides following serious business recessions indicates deep-seated feelings of hopelessness and strong self-depreciating attitudes that were at the root of the suicidal process.

Illness. Poor health and illness tend to activate self-critical thoughts about one's body integrity. Perceived bodily weaknesses and a deterioration in physical fitness are often the target of self-deprecating thoughts. Furthermore, people suffering from chronic illness may attack themselves as malingerers or as contaminating or other such pejorative words. Even people in good health, facing yearly physical checkups, frequently torment themselves with hypochondriacal thoughts:

> The doctor is going to find something terrible this time. You probably have cancer and he'll have to break the news to you. Why go, anyway? It's better not to know.

The depression and irritability that accompany ill-health are usually intensified, or may be directly caused, by negative cognitions, such as: "You're always sick"; "You're always complaining about your aches and pains"; "Nobody wants to be around a sick person like you." Illness can also trigger morbid ruminations about death, thereby increasing one's feelings of despair and futility about life.

Rejection. Rejection activates the "bad child" image wherein a person assumes that he is at fault and therefore deserves to be rejected. It is extremely difficult to remain objective in one's self-appraisal and to maintain good feelings when one is being rejected. Thus, negative experiences and interpersonal hurt cause most of us to feel unlovable. Individuals frequently interpret rejection as concrete evidence that they are undeserving of love, are inferior, boring, sexually unattractive, or are afflicted by a myriad of other negative qualities attributed to them by the voice. Rejection and subsequent feelings of worthlessness turn a person against himself, even when these self-critical thoughts are unrealistic and contradict objective analysis of the situation. Furthermore, even when critical thoughts have some basis in fact, they do not justify hostile attitudes toward self. A compassionate attitude toward oneself would allow one to make changes in those characteristics that are changeable, which is generally the case, or to accept one's traits when change is not possible.

Personal interactions with a person who is critical or insensitive will catalyze an individual's own self-attacks. Thus, certain people or personalities have a toxic effect, while others who are compassionate and accepting tend to have positive effects. Having contact with people who are judgmental, condescending, or evaluative can be damaging psychologically, because these people tend to support one's own negative, judgmental view of self. Having their motives misunderstood or actions misconstrued by paranoid individuals validates a voice in many people. It is difficult to remain unaffected by individuals close to us who hold on to a critical view about us. Often a person prefers to accept the negative evaluation and treatment in order to hold on to the relationship.

Positive Events That Arouse Voice Attacks

Self-critical thoughts that interrupt the pursuit of goals may be activated by positive experiences and good fortune as well as by negative events.

Unusual achievement. Many people feel anxious or nervous when they receive public acknowledgment for an unusual achievement or success. For example, many patients who had assumed positions of leadership, as well as those who had achieved a significant success in their field of endeavor, reported that they subsequently behaved in ways to undermine these achievements. In their sessions, they were able to trace their self-defeating actions to thought patterns that had made them self-conscious about their success or their position.

One man, a chemical engineer whose company had been awarded a large grant for new research, was put in charge of the project. He began to experience considerable discomfort and felt as if he were critically observing his every move. As he entered his new laboratory each morning, for example, he "heard" a snide, sarcastic voice making comments such as:

> Pretty neat setup. Let's see what big discovery you're going to make today.

In another case, an executive, despite evidence to the contrary, told himself that he was authoritarian and disliked by his staff. He "listened" to a voice telling him:

> You're so bossy and presumptuous—why should people take orders from a person like you? You don't know any more than they do. You're just faking it.

Guilt reactions to significant accomplishments. Individuals often experience feelings of guilt when they achieve a greater degree of success than friends, associates, or particularly their parent of the same sex. Their guilt reactions usually involve some form of giving up their new success by sabotaging their achievements. In one case, a lawyer, whose father had twice declared bankruptcy, decided to apply his knowledge of corporate law to business finance. He was eventually made president of a large corporation and awarded a generous bonus for his contribution to his company's growth over the previous year. At this point, he began to behave self-destructively in ways that seriously undermined his authority. He identified a voice that he felt accurately reflected his father's view of his success. These self-critical, belittling thoughts made him feel guilty about his rapid rise to the prestigious position he had worked hard to attain:

> Why do you think *you* can be successful? You act like you're superior to us, showing off. You're not that different from your family. You're not so great! Just take your place and stop acting like such a big shot.

Later, when this type of thinking had a detrimental effect on his performance, he attacked himself for his failures. Ironically, then he had guilt feelings about his trouble at work and felt "he was letting his family down." Voice attacks are often contradictory, double-edged, and illogical, revealing the underlying hostility toward self. This patient was suspended in a state between two types of guilt—guilt about surpassing his father, who had failed in business, and guilt about regressing to a less mature level of functioning. Voices expressing both forms of guilt tormented him, first deriding him for his success, and later castigating him for his inadequacies.

Voices following success in personal relationships. Many men and women reported a deterioration in their personal relationships following periods of unusual intimacy and tenderness. These events precipitated a flow of negative thoughts, some self-critical and others critical of their partner. Both parties tended to hold back, on an unconscious level, shared pleasurable activities, sexual responses, or special traits and behaviors that had been admired by the other. One patient reported "listening" to a voice that told her: "Why spend all your time with him? What about you? You need some time to yourself." She realized that she had distorted her husband's requests to share activities that the couple had previously enjoyed in response to a voice "telling" her that her husband was a bossy, demanding person. It was generally observed that critical, "picky" thoughts and misperceptions of one's mate were activated following a time when the partners had been especially close, both sexually and emotionally.

Circumstances Arousing Performance Anxiety and Voice Attacks

Stressful situations such as unfamiliar social settings, meeting new people, or applying for a job, are capable of activating an individual's self-attacks. In interviewing for a new job, several of our subjects reported that they felt under considerable pressure to perform and told themselves:

Take it easy. Don't be so nervous! Just relax!
You'd better be good. Get a smile on your face! Don't slouch.
Straighten up. Look confident.

As noted earlier, both men and women have a strong tendency to worry inwardly about their performance during lovemaking, particularly with a new partner. Self-attacks about one's performance interrupt the smooth progression of feelings. Men and women have reported telling themselves:

You're not touching (him, her) sensitively. You're moving too much (or not enough). You're too slow to reach a climax (or too fast).

Attempting to make a favorable impression on authority figures creates tension in many individuals. One man who was highly perfectionistic nonetheless had a consistently poor work record. He told his therapist that he felt his projects were under constant scrutiny by his superiors. He closely monitored his own behavior and judged every move with such thoughts as:

You're so slow! Look how long it took to complete that project! It's probably full of errors. They're going to find something wrong with it. You've got to be more efficient. You've got to work faster.

The patient expressed considerable anger while verbalizing this demanding, punitive voice.

Even in its mildest form, the voice interferes with an individual's ability to function adequately. This phenomenon is obvious in competitive games and sports activities. Most athletes are familiar with an internal running commentary that increases performance anxiety and typically contributes to errors or failures. Slumps of many professional ballplayers undoubtedly can be attributed to the cycle of: (1) the player becoming preoccupied with the voice's warnings and predictions of failure; (2) an increase in the level of anxiety and a corresponding drop in performance level; and finally, (3) humiliation and self-castigations by the voice, with a further deterioration in performance. Once demoralized by consistently poor performances, the player has difficulty breaking this cycle and interrupting the ongoing flow of self-critical comments.

VANITY AS COMPENSATION FOR THE NEGATIVE SELF-IMAGE

Inflated views of the self associated with vanity are compensations for underlying feelings of worthlessness and self-hatred. In areas where there is a pressure to perform and there is underlying uncertainty in the form of critical voices, an individual's vanity is likely to come into play. This aggrandized view of the self is represented by a flattering, "positive" voice that sets the individual up for subsequent self-recriminations.

One patient, an artist whose mother had told him that he had unusual talent, revealed a voice that reiterated her exaggerated praise. Whenever he sold a painting, he found himself congratulating himself silently and becoming very expansive. At this point, the patient typically began to feel increasingly anxious and pressure himself to produce and market his work. If, for a time, he was unsuccessful in selling his paintings, his self-doubts surfaced, and he would rip into himself:

> You'll never earn a living as an artist! You're a fool. You have no originality, no talent. Why don't you go out and find a *real* job?

MANIFESTATIONS OF THE VOICE

The Voice and Withholding Behavior

Many of our patients described a voice urging them to hold back their performance at work, especially when they perceived, rightly or wrongly, that their efforts went unrecognized by management. They reported self-statements such as: "Why should *you* do all the work, while *they* get all the credit? Why didn't *you* get a raise instead of so-and-so?"

We found that people frequently exaggerated the importance of minor mistakes and castigated themselves with thoughts such as:

> You never do anything right! You can't handle the responsibility of this job. You can't keep up the pace. Now they know how incompetent you are. You're not right for this job and you just proved it!

These voice attacks make people overanxious or cautious and may actually interfere with their productivity.

The Role of the Voice in Stifling Spontaneity

In general, the voice plays a prominent part in maintaining a posture of withholding. In all areas of endeavor, the voice warns people against being spontaneous and enthusiastic in the same derisive tone that their parents once used:

> Don't get so excited. What's the big deal anyway? Don't make a fool of yourself.

In personal relationships, the voice has been found to be influential in maintaining a posture of pseudo-independence and aloofness in each partner:

> Don't get too involved. Don't put all your eggs in one basket. Keep it casual. What do you need him (her) for? You got along fine before he (she) came along.

The fear of being depleted or drained, both physically and emotionally, can be aroused in patients suffering from severe emotional deprivation in childhood. Enthusiasm, vitality, and spontaneity are dampened or totally shut down in those individuals whose behaviors are regulated by too many of these seemingly self-protective thoughts.

When people have generous impulses, they frequently tell themselves: "Don't get carried away. They don't want (need) anything from *you!*" Many people are plagued by indecision when purchasing gifts for friends or loved ones. They reported thinking:

You have such poor taste.
It's not good enough.
She won't like it. Or,
What did he ever do for *you?* Why should you buy him a gift?

The Dual Focus of the Voice

We have observed that the voice not only serves the function of attacking the self, it is also directed toward others. Just as individuals have a split view of themselves, they also possess diametrically opposed views of the people in their lives. Both contradictory viewpoints—toward self and toward others—are symptomatic of the deep division existing within all of us. At times we view our loved ones with compassion and affection, while at other times we think of them in cynical or disparaging terms. Generally, negative views of others tend to correlate with self-depreciating attitudes. Indeed, a preponderance of angry thoughts about important relationships indicates the ascendancy of the voice process. When an obsessive attacking thought process is directed toward others, it is an important diagnostic sign, as these external attacks are generally accompanied by feelings of strong self-hatred and are very often symptomatic of regression. In studying the dual nature of the voice, we also noted that whenever people were "into their voice," that is, basing their actions on a hostile view of themselves, their interactions with others tended to be angry, intrusive, or objectionable.

In sessions, patients often alternated between expressing self-attacks and verbalizing harsh or suspicious attitudes toward others. In their everyday life, people tended to vacillate between castigating themselves for failures and blaming someone else. It became increasingly evident to us that critical, judgmental views of other people were inextricably tied to self-attacks by the voice.

We observed that people anticipate rejection from others

based on the dual aspect of the voice. For example, both attacks on others and attacks on oneself serve to alienate the person from close associations. In the first instance, patients reported that they predicted rejection at various stages in their relationships with such self-depreciating statements as:

> He's losing interest in you. No wonder—*you* have nothing to offer a man like him. You've never been able to hold on to a man before; what makes you think *this* relationship will be any different?

Or:

> Why should she like you? *You're* not in her class. Why would she go out with a creep like you?

In the second instance, we found that individuals were suspicious and attacking of others on the basis of their negative beliefs, thereby distancing themselves and avoiding close involvement. Men and women reported such representative thoughts as:

> She said she really loves you? Well, don't believe her. She's erratic, two-faced. She tells every man the same thing. She's leading you on, you idiot. One of these days, she'll be gone and you'll look like a jerk.

Or:

> He treats you like a sex object. He has no genuine caring feelings for you. He's not interested in making a real commitment. Don't be a victim!

Sexism and stereotypic attitudes are extensions of these hostile thoughts. These sexual stereotypes frequently dictate behavior in relation to members of the opposite sex. Many women have negative attitudes toward men. "All men want is sex. They don't want love, marriage, or a family. They're uncommunicative. They don't want to share themselves with a woman." Many men hold cynical views about women: "They're overemotional, touchy, and jealous." These negative, stereotyped attitudes have a detrimental effect on couple relationships, particularly if the underlying negative thought process is largely unconscious (Firestone, 1984).

In some patients, the tendency to distort others or to view them with suspicion is more pronounced than feelings of inferiority. These individuals exhibit a basic paranoid or victimized attitude toward life. On the other hand, patients who base their behavior more on their low opinions of themselves than on their hostile views of other people more often display symptoms of depression.

A paranoid orientation stems from the projection of one's voice onto others, as well as the attribution of one's own negative qualities to other persons in the interpersonal environment. Whenever feelings of self-hatred become intolerable, patients tend to deny the existence of the undesirable qualities that they hate in themselves and displace these traits onto others. Further, when the voice process is operating below the threshold of awareness, there is a strong tendency to *project the voice onto other people and see them as judgmental and critical.* One subject who was very ambivalent toward women described the process of projecting his voice:

> Whenever I meet a woman for the first time, I *know* that she is thinking certain things about me. I don't just "think" or imagine women see me in a negative light. I feel absolutely certain of it.
>
> I believe that women, in general, think I'm boyish, not to be taken seriously as a man—a pal, maybe, or someone to joke with, but definitely not a man.
>
> It's difficult for me to take back these projections and to see that *I'm* the one who is thinking this way about myself. Most of the time I act in a way to get that kind of response from women, a response that fits in with the negative ways I've defined myself.

If the subject had remained unaware that his beliefs about women were projections of his own self-attacks, he would have found it difficult to identify the underlying causes of his self-defeating behavior. Furthermore, he would have had a tendency to continue acting out feelings of inadequacy, that influenced a hesitant, tentative approach to women and insured rejection. These dynamics confirmed his negative image of himself as a man.

The tendency to project one's voice attacks onto another person is especially evident in couples. In addition, there may be mutual withholding and acting out of undesirable behaviors on the part of one or both members, which tend to validate the other's cynical view.

It has been our clinical experience that both negative views (of the self and of others) contribute to a basic posture of isolation and alienation by influencing an individual to avoid relationships that would challenge his or her negative self-image and feelings of unlovability. In helping individuals to develop closer ties, it is beneficial for them to recognize their voice attacks on others and to expose them rather than to act them out.

The Voice as Distinguished from the Hallucinated Voices in Psychosis

It is important to note that the "voice" occurs as an actual voice in psychotic hallucinations. The hallucinated voices in schizophrenia are exaggerated manifestations of the voice in neurotic disorders. In psychotic states, the voice has been externalized and is experienced as real sensation, seemingly originating in the outside world. The psychotic patient actually hears commands, directions, criticisms, and judgmental pronouncements as in a real conversation. The schizophrenic patient's ego is in an extremely weakened state, and he will frequently act upon these commands in a maladaptive fashion, often regardless of the consequences. The patient is almost totally at the mercy of, or completely "possessed" by, the alien point of view described throughout this chapter. Bizarre behaviors, as well as inappropriate generalizations, decomposition of concepts, idiosyncratic symbolism, and blocking may indicate the profound intrusion of the voice into the patient's cognitive processes.

The character of the "voices" in psychosis and in neurosis are similar in many respects. The hallucinated voices heard by schizophrenic patients have a parental quality that is very similar to the judgmental character of the neurotic patient's self-critical thoughts and negative self-appraisals. Frequently, auditory hallucinations take the form of mothering or controlling statements. For example, they may be heard as commands to perform certain actions. Later, the patient may hear voices saying "shame on you," after he acts out the bizarre or self-destructive behavior.

Many schizophrenic patients refer to themselves in the third person, almost as if they were doting mothers or fathers. They may reply when asked how they feel, "Oh, he feels all right"; or with other responses that indicate an extreme degree of depersonalization. In the schizophrenic, the self is being treated as an object by the patient's voices, in a style comparable to the way the self is attacked by the neurotic patient's voice. However, the extent to which the process of depersonalization has taken place is far greater in the schizophrenic patient.

Psychotic patients, in believing that others hate them and accuse them, also imagine that they hear voices degrading them, ordering them to perform strange or self-destructive acts. Often it may be ascertained from these patients that the voices remind them of parental orders or reprimands.

THE VOICE PROCESS AND VALUE SYSTEMS

Although I know very little of the Steppenwolf's life, I have all the same good reason to suppose that he was brought up by devoted but severe and very pious parents and teachers in accordance with that doctrine that makes the breaking of the will the cornerstone of education and upbringing. . . .

Instead of destroying his personality they succeeded only in teaching him to hate himself. It was against himself that, innocent and noble as he was, he directed during his whole life the whole wealth of his fancy, the whole of his thought; and in so far as he let loose upon himself every barbed criticism, every anger and hate he could command, he was, in spite of all, a real Christian and a real martyr.

Herman Hesse
(1927/1929, p. 9-10)

Although injunctions of the voice may at times appear to be synonymous with values and moral considerations, I do not conceptualize the voice as constructively influencing an individual's morality. The voice acts as an agency in the personality that *interprets* moral standards and value systems in a punitive manner of self-attack and recrimination. Furthermore, the voice process is contradictory, first instigating destructive actions, then condemning them. In their most pathological form, self-attacks of the voice ultimately can lead to suicide, while suspicious, paranoid voices about other people sometimes culminate in homicide. Thus, it is difficult to fit behaviors that are controlled by the voice under the rubric of moral standards or a value system.

The voice process supports self-denial and the renunciation of natural drives and wants through a distortion of conventional values and mores. These distortions arise because many patients have been taught as children to conform to unnecessary prohibitions at the expense of self; they have learned to be selfless and to feel guilty for having wants and needs. The child blames himself for feeling deprived and later assigns this sense of badness to real behavior that conflicts with moral values.

Concomitant with learning moral precepts, children are also in the process of introjecting their parents' rejecting attitudes in the medium of the voice. Therefore they tend to associate these internalized values with the destructive admonitions of the voice and to confuse the two processes. People typically equate the attacking *process* with a particular criticism or evaluation that is valid, as though it were proper to accuse themselves and despise themselves for being inadequate or for making mistakes. For example, many patients come to therapy exhibiting an extremely moralistic, judgmental attitude toward themselves, which they use in conjunction with their own moral code to punish themselves. If they resolve to change a specific negative behavior or habit pattern and subsequently break their resolution, they punish themselves with thoughts such as: "You have no will-power. You'll never change—you make resolutions, then just break them. You're hopeless." This style of thinking demoralizes people and engenders hopelessness about gaining control over actions they want to change.

In my work, I attempt to show patients that it is maladaptive to punish or hate themselves for making mistakes or for possessing negative traits or personality characteristics. I sometimes cite the example of a patient with a below-average I.Q. who continually berated himself for being "stupid, an imbecile, a misfit, a totally despicable person." The fact that he really was backward did not justify his calling himself names. His actual retardation did not merit his self-attack or account for the hostility toward himself. The degrading, punitive quality of the voice—the tone in which this patient maligned himself—is a major characteristic that distinguishes it from a healthy conscience or ego-ideal. We have determined that there also is a persecutory element to the voice, a belittling, parental aspect that goes far beyond what would normally constitute moral guidelines and ideals.

CONCLUSION

For more than 12 years, my professional associates and I have been exploring manifestations of the voice in normal and neurotic subjects. We have discovered that, more often than not, people adjusted their behavior in response to their negative views of themselves. Struggling against their self-critical thoughts had become extremely debilitating for these patients because of the energy required to defend themselves against intrusion of the voice. Moreover, we found that more seriously depressed patients were frequently unable to distinguish between their own point of view and negative, judgmental appraisals of themselves based on the voice.

During sessions when patients have verbalized their self-accusations, their guilt and remorse, and their negative perceptions of themselves, I have been impressed that these destructive elements are present in every individual, opposing the natural evolution of self. As such, the voice is antithetical to the emerging personality of the individual. Human beings, like flowers or plants, are able to develop their full potentialities only under ideal conditions, and are stunted in their growth if the surrounding atmosphere lacks certain vital ingredients. Unfortunately, they are also capable of *incorporating harmful elements from their early environment, a process that seriously restricts their natural development as unique individuals.*

In the therapeutic enterprise, the artistry lies in sensing what is natural to each patient's self and what is alien and detrimental to that self, in not prejudging or placing arbitrary constructions on the emerging self, but becoming attuned to it and allowing it to grow. The other, equally important, task of therapy lies in helping to expose the voice whenever the patient is seen to be living out a destructive or alien point of view based on his past associations, thus renouncing his real self. Throughout our work over the past several years, we have become increasingly sensitive to the conflicting aspects of the self that exist in every individual. In the following chapter, we will describe how we arrived at the concept of the voice and related hypotheses. We will trace our growing knowledge of the destructive elements of the personality as it evolved during the years of investigation and discovery and will discuss the development of therapeutic procedures to contend with these elements.

3

Historical Development of Voice Therapy

Now I know (Dr. D. told me) that the voice is me, Elizabeth. I am not having auditory hallucinations. . . . The voice comes out of my head. I don't argue with him. Of course the voice comes out of my head, but the voice isn't me. Oh, no, not me, not in a million years. Nobody understands this. But I know now that *the voice is a separate entity that happens to reside in my head* [italics added].

Elizabeth Ikuru (1985)
The Voice Inside Me

This account, written by an unusually articulate and intelligent woman diagnosed as suffering from a bipolar affective disorder, provides us with a graphic description of the voice. Drugs relieved the patient's distress for brief periods of time, yet the voice invariably returned, with its insistent, overpowering demands that she physically abuse or mutilate herself as punishment for being "bad." After several years of treating her symptoms, her doctors still knew very little about her voice or her self-destructiveness. Why, after living a fairly stable, well-adjusted life for 27 years, did this woman suddenly develop a severe form of micro-suicidal behavior in response to an internal voice?

Although certain aspects of the self-abusive voice described by this patient have been delineated in the literature, much remains to be learned about its origins and its relation to the ego and ego-functions. In the following pages, we will describe a fascinating and compelling process of discovery that we have been involved in for many years in an effort to understand the voice. We will examine and analyze clinical material from which we derived our developing hypotheses. Finally, we will discuss a number of hypotheses concerning: (1) the probable sources of the voice; (2) the function of the voice as a defense mechanism in neurosis; (3) the affect associated with the voice; and (4) the resistance to changing the negative view of self.

INITIAL INVESTIGATIONS OF THE VOICE PROCESS

Very early in my clinical practice, my colleagues and I became aware that people appeared to be abnormally sensitive to certain kinds of feedback. They would become angry and defensive when confronted with information about themselves that they mistakenly interpreted as critical or negative. We observed that most individuals prejudged themselves in ways that were characteristically self-punitive. Therefore, any external criticism or judgment, whether mild or harsh, was capable of activating *self*critical associations. It seemed important to try to better understand the types of interactions, events, and feedback that appeared to arouse these self-attacks.

In 1973, several of my associates and I formed a discussion group with the goal of systematically studying our reactions to confrontation and feedback. As the group progressed, we observed that we tended to overreact to feedback that corresponded to our own negative self-evaluations. We came to the conclusion that an observing, critical thought process existed in each of us that was stirred up by certain kinds of external criticism. These preliminary explorations captured our interest and led to further investigations of the mechanism of self-attack.

Concurrently with the ongoing therapists' group, we were studying the manifestations of this inimical thought process in our patients. First we suggested to our patients that they note the situations or events that typically made them feel anxious or depressed. Then we asked them to recall what they were telling themselves in those situations. These patients provided numerous examples of their self-punishing or self-disparaging thoughts. They were especially aware that self-attacks increased their nervousness and agitation when they were already under stress as, for example, in unfamiliar situations. While saying their self-critical thoughts *out loud,* they learned that it was not so much the adverse circumstances or events in their lives that caused them discomfort; rather it was the voice's *interpretation* of these events. In discussing their self-critical views with the therapist, our patients were impressed that these negative thoughts were very different from their usual self-appraisal, i.e., when they were *not* feeling depressed.

In these early sessions, we were surprised at the ease with which these patients not only grasped the idea of an internal self-attacking thought process, but applied this idea to their everyday lives. Once they caught on, they seemed fully familiar with the countless ways that they habitually criticized and castigated themselves. They were surprised, however, to discover the degree to which this process of running themselves down had undermined their ability to function effectively or to find satisfaction in their personal relationships. In sessions, when they allowed themselves to give full vent to their feelings of worthlessness and hostile self-reproach, they were able to connect these feelings to specific self-critical thoughts.

After isolating the content of this hostile thought process, our patients began to separate it from a more realistic view of themselves. They found that it felt more natural to verbalize their self-accusatory thoughts as statements spoken in the second person, e.g., "*You're* this or that." The patients began to adopt this way of verbalizing their thoughts without prior instruction or suggestion from the therapist. Thereafter, they tended to state their hostile self-attacks in a form as though they were addressing themselves as an outside person.

To illustrate, a twenty-seven-year-old patient happened upon this method of verbalizing her feelings in the course of a therapy session. The woman, an attractive model and actress, was plagued with self-doubts about her acting ability. In attempting to

give words to the discomfort she felt in front of television cam-
eras, she began speaking as though she were a mother com-
menting about an awkward child:

> When I'm in a scene where I have to move around the set, I
> keep reminding myself to be sure and do it naturally, like, "Care-
> ful how you're walking. You're too stiff. Watch out for that turn—
> do it more slowly, deliberately. C'mon, head up higher, look
> proud, don't slouch!"
>
> If I start talking to myself like this, sort of under my breath, I
> get *really* down on myself, especially if I happen to catch a glimpse
> of myself in one of the TV monitors. I start telling myself, "Look
> at your arms hanging there. *Do* something with your hands—you
> look so awkward, like you're playing a part. You're *supposed* to
> look *natural*. This is a joke, you trying to be an actress. You can't
> do it. You just don't have what it takes!"

The patient was shocked at her tone of voice as she verbalized the critical commands she was giving herself. She told the
therapist that she never would have tolerated anyone else talking to her in that degrading tone, yet she customarily accepted
this style of abuse *from herself*.

In the therapists' group, we were also experimenting with
techniques of verbalizing our self-depreciation. We discovered
that formulating our harshly judgmental thoughts in the second
person had considerable emotional impact and led to valuable
insights. We found that, once articulated through this mode of
expression, the specific thoughts could be effectively evaluated
and countered.

We observed that this method of identifying our self-critical
thoughts was often sufficient in itself to start the process of
change. Repeated exposure of the voice in brief sessions utilizing this nondramatic or analytical technique had a considerable
therapeutic effect.

The therapists in the group were very excited as they became aware of the implications of this new procedure. They applied their growing knowledge to many subjects. In one very
interesting application, they utilized this method of self-investigation to analyze their oversensitive countertransference reactions to patients' negative transference. This enabled the

professionals to achieve better understanding of their own pain and irrational suffering.

At this point in our explorations, a number of patients or subjects began referring to their self-depreciating thoughts as "the voice" or "my voice." This term accurately described the negative thought process as they experienced it; that is, as different from their usual way of thinking. The term "voice" appeared to reflect their perception of these self-attacking patterns of thought as being directed toward them verbally from an outside source. My associates and I also began referring to this system of negative cognitions as the "voice" to indicate its separate, functional autonomy as a corrosive, self-destructive force within the personality that could be verbalized or "voiced" through the procedures described above.

DRAMATIZATION OF THE VOICE

From 1977 on, we conducted more structured investigations of the voice process. Again, professional associates and other volunteers served as subjects in these pilot studies, which generally took place in a group setting. The clinical material we gathered from this experimental group and from our continuing work with patients contributed significantly to our growing knowledge of this systematized pattern of negative thinking and feeling. By far the most surprising phenomenon we observed during this period occurred when the participants in this new group began to express themselves more emotionally in the course of verbalizing their self-attacks. They sensed the anger and hostility behind their feelings of low self-esteem and depression, and spontaneously began to express varying degrees of rage in conjunction with the thought content of the voice.

Subjects began to blurt out intense, vindictive statements against themselves in powerful, passionate language and with strong negative affect. For example, one subject loudly condemned herself for being overweight with this bitter diatribe:

You're disgusting! Look at yourself in the mirror! You pig! No one can stand you. You'll never lose weight. You have no willpower, you creep! You're a failure, do you hear, a total failure!

Following this outburst, the woman recognized that she typically expended a great deal of energy in an internal dialogue consisting of a rapid succession of self-admonitions similar to the vicious self-attacks she had just verbalized. In subsequent meetings, she expressed this material in a sarcastic tone of voice quite unlike her usual mode of expression. She assumed a style that could be described as lecturing or sermonizing, together with snide innuendos and name-calling, a style she immediately identified as her mother's style of addressing her. In one session, the woman remembered that her mother had repeatedly told her as a child that she was "like a leaf in the wind," that she had "no willpower or ideas of her own," among other railings strikingly in key with her own self-attacks.

This pattern was obvious to many others. More and more subjects identified their self-criticisms as statements they had heard one or both parents make to them during their developing years. Others recalled parental attitudes they had picked up in their parents' tone of voice, body language, or other behavioral cues—attitudes that appeared to be directly related to the subjects' specific self-attacks. For example, one young man remembered that, though his father had never expressed his anger to him in actual words, he had projected hostility by his absolute disregard of his son as a person. By his indifference, the father had treated the son as a nonentity in the family. We need to emphasize here that in all these instances, both subjects and patients arrived at their own interpretations of the clinical material. Their conclusions about the sources of their derogatory self-statements did not reflect an a priori interpretation of the material by the therapists.

In the patient population, as well as in the experimental group, we observed that remarkable changes were manifested in an individual's physical appearance and expression during voice sessions. These changes were particularly notable when there was a powerful cathartic release of feeling during verbalization of hostile self-criticism. The subjects' bodies assumed postures and mannerisms that were uncharacteristic of their own style. In scrutinizing our subjects' behavior, we noted that the expressions we observed were very similar in style to their parents' mannerisms; in particular, to those of the parent of the same sex. It was as though the parental figures lived inside the subjects and could be brought out by this method.

Phrasing and speech intonations underwent basic transformations and often took on the regional accents of the parents. This was especially obvious when the subjects' parents happened to be of foreign background. Sometimes entire phrases and colloquial expressions were blurted out in their parents' idiom. At this stage in our studies, we began to videotape sessions of our experimental groups in order to document these dramatic changes in subjects' appearance, mannerisms, and speech patterns.

The material uncovered by subjects during these sessions touched on themes that were central to their lives. The issues brought to the surface involved basic psychological defenses that had existed in their personality structure since childhood. In general, a wealth of unconscious negative thoughts and feelings was unearthed by the participants in the experimental group. While dramatizing the voice, people had powerful insights, enabling them to identify and understand the origins of their self-limiting behavior and feelings of self-hatred.

From the clinical data we were accumulating, we began to understand the connection between the subjects' verbalizations and negative parental statements and attitudes assimilated by them as children. We hypothesized that what we were witnessing were manifestations of these parental warnings, directions, labels, definitions, and feelings. Furthermore, the negative attitudes toward self expressed by our subjects appeared to have been incorporated into the subjects' own thinking process early in life, during the formative years.

In the office setting, our patients were able to identify the thought content of this disparaging, angry point of view toward self and to express outwardly some of the repressed rage they had turned inward on themselves. They became aware of the extent to which they had accepted this critical view of themselves at face value. They became cognizant of how they maintained certain undesirable behaviors in order to validate the "bad child" image they had assimilated originally in their family constellation. Expressing the emotions associated with specific self-accusatory thoughts shattered deeply held misconceptions of self, relieved feelings of guilt and remorse, and led to increased feelings of compassion for self in most patients.

The release of feelings that accompanied these penetrating exposures of the voice process relieved patients of the tension and anxiety caused by suppressing intense emotions. Afterward, patients reported feeling much more relaxed and at ease. Although they experienced painful regressive feelings during the sessions, these did not persist, and patients returned to a normal functioning mode following the sessions.

The technique of expressing the voice dramatically became an important part of our procedure because it represented a more direct pathway to deeply repressed material in the patient's unconscious. In addition, we felt that this method had potential as an important research tool with which to study the unconscious cognitive processes involved in severe neurotic disorders, depression, and self-destructive or suicidal behaviors.

DEFENSIVE FUNCTIONS OF THE VOICE

Later in our investigations we discovered that there seemed to be two important aspects of the voice process: a protective, parental quality that acts to stifle one's enthusiasm, spontaneity, spirit, and sense of adventure, and a malicious or hostile quality that issues directives to mutilate the self emotionally and/or physically.

(1) We noted that the voice had overtones similar to those of an overprotective parent, cautioning, directing, controlling, and advising people in a manner that seemed at first glance to have their best interests at heart. For example, a common "advisory" self-attack was:

> Don't get too hooked on her (him). What if she (he) breaks up with you? Why go through all that agony just for a few weeks on cloud nine?

In contemplating pleasurable activities, many people warned themselves about possible dangers:

> Why blow so much money on this trip? You can't trust the brochures. Your French is hopeless. What if the plane gets hijacked? With the shape the world's in, why go anywhere.

In one case, an older patient decided not to build the house he had always dreamed of. He listened to a voice reminding him of his age:

> Why start something you probably won't be around to finish? Do you think you can take all the frustration of dealing with a big construction job? With all your money tied up, how are you going to handle a medical emergency?

These apparently self-protective voices functioned to block people's desires before they could be translated into positive action. While these inner warnings all had some basis in reality, we determined that the *process of denying one's wants on an unconscious level* (which, in effect, was the end result of heeding these subliminal voices) was generally detrimental to an individual's well-being. The majority of these individuals were not making rational *conscious* choices based on practical considerations, but were turning their backs on strong motives and wants. Their decisions were based on an unconscious negative thought process that utilized both fact and fantasy to support a theme of self-denial. In "listening" to the voice, these people were interfering with basic expressions of self and diminishing rather than enhancing a sense of personal identity.

Even in situations where caution is advisable, we determined that the voice functions to stifle a person's enthusiasm and spontaneity. It is this factor, rather than the specific warnings of the voice, that damages people's spirit and sense of adventure. Indeed, many subjects reported "listening" to a voice that ridiculed them for being excited. They remembered being subdued as children by parents who made fun of their youthful exuberance. The derivation of this self-protective function of the voice became apparent when subjects repeatedly connected their derisive internal warnings to parental attitudes.

(2) In our investigations, we observed that what initially appeared to be an abnormal defensive process soon became, when carried to its limits of expression, a powerfully hostile force, even

in comparatively normal subjects. The pronouncements of the voice, even when self-protective or accurate, were malicious in their attitude toward the individual. As our subjects explored this process in greater depth and fully expressed the intensity of the negative affect associated with their self-critical thoughts, they discovered that their voices were sneering, sarcastic, and even savagely angry. For example, a man whose father had been extremely rejecting and at times physically abusive, expressed this attack on himself:

> Go ahead—why don't you just smash your hand! Just get yourself off the earth! You don't deserve to live! You're a reject. You're not a man! You're just a poor excuse for a man!

This series of thoughts, containing injunctions to harm himself, corresponded to this subject's apparent disregard for his own safety in his work as a machinist and was directly related to his accident proneness.

When we first heard our subjects verbalizing these commands to injure themselves, we were shocked by the unexpected depth and magnitude of the rage they expressed. We were disturbed by the violence and the range of the voice's destructive commands, as were the participants in our group. It was very difficult to believe that relatively well-adjusted individuals could harbor this degree of intense anger toward themselves. It was obvious to us that the murderous rage that we were tapping when our subjects dramatized the voice typically remains below the level of awareness in most people.

In other cases, manifestations of this internalized rage assumed a more subtle form. To illustrate, one woman who lived alone and was abnormally reserved and reticent reported that she "heard" a voice that told her to be unobtrusive in social interactions.

> In social situations, I tell myself: "Just be quiet. Nobody wants to hear what you have to say. Don't bother people. Just stop talking. Don't say anything more. *Just shut up!* [spoken loudly with intense anger.] Don't talk to me, don't bother me. I never wanted you, you little bitch!"

The patient reported that she had always held a deep conviction that she was undeserving of love or respect, a belief that corresponded to the suppressed anger she had turned against herself. It was obvious that she had incorporated extremely rejecting attitudes toward herself from her mother.

In this session and others where a number of subjects exposed these malevolent directives to mutilate or annihilate the self, strong feelings of compassion were aroused in fellow participants. People could not help but identify the vicious tone of voice with which these individuals expressed previously repressed anger and bitterness. The quality and tone of these self-attacks struck familiar chords in each person, even in those subjects who had not verbalized their voices with this degree of intensity or blatant self-destructiveness.

It was becoming increasingly evident that most subjects harbored deeply repressed rage and hostility toward themselves, to a degree far beyond what they would have imagined, or even what we as therapists had believed possible. The extent to which people's voices acted to invalidate basic parts of the self was of deep concern to us. We developed a better understanding of the damage that these individuals had sustained in their early years and how the process of self-attack functioned to perpetuate this damage into the next generation.

The connection between this internalized hostility, as exemplified in the two cases above, and in destructive acting-out behavior such as substance abuse, accident proneness, or withdrawal from social contact, became more obvious. Indeed, we observed that several of our apparently "normal" subjects at times did behave in ways that were potentially dangerous or detrimental to their physical health. Many others tended to turn to isolated activities whenever their actions were being influenced by a voice "telling" them to stay in the background or to be unobtrusive, as in the case of the woman described above. We learned that, as a result of "listening" to the voice, an individual tends to deny his wants and turn against his goals and priorities. We concluded, based on these observations, that the voice functions as a regulatory mechanism, mediating self-destructive behaviors and self-limiting life-styles.

Finally, we found that people whose behavior patterns were

primarily influenced by the voice had very little compassion for themselves. Indeed, genuine feelings of warmth and affection are notably diminished in individuals who act primarily in response to the dictates of this destructive thought process. We conjectured that the emotional deadness or blandness and corresponding lack of positive affect we observed in these patients was somehow a function of the extent to which the voice prevailed over their rational thoughts of self-interest. We noted that the voice operates as an external punitive judge of the self, which it treats as a hated object. It seemed that this maladaptive cognitive process functions as a depersonalized, anti-feeling entity. At the same time, however, it is accompanied by varying degrees of *negative* affect.

TWO POINTS OF VIEW

The more we examined our clinical material, the more we became aware that people possess two radically different, almost mutually exclusive, points of view of themselves, of others, and of the world they live in. Moreover, they tend to move in and out of these modes, many times with little or no awareness of the transition.

The degree to which people's behavior is mediated by the voice generally determines the state of mind that they are in at any given time. The process is circular in that as individuals act out behaviors they disapprove of, they become more guilty and inward. Their inwardness and isolation, in turn, have the effect of making them more susceptible to voice attacks.

We observed that the more an individual bases his actions on the prescriptions and admonitions of the voice, the more he appears to be subsumed by an alien personality, often quite divergent from his own. This phenomenon has been especially evident in our experimental population, composed of individuals with high ego-strength and a low degree of pathology. Our subjects' acquiescence to the hostile point of view as manifested in their real life interactions was very obvious to the other participants in the group, if not always to the subjects themselves.

An individual tends to display differential behavior, personality characteristics, and facial expressions that correspond to the contrasting points of view. For example, one subject in our experimental group appeared to possess two almost completely different personalities, depending upon which point of view was dominant. The man, acknowledged by friends as being very likable, humorous, and extroverted when he was "himself," at other times would become extremely petulant, irritable, and almost unapproachable. Furthermore, his looks and general demeanor changed dramatically between the two states.

For years, this man had explained away the profound changes in his personality as simple moodiness. When he made an effort to stop acting out his irritability on family members, he was able to identify the negative thought patterns underlying his destructive behavior. He uncovered deep feelings of animosity toward himself as well. His voices were extremely self-accusatory and self-righteous, condemning self and others for their "bad habits" and irresponsible behaviors. It is important to note, however, that this man was not really conscious of *thinking* negatively about others or about himself when in the past he automatically acted out his hostility. Indeed, acting on his voice had served to submerge it. Only by controlling his hostile behavior was he able to bring his judgmental, punitive thoughts more into consciousness.

As our subjects became more aware of their inconsistencies and ambivalent attitudes, they became uneasy about the intrusion of the voice into their everyday lives. They were disconcerted and frightened to learn how deeply divided they were. Most people are very resistant to experiencing internal conflict, and desperately attempt to maintain a sense of unity, albeit false. In an effort to achieve integration and appear more consistent in their behavior and attitudes, they frequently side with the alien point of view. For example, one woman, who had vacillated for months in her attitudes about having a child, finally concluded that motherhood would not fit in "with her easy-going, relaxed life-style." On closer examination, however, her arbitrary decision was found to reflect a deeply held belief that she could not be sensitive to a child. She believed that other women were capable of being good mothers, but that she was not. Unable to tolerate her self-doubts and ambivalent feelings past a certain point, she had settled the internal conflict with superficial rationalizations. Following her decision, she was no longer actively troubled by thoughts telling her she would be a "bad mother." Unfortunately, submerging her real point of view led to symptom formation. She regressed to a more immature style of relating to her husband and felt guilty and depressed.

Definition of the Natural Point of View

As we discovered the extent to which the alien, imposed point of view intruded itself into our subjects' thoughts, feelings, and behavior, the question arose as to what constitutes an individual's "natural" point of view and what elements can be attributed to the alien view. Are the negative, harsh, judgmental attitudes an integral part of one's personality that need to be accepted as aspects of the real self and further integrated? Who has the right to ascertain what is "normal" and "natural" for human beings and what is alien? Aren't all internal processes a part of the person? The author suggests that these fundamental questions about human nature may be partially answered by considering basic needs inherent to all human beings.

It is generally accepted that as individuals satisfy their needs at one level, e.g., the survival needs for food, sleep, and rest, they move to the next level of needs for social contact, productive work, and other self-actualizing activity. In *Explorations in Personality,* Henry Murray et al. (1938) lists and explains some 30 psychological needs including the need for achievement, acquisition, affiliation, autonomy, blame avoidance, nurturance, play, recognition, sex, understanding. One can hypothesize that in his natural state, man would tend to seek satisfaction and fulfillment as he moved upward through the hierarchy of needs and, conversely, would not do so if he were acting *against* himself.[1]

Therefore, when a patient is consciously or unconsciously renouncing one of the more basic survival needs, as for instance when the anorectic patient refuses to eat, we have reason to assume that he or she is *not in the right frame of mind,* i.e., is not acting in his or her own self-interest. Similarly, on a higher level, when people set goals for themselves based on individual, and highly personal, wants and desires, then move *away* from these goals rather than toward them, it can be assumed that they no longer are acting in their own self-interest. Indeed, we contend that they are following a line of reasoning or logic other than their own. Many people, however, tend to blame external circumstances, other persons, or even fate, rather than recognize that their actions are antithetical to an ongoing pursuit of their natural wants and needs.

DYNAMICS OF THE VOICE

Lastly, in studying the concept of the voice, we related our findings to a basic theoretical orientation that explained the dynamics involved. We considered such matters as: (1) the function of the voice in supporting the patient's resistance to changing his negative view of self; and (2) the connection between the concept of the voice and the dynamics of identification and introjection.

Resistance to Changing the Negative View of Self

When the voice has gone unchallenged since early childhood, it becomes the basis of the negative self-concept. In listening to the voice, accepting it, and habitually believing it, people eventually become what their voice tells them they are. For example, a woman who was defined in her family as "the plain one," now, despite pleasing features, leaves one with the impression that she is unattractive, even homely. She traced her self-consciousness about her appearance to specific negative thoughts about her looks, dress, and posture. Paradoxically, in therapy, this patient was stubbornly resistant to changing her basic negative evaluation of herself. Her behavior indicated that she preferred to maintain her *family's* definition rather than go against this negative view.

Our clinical experience has demonstrated that when patients begin to feel loved or acknowledged by a significant person in their lives for specific qualities that contradict their negative self-image, they frequently regress and reestablish their defenses. Certain aspects of negative transference phenomena can be explained by this adverse reaction. The patient, in feeling understood and accepted by the therapist, initially has a positive response. At the point, however, where the therapist's warmth and empathy begin to challenge fundamental beliefs making up the patient's negative self-concept, he or she becomes angry at the therapist and resistant to the therapeutic process.

These adverse reactions can be observed in everyday life. For example, many people cannot accept compliments or genuine acknowledgment of qualities that contradict basic misconceptions of themselves. One subject, who had published a number of books noted for their compelling narrative style, was nevertheless critical of his work and could not identify with an image of himself as an author. When complimented, he usually replied with a caustic or self-depreciating remark.

The author contends that the tendency to shrug off or disdain compliments represents a relatively minor manifestation of a more fundamental resistance. As previously noted, many individuals have negative reactions to positive experiences and refuse to believe in themselves. An interesting symptom of people's tendency to discount their achievements has been documented in the literature by Harvey (1984) in her work with the "impostor phenomenon." She writes:

> The impostor phenomenon, [is] a hidden symptom associated with high levels of anxiety, and [is] characterized by an intense, subjective experience of . . . role-related fraudulence. (p. 16)

The subjective feeling of having fooled others or of feeling undeserving has been reported by many of our own subjects, particularly when they believed they "should" have been proud of their accomplishments.

The author suggests that the impostor phenomenon is an external manifestation of the patient's underlying resistance to changing his or her basic identity. Individuals are extremely resistant to restructuring deeply entrenched *negative* beliefs about the self, misconceptions that, if seriously challenged in therapy, would disrupt core defenses and arouse intense anxiety.

The Dynamics of Identification and Introjection

In investigating the reasons that patients are so strongly opposed to changing these highly personal "*dis*beliefs" in themselves as decent human beings, we devoted considerable effort to understanding the origin of the intense fear underlying this resistance. A more elaborate analysis of our clinical material has led us to a deeper insight into the genesis of this fear.

Briefly, the empirical data documented thus far suggest that *the voice is a representation of negative parental introjects that significantly affect our perception of ourselves*. Thereafter, the voice functions to tie individuals to their parents in the sense that, even though physically separate or geographically distant from the family, adults still possess an internal parent that directs them, controls them, and punishes them. These voices, albeit unpleasant, serve the function of maintaining the fantasy bond and shield the individual from experiencing his aloneness, sense of separation, and death anxiety. Interestingly enough, Sigmund Freud (1926/1959) arrived at an intuitive understanding of the role played by the internal parent. He commented on the security provided by the "introjected parents" in one of his last writings:

> I am therefore inclined to adhere to the view that the fear of death should be regarded as analogous to the fear of castration and that the situation to which the ego is reacting is one of being abandoned by the protecting super-ego [introjected parents]—the powers of destiny—*so that it has no longer any safeguard against all the dangers that surround it* [italics added]. (p. 130)

In essence, the patient is terrified of losing the internal parent, represented by the voice. The irrational fear of disrupting the illusory connection or fantasy bond with the family and the dread of reexperiencing feelings of infantile frustration and a primitive sense of helplessness are at the core of resistance.

NOTES

[1]See also Maslow's (1954) exposition of *The Role of Basic Need Gratification in Psychological Theory* where he states that "the most basic consequence of satiation of any need is that this need is submerged and a new and higher need emerges" (p. 108). Maslow stresses the limitations of "gratification theory," writing that it "is obviously a special, limited, or partial theory" and that "basic need gratification differs from neurotic need gratification in important respects" (p. 108).

3/22/88

4

Introjection, Negative Identification, and the Voice—A Developmental Perspective

A most curious phenomenon of the personality, one which has been observed for centuries, but which has not yet received its full explanation, is that in which the individual seems to be the vehicle of a personality that is not his own. Someone else's personality seems to 'possess' him and to be finding expression through his words and actions, whereas the individual's own personality is temporarily 'lost' or 'gone' . . . .

There seem to be all degrees of the same basic process from the simple, benign observation that so-and-so 'takes after his father', or 'that's her mother's temper coming out in her', to the extreme distress of the person who finds himself under *a compulsion to take on the characteristics of a personality he may hate and/or feel to be entirely alien to his own* [italics added].

R. D. Laing (1960/1965, p. 58)

The phenomenon noted by Laing accurately portrays key

aspects of the voice process as depicted in our work. Its mystery can be explained by the fact that human beings are capable of incorporating into themselves an image of their parents as the parents were when they were the most defended, the most aggressive, and the most feared by the child. These parental introjects have a basic autonomy within the personality and may ultimately dominate the scene, as it were.

IMITATION

Children tend to take on an image of being the "bad, weak child" while maintaining an image of the parent as being good and powerful. In order to justify and hold on to a sense of "badness," they may continue to perpetuate in their personality traits and characteristics that they feel are objectionable. In addition, there is a compulsion to imitate personality traits of authority figures, even though these traits are seen as negative or undesirable. This process is influenced by conditions of neglect, emotional deprivation, overt and/or covert rejection, and abuse.

To illustrate, a college math professor who was characteristically relaxed and decent in most interactions with his family, nonetheless was perfectionistic and punitive in relation to his children's intellectual achievements. According to my patient, his father would suddenly lose his temper, explode, and berate him for poor academic performance. Although these expressions of anger were not typical and occurred infrequently, they had a profound effect, and these negative encounters were in the foreground of his perception of his father. Paradoxically, as an adult, he displayed the same rigidity and intolerance for imperfection that characterized his father's attitude when angry and defensive. Unfortunately, children tend to incorporae the parent at his or her worst, i.e., at extreme times of tension and abuse. Therefore, parental introjects may not be truly representative of parental attitudes on the whole.

The mechanism of imitating and self-parenting is made up of two important psychological processes, *introjection* and *identification,* which are vital in the developmental sequence.

Identification

The process of incorporating the image of the rejecting parent and introjecting hostile thought patterns is related to the phenomenon of "identification with the aggressor," described by Bettelheim (1943/1979).

> The old prisoners' identification with the SS did not stop with the copying of their outer appearance and behavior. Old prisoners accepted Nazi goals and values, too, even when these seemed opposed to their own interests. (p. 79)

When children are in too much pain psychologically, they attempt to avoid the full experience of their distress, i.e., when the pain becomes intolerable, they no longer identify with themselves. When they feel the most threatened and fearful, they generally identify with the person who is the source of their suffering in an attempt to possess that person's strength or power. Children assume the qualities of the parents through this process of identification, and, at the same time, assimilate their hostile, critical attitudes. Furthermore, in forming an imagined connection or fusion with one's parents, one becomes at once the weak, bad child and the strong parent, the transgressor and one's own severest critic. This process serves to reduce anxiety and supports the illusion of safety and independence.

Introjection

The process of introjection is in itself benign. According to David Rapaport (1951), it is crucial to the development of reality-testing and secondary process thinking. In describing the dynamics of the child's developing thought processes, Rapaport points out that the parents are the infant's first "social relationships." He states that when the developing individual becomes aware of being separate from this first love-object, he forms an internal image of the object in his mind. Rapaport's formulations are somewhat analogous to the author's concept of the primary fantasy bond. An intrinsic part of this illusory connection involves the child's introjection of the parents' negative attitudes and qualities, which he takes on as his own. Rapaport writes:

> When reality obliges him [the infant] to give up these objects, they are not given up intrapsychically: in fact, their intrapsychic existence only then really begins. . . . This process is conceptualized as *introjection*. (p. 724)

According to Rapaport, final integration of these parent introjects into the personality can take two directions: one in which the more positive traits of the parents become integrated into the ego and contribute to ego strength, and another one where "the individual [is able] to *see himself with the eyes of others*" (italics added) (p. 725). According to this psychoanalytic view, the observing superego or ego-ideal becomes the repository of the judgmental, defensive, and sometimes hostile facets of the parent's personality.[1] Thus, the process of introjection, so necessary for higher-level learning, is also responsible for the inclusion of a systematized "parental" point of view within the self. This introjected view militates against the individual's unique personal aspirations as well as opposing drives or motivations to fulfill basic wants and needs.

The relationship of the introjected object to other structures of the personality has long been the subject of controversy in psychoanalytic circles. Some theorists have proposed that these introjects are precursors of the superego[2], while others see them as evolving into the punitive part of a split-ego, e.g., the "antilibidinal ego" (Guntrip, 1969).

Guntrip interprets the views of Fairbairn in relation to the destructive forces within the developing personality as follows:

> We view the libidinal ego as in bondage to guilt or fear, that is imposed by an *antilibidinal ego* [italics added] which in part represents the frightening or accusing parents who have themselves disturbed the child. (p. 202)
>
> *We must regard the hard core of personality 'illness' as this persisting structuralized version of intolerance and rejection, through fear and later guilt, of the originally disturbed child, now existing as the deepest repressed immature level of the personality.* (p. 190)

Guntrip links the punishing ego-function to depression and suicidal behavior:

> In depressed and obsessional persons the central ego [conscious, coping ego] may be all but captured by the antilibidinal ego. (p. 189)
>
> The degree of self-hate and self-persecution going on in the unconscious determines the degree of the illness, and in severe cases the person can become hopeless, panic-stricken, and be driven to suicide as a way out. (p. 190)

We tend to agree substantially with this latter position and contend that the emotionally charged negative traits, attitudes, and thoughts, incorporated from the parents, are never fully integrated into the ego; instead, they act to divide the self and form the basis of the voice process in the developing personality. It is important to remember that negative parental views are transmitted to the child primarily on an unconscious level. Later, the child takes on the destructive viewpoint toward himself without recognizing that it is *not* his own point of view.

It is more important to recognize the extensive effects of the process of introjection and the associated hostility toward the self than to hypothesize about or categorize the structures involved. Essentially, the more an individual sees himself through the eyes of a parent who had overt or covert hostility toward him, the more he will be predisposed to self-destructive thoughts and behavior.

Our clinical material supports the hypothesis that the voice represents the introjection of an imposed set of thought patterns and attitudes and is based on the powerful *negative identification* with one's parents. Resistance to changing negative self-evaluations that have become a basic part of our identity stems from the deep fear, even terror, of disrupting this form of internal security. Many patients, for example, reported having the illusion of feeling parented in listening to the voice. The harangue, however unpleasant or negative, gives them a feeling of security. Separation from the internalized parent or voice through identifying self-attacks temporarily leaves people feeling empty and alone and is analogous to separation from the actual parents. It disrupts the fantasized connection with the family and precipitates anxiety states that must be carefully worked through in the course of psychotherapy.

THE RELATIONSHIP BETWEEN THE VOICE PROCESS, MELANCHOLIA, AND SUICIDE

The mystery surrounding the ultimate form of self-destruction has long occupied the minds of theologians and men of science. Seventy-five years ago, Sigmund Freud (Nunberg & Federn, 1967) commented on the puzzling phenomenon of suicide at a 1910 meeting of the Vienna Psychoanalytic Society, which was devoted to a discussion of childhood suicide:

> The approach to the complex [problem] of suicide from a study of the ill lies in *melancholia,* and at the moment nothing is known about its nature; its mechanism, especially, has not been studied at all. (p. 505)

Later, in writing more definitively about the dynamics of melancholia, Freud (1921/1955) stated:

> A leading characteristic of these cases [of melancholia] is a cruel self-depreciation of the ego combined with relentless self-criticism and bitter self-reproaches. (p. 109)

Freud's statement hints at certain clues to the dynamics of depression which later psychoanalysts were to follow in their ongoing search for answers to the suicide problem. However, despite concentrated efforts by these clinicians to pinpoint causative factors, the mystery of suicide has continued to perplex us.

A number of suicidologists, in examining the "mechanics of melancholia" referred to by Freud, have come across signs that, if properly investigated and understood, could significantly advance our knowledge of suicide and self-destructive behavior. For example, in the final chapter of *Definition of Suicide,* Edwin Shneidman (1985) comments briefly on two themes that, while not necessarily characteristic of all suicidal episodes, are found in *most of them:*

[1] A common psychodynamic thread—probably ubiquitous in cases in which a parent of the suicidal person has committed suicide—is the problem of *negative identification*. Negative identification has to do with the powerful unconscious emulation, patterning, modeling or copying of "negative" or generally undesirable traits or features in the person who is being copied. (p. 237)

[2] If there are common psychodynamic themes in suicide, they probably relate to omnipotence and loss. . . . At the moment of committing suicide, the individual may feel he controls the world—and by his death can bring it down. At least he controls his own destiny. (p. 237-238)

*   *   *

In our work, the importance of these two themes in the development of suicidal ideation, depression, and self-destructive behavior will become apparent. The first theme, "negative identification," relates to the psychological process of introjection.

The second theme, the illusion of having control over life and death, represents a powerful defense against death anxiety. This defense manifests itself not only in overt suicide, but in many forms of partial or *micro*-suicide.

The dynamics underlying human self-destructive behavior are not instinctual. However, faced with an awareness of their mortality, people may choose to turn against life and against themselves in order to gain an illusion of mastery over death. Through a process of progressive self-denial, they tend to deny themselves experiences that would enhance life and give it value. The prospect of losing one's life and losing all consciousness through death can be so unbearable that the process of giving up provides some relief from the anguish.

Otto Rank (1936/1972) was well aware of this process and wrote extensively about it:

The freeing of instinct from repressions causes fear because life and experience increase the fear of death. (p. 133)

[Man] seeks in his own way to buy himself free from his guilt. He does this through a constant restriction of life (restraint through fear); that is, he refuses the loan (life) in order thus to escape the payment of the debt (death). (p. 126)

Both themes, "negative identification" and the illusion of omnipotent control, are closely linked to the voice process elaborated in our work. To relieve fear of separation and abandonment, the infant forms an imaginary connection—a fantasy bond[3]—with the mother[4] and, in the process, incorporates the image of the mother into itself. The infant or young child develops the illusion of being at one with the mother, and at the same time, takes on her fears, anxieties, and defenses as his own. In other words, the child not only identifies with the positive characteristics of the parental figure; he also identifies with the parent's defense system and his *negative* traits. This process of incorporating rejecting parental attitudes toward the self occurs to varying degrees in every individual. The extent to which the imposed point of view becomes pathological depends partially upon the degree of deprivation and separation trauma experienced by the child.

Illusions of omnipotence are also prominent in childhood and come into play later as the child attempts to relieve anxiety states aroused by his growing awareness of the concept of death, the ultimate separation. Furthermore, the child's defenses against emotional deprivation and rejection, including loss of feeling, addiction to internal sources of gratification, and the incorporated negative point of view, are now applied to death anxiety and are actually reinforced and strengthened by this new consciousness of mortality.

These defensive processes, i.e., negative identification and illusions of omnipotence, are interrelated in the sense that both protect the child against anxiety and pain early in life but later on severely restrict his adult life. In extreme cases, these defenses can kill. They kill by destroying an individual's natural wants and aspirations through the gradual ascendancy of the imposed, alien point of view described above. The absence of desire, interest, or motivation to pursue desired goals can make the alternative of suicide appear to be the *only* solution to someone who is profoundly upset and in emotional pain.

Consider, for example, the thought process this teenage girl [quoted by Breskin (1984)] revealed after twice attempting suicide:

"It was a black cloud of depression. It envelops you. You cannot get out. You don't think life will ever get better. You can't conceive of it. You can't imagine it. . . .

"And you're gonna die anyway; life's this long corridor with all these doors, and death is the last one, so why not now? It's so painful to live that it seems less painful to die.

"I felt great satisfaction. I felt great calmness. It was real decisive. I was finally taking fate in my own hands. I had some control. As opposed to being a victim." (p. 78)

This teenager's motives for attempting suicide illustrate the themes just described: first, a destructive point of view consisting of hopelessness, self-hatred, and cynicism about the world, as well as an absence of goals, other than the desperate desire to escape unbearable emotional pain; and secondly, an illusion of omnipotent control brought about by the decision to end her life.

What is *missing* from this girl's account is an awareness that her depression, as well as the actions she took to try to escape the pain of this depressed state, were being constantly regulated, influenced, and controlled by an alien point of view, imposed originally from without, yet existing now within her own mind—a systematized thought process, bent on destroying her. More significant is the fact that a relationship exists between this hostile, subliminal thought process and actual suicide. Furthermore, to varying degrees, the incorporation of a covertly rejecting parental point of view has a profound negative effect on *every* individual in terms of his or her overall adjustment. Unfortunately, most people are largely unaware of being so divided or set against themselves. They remain only partially conscious of the fact that they possess a hostile, self-denying, and self-attacking point of view and therefore continue to be restricted and controlled by early influences.

NOTES

[1]Rapaport contends that this "observing" or "self-reflective" part of the personality can later become distorted or disturbed:

Introjection and identification thus enable us to take over, as our own, the feelings and reactions of other people, and later their thoughts also—both *those directed specifically towards us* [italics added] and those more general. (p. 725)

[This] reflective self-awareness . . . may become charged with drive-cathexes (libidinized) and thus take on the aspect of symptom: pathological generalizing on the one hand, and pathologically distorted or exaggerated reflectiveness on the other, arise. (p. 707)

²See Samuel Novey's (1955) paper, *The Role of the Superego and Ego Ideal in Character Formation* and Drew Westen's (1986) paper, *The Superego: A Revised Developmental Model.*

³Fantasy Bond—defined in the author's writing as an *imaginary connection,* originally formed between the infant or young child and his or her mother to compensate for emotional deprivation in the early environment. It should be distinguished from the concept of bond or bonding as used in the positive sense, as in maternal-infant bonding.

⁴The term "mother" is used here to connote the primary caretaker, female or male.

5

Origins of the Voice

The voice originates in the abuses of childhood. From the diverse, albeit interrelated, discoveries documented in the preceding chapters, we concluded that the voice represents the introjection of an attacking, condescending, parenting process, acquired in the social matrix of the family. The authors believe that the voice is the intrapsychic mechanism primarily responsible for the transmission of negative parental traits, behaviors, and defense patterns from one generation to the next. Its function in perpetuating mental illness, self-destructiveness, and child abuse through succeeding generations may be as significant to human development as the transmission of the parents' physical characteristics by the DNA molecules carried in the genes.

THE VOICE AND CHILD ABUSE, A CYCLICAL PROCESS

The child who is harmed physically, denigrated emotionally, or seriously neglected, does not know how to love or to care, and grows up with a poor self-image and a mistrust of others. . . . [For example,] this young woman will no more be capable of proper child rearing than her mother was. . . . [She] identifies her child with herself. . . . Thus, she externalizes and projects her hostility onto her child.

Marvin Blumberg (1980, p. 353)

Damaging effects of the introjected parent are evident in the high incidence of child abuse in our society. Indeed, no subject is of greater importance or concern than this destruction of children. The repetition of child abuse, both physical and mental, through successive generations, occurs despite parents' best intentions and resolutions.

Physical child abuse resulting in actual harm to the infant's or child's body has been found by some researchers to be the culmination of a compelling drive to act out internalized rage assimilated by the parent during his or her own childhood. If this internalized anger is not uncovered in "depth" psychotherapy, repeated incidents of physical child abuse are inevitable. The author hypothesizes that the determining factors in child abuse are: (1) the traumatic experiences in childhood suffered by the child abuser; (2) the repression of these painful events that serves as a defense mechanism to preserve and maintain the idealized image of the child abuser's parents; (3) the introjected parental hostility that underlies the system of negative thoughts and self-attacks that we term the "voice"; and (4) the compulsive acting out of this self-hatred on the abuser's children.

In the years following Henry Kempe's (Kempe, Silverman, Steele, Droegemueller, & Silver, 1962) essay on the "battered-child" syndrome, the problem of physical child abuse has been the focus of national attention and public concern. *Any* incident where force is utilized by a more powerful adult against a vulnerable child, whether it be physical abuse or sexual exploitation, constitutes a reprehensible violation of another person. Although physical and sexual abuse are tragic events that are obviously traumatic to children in their development, these acts are statistically less frequent than the abuse of the child's spirit through psychological and emotional trauma. Extreme cases of physical and sexual abuse probably occur more often than most people think,[1] yet focusing on these blatant expressions of parental mistreatment can obscure the more prevalent and less well-defined incidents of emotional violence perpetrated on children.

The problem of emotional abuse of children is of serious proportions. It is widespread in the population and not restricted to socially deprived or maladaptive families.[2] Unfortunately, it exists in a large majority of "normal" family constellations.

We can define *emotional child abuse* as those parental thoughts, feelings, attitudes, and behaviors, antithetical to the child's emerging self, that either exist covertly or are acted out overtly in parent-child interactions.[3]

The role of the voice in perpetuating the cycle of psychological or emotional child abuse is apparent. To whatever degree individuals have introjected their parents' hostile and punitive attitudes toward themselves, they will continue to hate and punish themselves and eventually their own children. The angry affect associated with the voice provides the powerful impetus behind a person's unconscious compulsion to act out destructive feelings on his or her children. In general, parents repeat the specific forms of emotional abuse inflicted on *them* as children.

The author believes that the problem of emotional and mental abuse has not been stressed sufficiently by most professionals. There have been some notable exceptions; primarily Alice Miller and John Bowlby, among others. In her book, *Thou Shalt Not Be Aware,* Alice Miller (1981/1984) has repeatedly emphasized the importance of recognizing the emotional damage sustained by children in their psychological development.

It is important to point out that guilt or blame for the trauma of childhood cannot be assigned to one person or group of persons: parents were once the abused children about whom we are writing. The fault or blame lies in the fact that, under normal circumstances, the rage and hostile thoughts underlying rejecting or abusive child-rearing practices are generally inaccessible, thereby guaranteeing their compulsive repetition. Furthermore, because of the tremendous guilt parents feel about their angry or sadistic *feelings* toward their children, there is extreme defensiveness and dishonesty within the family. Parents are obviously very reluctant to expose these unacceptable feelings. Therefore, much of this material remains repressed, and episodes where these angry feelings or hostile attitudes are acted out are quickly relegated to the unconscious mind.

The problem of emotional child abuse is also complicated by the fact that many of our traditional child-rearing practices tend to support attitudes toward children that perpetuate this damage. For example, many books on child-rearing advise parents to "act" or "talk" with their children by playing out roles that are not representative of the parent's genuine feeling at any given moment. Also, these books suggest that parents act in ways to deceive the child through manipulative strategies. They encourage role-determined behavior and communication, which contribute to duplicity and distrust among family members.

REPRESSION AND THE INTROJECTION OF PARENTAL ATTITUDES

In the course of rigorously examining manifestations of the voice process, we discovered that the effects of painful traumatic experiences in childhood are incorporated in the form of hostile thoughts and attitudes toward ourselves. Perhaps the most tragic consequence of our identifying with the parental aggressor is our propensity to later unconsciously reenact these painful experiences with our own offspring.

Obviously, parents vary in their responses to their children. However, children selectively attend to those qualities in their parents that are the most malignant and punitive because these are so hurtful. As described earlier, children introject these negative traits in an effort to allay their intense anxiety when they are under unusual stress. Subsequently, they no longer identify with the child in themselves but with the powerful parent *hating the weak child, especially the child in pain.*

The persistence with which this introjected negative caricature of the parent endures over time, on an unconscious level, and is used to punish oneself and others is a remarkable psychological phenomenon. As previously noted, Bettelheim's (1943/1979) concept of "identification with the aggressor" has important implications for understanding the origins of the voice process.

> Often the SS would enforce nonsensical rules, originating in the whims of one of the guards. . . . There were always some old prisoners who would *continue to follow the rules and try to enforce them on others long after the gestapo had forgotten about them* [italics added]. Once, for instance, a guard inspecting the prisoners' apparel found that the shoes of some of them were dirty on the inside He ordered all prisoners to wash their shoes inside and out with water and soap. The heavy shoes, when treated this way, became hard as stone. The order was never repeated. . . . Nevertheless there were some old prisoners who not only continued to wash the inside of their shoes every day but *cursed all others who did not do so as negligent and dirty* [italics added]. (p. 80-81)

Similarly, many parents tend to forget or repress painful attitudes and restrictions imposed on their children, yet children are left with vestiges of their parents' anger and vindictiveness, often revolving around the enforcement of unnecessary rules. The internalized rage and hostility is indelibly imprinted on the child's psyche, to be unleashed later on his or her children.

All children suffer trauma and rejection to some degree in their developing years and incorporate a self-hating process in the form of a voice or internal dialogue. In our work with patients in a Feeling Release Therapy, we documented considerable clinical material supporting this thesis. Later in our study, we observed that there was a correlation between repressed childhood experiences and specific negative thoughts, attitudes, and "voices" that later predominate in the adult's inner world.

THE UNIVERSALITY OF CHILDHOOD TRAUMA

Evidence From Feeling Release Therapy

My associates and I had the opportunity, over a 5-year period, from 1971 to 1976, to work with approximately 200 patients, volunteers, and associates utilizing the techniques of a Feeling Release Therapy.[4] At critical times in therapy when patients were close to important feelings, our method was to ask them to breathe deeply and make loud sounds on the expulsion of breath. Utilizing these techniques, we found that a large majority of our patients expressed intense feelings of pain, rage, and sadness that reawakened emotional events from their childhood. After these acutely painful episodes, the patients generally experienced a flood of powerful insights and were able to integrate their new awareness. The meaning of their present-day neurotic symptoms and behaviors was apparent to our patients without therapeutic intervention or interpretation. Our methodology was similar in many respects to those of Arthur Janov's (1970) technique as reported in *The Primal Scream,* and the phenomena were much as he described them.

In analyzing our results, we found that, with rare exceptions, every subject indicated a considerable amount of deep-seated pain and sadness that he was continually suppressing. They were largely unaware of these underlying feelings in their everyday lives. It appeared that virtually no one had escaped childhood without being scarred to some extent in early family interactions. We concluded, along with Janov, that most people maintain a defensive posture and arrange their lives in order to protect against ever having to feel their pain or become aware of it. Yet this pain affected all of their interpersonal responses, shaped their lives, and controlled their destiny.

Many interesting findings relevant to child development were revealed by parents in our sample. A number of patients reported that they averted these painful "primal" emotions by remaining distant and unconsciously avoiding genuine contact on a feeling level with their offspring. They recognized that especially close personal interactions tended to reawaken repressed feelings of sadness and pain. Many patients who participated in this Feeling Release Therapy found themselves relating on a deeper, more personal level with their offspring after moving experiences in their sessions. Regaining their own feelings led to more compassionate responses in general.

In working with people who were involved in this innovative therapy, my associates and I became acquainted with important facets of each person's inner life and personal history. In our work, we didn't ask or directly encourage people to relive their childhood experiences; rather, these experiences emerged from the release of feeling and from the physical expression of sadness and anger. In other words, there were no instructions to patients to regress or to attempt to remember these early experiences. If one can generalize from our sample, it appears that human beings retain these traumatic incidents together with associated negative voices based on their early lives. They retain these experiences in the form of memories that become conscious when there is a strong emotional release.

A Case Study—Carol

A mother of three children, Carol had tended to live her life through her husband's accomplishments. She hoped to gain a greater sense of self and to become more independent in her relationship with her husband through participating in Feeling Release Therapy. Although she tended to be somewhat unspontaneous in her emotional responses, her basic personality was intact with no symptoms of serious psychological disturbance. Carol recorded her impressions in a journal immediately following each session, providing a vivid portrayal of the personal interactions in her family that had caused her distress. One of her first sessions revolved around a strong sense of feeling rejected and being treated as an "object" by her parents.

> I could see from the start of the session that I was in a crib and that I was a baby. I yelled and screamed to get attention. I *really felt* like a baby. I wanted someone to come and pick me up.
> Suddenly I realized there were many people standing around my crib staring at me. I didn't like that, and I screamed at them. Then I saw that my mother and father were standing in the circle around me. They were showing off their baby to friends. They didn't pick me up, just obseved me. They never ever touched me (that was the feeling). I cried a lot. No one ever loved me. Now I feel that I have to do and say the right thing to be loved. I watch carefully what I say, so it comes out flat. Also, I worry a lot about how I look.

In another session, Carol realized that by denying her parents' limitations, she blamed herself for their rejection of her and came to see herself as bad. She connected her present emotional blandness and subservient posture to strong memories of her mother's effort to smother or stifle her exuberance and "loudness." Later in the same session, she recalled that she had been unable to relate easily to her own children, but was constantly tense and on guard lest they disturb the peaceful atmosphere in her home.

> I remember having difficulty breathing, and I could not talk. I felt that my mother was telling me that nice girls don't act that way, that I should be quiet and not say anything, not bother her.
>
> I saw myself as a little girl, standing looking down at the ground, looking defeated and pathetic, wearing a dress too long, with long stringy hair. I attacked myself for being a coward, for not looking at them, for not standing up to them—I hated her for being a coward, for condemning me to being a coward.
>
> I remembered some things that made me feel very ashamed. I remembered holding my baby and feeling anxious. I was ashamed at feeling anxious, afraid that the baby might have felt my anxiety. I felt like a bad mother. I wondered if that feeling of anxiety had been passed to me by my mother.

These excerpts indicated that the patient had introjected her mother's view of her as being a burden. She hated herself for being cowardly in trying to get love by selling out on her own point of view and continually deferring to the wishes of others. Another pattern of self-critical thoughts centered on her perceived inadequacies as a mother. She felt anxious, guilty, and self-hating for holding back affection from her own children and for condemning their expressions of spontaneity, much as her own mother had done to her.

The case cited above is representative of many others that were documented during our ongoing work using the methods of Feeling Release Therapy. We found no major qualitative differences between our patient population and a group of professional associates and volunteers with respect to their painful emotions and the reliving of childhood trauma during the sessions. In other words, there were not two categories of people,

neurotic and normal, those with pain and those without it—
everyone in our sample population possessed repressed pain, and
everybody's life was directed toward the avoidance of it.

MANIFESTATIONS OF CHILD ABUSE PERPETUATED BY THE VOICE

> I consider many adults (including myself) are or have been, more
> or less, in a hypnotic trance, induced in early infancy: we remain
> in this state until—when we dead awaken, as Ibsen makes one of
> his characters say—we shall find that we have never lived.
>
> R.D. Laing (1969/1972, p. 82)

The dynamics underlying more subtle and indirect forms of
child abuse can best be understood by summarizing the cycle that
perpetuates the damage. As we have demonstrated, all children,
to some extent, suffer trauma and rejection in the developmental
process. They introject an internal parent represented by a destructive self-critical thought process or negative voice that can
be uncovered through the laboratory procedures of "Voice
Therapy." They carry this abusive voice with them through life,
restricting, limiting, and punishing themselves, and eventually
acting out similar abuses on their offspring. These, in turn, are
internalized as punitive, self-critical voices by their children, thus
completing the cycle.

In analyzing case material relevant to this process, we will
discuss the specific self-attacks associated with trauma reported
by individuals participating in Voice Therapy sessions. This data
was made available primarily by volunteers. They were not patients at the time of these studies, nor could they be considered
to be child abusers in any sense by generally accepted definitions
of the term. To the contrary, they were average parents with a
special concern for their children's well-being.

In these cases, we will be describing people's recollections
of the hurtful treatment they received as children, as well as the
hostile parental attitudes and feelings they incorporated under
adverse conditions. We will show how these internalized self-at-

tacks were acted out later in abrasive and insensitive interactions with *their* offspring. Before describing this clinical material, it would be valuable to elaborate incidents of psychological child abuse revealed by these individuals.

Patterns of Emotional Child Abuse

Parental behaviors that incidentally stifle the child's spirit are assumed by many people, lay and professional, to be an inherent part of traditional or "normal" child-rearing practices. This assumption itself is indicative of a prevalent stereotypic view in our society of both children and parents. The fact is that when parents base their interactions with children on the hostile attitudes of their voice, they necessarily behave in ways that are detrimental to the emotional well-being of their children; however, they are generally unaware of the profound suffering they are causing. Indeed, the parents' voice attacks are externalized and are directed toward anyone who would be vulnerable to them, toward anyone who would *need* them, or toward anyone who would value them. Because the voice is an incorporated attack on oneself, it is an attack also on one's interests, one's close associates, and particularly one's offspring.

The function served by the family in conventional society is that of protecting the physical lives of children and nurturing their bodies, while at the same time unintentionally stripping their minds of dignity and attempting to deaden all but socially role-determined feelings. Children are taught to adopt the defenses of the parents in order to continue to protect the parents from unwanted stimulation of repressed primal feelings. They must continue to soothe and safeguard the parents throughout their relationship with them lest they disturb their parents' defenses.

Parents suppress and deride the feelings of their children in a wide variety of ways—varying from their insistence on false cheerfulness or stoicism to the somewhat sadistic teasing of their children in sensitive areas. Often they ridicule the children's enthusiasm and excitement about life, thereby damaging their spontaneity. Furthermore, they condescendingly view children's activities and interests as immature and unimportant. As an example, parents often tease young people about their close attachments, labeling them "puppy love." Many times they categorize and pigeonhole their children, defining them and establishing a rigid conception of their identity.

Children are often addressed in phony, syrupy voices, for example, in a tone of voice used by many schoolteachers with young children and by many nurses with their patients—a voice loaded with condescension and cut off from real feeling. Patronizing, belittling attitudes toward the child lead to voices that run down the individual: "Who do you think you are, anyway?" "Who wants to hear your opinion?"

Parents have a tendency to violate boundaries between themselves and their children, speaking for them, intrusively touching them and fussing with their clothes, etc. Their overzealous attempts to control bodily functions as well as emotional expressions tend to drive their children toward secrecy and an isolated, inward existence.

Parents believe, on a deep level, that their children belong exclusively to them. Many take an overbearing, proprietary interest in their offspring, whom they treat as their possessions. This sense of being owned by the parent virtually destroys a child's sense of self. Later the child feels guilty about choosing his own point of view and remaining self-directed or inner-directed.

Parents communicate with their children through a web of confusing mixed messages. Their verbal statements contradict their actions to a considerable degree. As studies have shown, double messages in seriously disturbed families destroy the child's sense of reality and, over an extended period of time, can lead to severe mental illness (Bateson, Jackson, Haley, & Weakland, 1956). Mixed messages and lies about life make one distrustful, as conveyed by voices:

> You can't trust anybody. People don't mean what they say. You can't afford to be vulnerable. Why take a chance on getting hurt again?

Threats of abandonment, loss of love, and other dire consequences for so-called "bad" behavior are the daily fare of many children. Serious depressive states have been attributed by many researchers to this form of emotional blackmail.

To compensate for withholding loving responses or a lack of love and concern, parents build up their children, exaggerate their importance, and feed off their accomplishments. They teach their children to rely on strokes of their vanity; consequently, children learn to seek out special treatment and dishonest buildup in preference to real acknowledgment and positive regard. In addition, many parents also build *themselves* up in the child's eyes by demanding unearned respect and hero worship.

Parents make their children feel ashamed of their bodies and natural functions to varying degrees through perpetrating distorted views of sexuality learned in their own families. Punitive or unaccepting attitudes toward the body or bodily functions lead to insecurity and distort a person's body image and overall sexuality. Voice attacks accusing oneself of being unattractive and unlovable or associating one's sexual feelings with bodily functions of elimination emanate from the same source. They lead to abnormal guilt reactions about sex and a "dirty" view of sexuality.

Many of our subjects revealed that they were misled about important issues such as birth, death, illness, sex, and that their views of other people were often distorted by paranoid or distrusting parents. Some were neglected, and others were forced to conform to many unnecessary rules and rigid standards of behavior. They were taught that what neighbors and relatives thought about them was more important than what they themselves as children, felt or thought. Many learned that one's image was more important than actual traits and characteristics, indeed, that impressions were more important than real issues of character.

Some individuals were so overprotected as children that they became abnormally fearful and had difficulty functioning as adults in many areas of their everyday lives. Others had been humiliated and degraded whenever they openly expressed their wants and desires to their parents. It appeared that many parents were afraid of "spoiling" their children by giving them what they asked for. Parents often had rationalized their withholding responses by insisting that they were preparing their children for living in the harsh, "real" world. Many subjects were the object of a parental paranoia that perceived the child as out to exploit them or take advantage.

Many children are treated impatiently and insensitively by parents who are intent on fitting them into a formal, socially approved style of relating. They are lectured and verbally abused by parents who feel that they are within their rights because they, as parents, are older and wiser. Later, these children tended to listen to a voice that told them: "You'd better fit in—you'd better not get out of line."

Many parents avoid relating to their children with genuine feelings; rather, they tend to act out behavior that they consider a mother and father is supposed to feel. They replace honesty and spontaneous expression with socially designated feelings and responses.

Parents who had grown up with a negative self-image covertly rejected their own children. Unable to care about themselves, possessing a negative view of their own bodies, and ashamed of their productions, they were incapable of loving or being tender to their children. In fact, they were more likely to project their negative self-image onto their children and punish them.

Several volunteers recounted incidents where they despaired of ever being able to please their parents or earn their approval. If they tried to improve their grades, for example, and brought home a good report card, their parents would point out the one "B," saying: "Why isn't that an 'A'?" These individuals were plagued by a voice that reminded them that no matter what they accomplished in life, it was never enough. They had introjected parental attitudes that caused them to be dissatisfied with life and could not take pleasure or joy in their achievements.

The destruction of the child's spirit is further augmented by certain religious ideologies that impose unnecessary limitations on many aspects of human fulfillment. The concept of "original sin" has been interpreted by clergy and laity alike to mean that people are born bad. This implied condition of innate evil or "badness" is accepted by children when they incorporate their parents' negative attitudes toward them. This form of thinking interprets original sin in terms of man's corrupt physical nature. This particular viewpoint degrades human sexuality and sees the naked body as sinful and dirty.

> This mistaken notion supports feelings of shame [about the body] that originate in the child's earliest experiences of the family. . . . Abnormal guilt reactions introjected by the child from defended parents [and supported by the concept of "original sin"] lead to serious limitations in adult relationships. (Firestone, 1985, p. 234–235)

A more secular interpretation of the concept of "original sin" is the "bad seed" conceptualization of the child. This view not only labels the child as inherently "bad," but goes on to judge him as irredeemably evil and corrupt. For example, in their book, *Crime and Human Nature,* Wilson and Herrnstein (1985), although stating that "criminal behavior, like all human behavior, results from a complex interaction of genetic and environmental factors," stress that "individuals *differ at birth* [italics added] to the degree to which they are at risk for criminality." They believe that "there is *some* psychological trait, having a biological origin, that predisposes an individual to criminality" (p. 70).

Case Studies

The following clinical findings illustrate several forms of emotional child abuse and the kinds of self-attacks emanating from the original trauma. The material is excerpted from videotaped Voice Therapy sessions[5] that took place in a group setting. A few cases will suffice to underscore the relationship between the voice and repetitive incidents of damage to children.

Wally, a forty-nine-year-old systems engineer, was raised by a rigid father with perfectionist standards—a man who valued scholarly achievement and athletic prowess above other ideals. In this particular session, Wally explores the reasons that he could not feel empathy or compassion toward a close friend, Dick, who had just expressed some painful feelings. As he talks, Wally also refers to his son, Danny, fifteen.

Tonight I noticed that I had a couple of voices. One of them was, Dick, when you were talking. I couldn't feel for you. And I tried to figure out why. And then I realized that I have a voice that says: "Don't you cry.

Boy, don't you cry!

I'll give you something to cry about! (angrily stated)

You're going to cry?

Yeah, well, I'll give you something to *really* cry about!"

It's like: "You're not supposed to cry." And I think it has something to do with another voice I hear:

"Get that smile on your face, goddammit!

Don't you look that way.

You'd better smile, buddy!"

But underneath that voice I think—and it's not even a voice— I just think, "I can't do anything. I can't help you." It's very painful. "I can't make you feel better."

I would feel it with Danny when he would cry, I would want him *to stop*. (spoken in an angry tone) It would be like a fury. But the real pain is that I have to turn away from your pain. I have to turn away from you crying. I can't help you.

I don't even know where it comes from. It's like a strong determination, "I'm *not* going to help you."

My father never helped me in anything, any battles I had with life or anything. He would just turn away.

I had another voice that said "You're not talking clear. You'd better talk right! If you don't talk right, just shut up. Don't say a goddamn thing!" or it says, "You'd better talk *better* next time."

There's a lot of pressure that I put on myself. *It all comes down to this fury that I feel against myself. Strong anger—and I feel it against my son.* (sad) I don't want to. . . .

Wally's son, Danny, had introjected the same demanding, perfectionist voice that plagued his father. He was hypersensitive to criticism and found it very difficult to take suggestions. He tended to overreact angrily and defensively to relatively minor events that might detract from a macho or masculine view of himself. In a family session, Danny spoke of this internalized anger:

> When I feel criticized, I attack people savagely in my mind. Really angry. It's different with each person. I have the goods on everybody. I know their worst qualities, and I think they're totally that way. But the whole time I'm also attacking myself. If I'm playing some kind of sport, I tell myself: "If you don't beat him, you're a jerk."

Susan, a thirty-seven-year-old psychotherapist, had grown up in a home where the family members rarely communicated with each other. Susan's mother had been extremely overprotective and intrusive on one level, yet on a deeper level, she had a great deal of unconscious hostility toward Susan which manifested itself in her impatience and occasional outbursts of temper. In describing her self-depreciating thoughts during one group session, Susan said:

> I have such a mean attitude toward myself. I have a voice that says: "Don't you have anything better to do than to sit around talking about your feelings? Who cares about how you feel, anyway? It doesn't matter how you feel."
> I could just feel it grinding in me, like someone was taking a stake and grinding it in me.
> "Who cares what you feel?
> You don't matter.
> There's other more important things.
> I don't care what you feel.
> Keep it to yourself!"
> It's really sarcastic. I know that that sarcasm comes out in me towards other people. *I know that I'm so intolerant or impatient with kids and what they feel.* This is where it comes from. There was no tolerance for my feelings or no importance on them in my family.

In both cases, the subjects' voices appeared to be associated with specific forms of maltreatment that they had received

4/5/88

as children. For example, Susan's parents showed no tolerance for or interest in her feelings or her emotional state. Today, she has a voice telling her that her feelings don't matter; and in turn, she is impatient with her own children when they try to express *their* feelings.

A number of participants attacked themselves for feeling unduly enthusiastic and optimistic. They traced these voices back to parental sarcasm and ridicule. One woman recalled her parents teasing her for being shy. Later she reported hearing a voice that she used to stifle her excitement whenever she stepped out of the role of being the "quiet, reserved" one in her family:

> It's embarrassing, but I remembered when I was a little girl, and when I felt bad, my parents used to make fun of me, because I would always pull my dress over my head. If I get my feelings hurt today, I'll slip into almost that same feeling of wanting to cover myself. I'll disappear—I just won't want to see anyone.
>
> Recently I've been very excited about using this therapy to develop myself further, but then I had a voice like:
>
> "This is so stupid. What if you had a real problem? What's this silly problem of letting your friends like you? What a stupid thing to waste your time on! What if you had other *real* problems?"
>
> I could feel myself sink, almost feeling foolish for being excited or foolish for wanting more, personally, in my life.

In one session, a thirty-two-year-old father of two young children faced the painful realization that he had projected his own feelings of self-loathing onto his children. The man had been raised in a household where family life had been chaotic and dominated by repeated scenes of spouse abuse. The man had grown up ashamed of his family background and of himself. In the following segment, he becomes aware that he has passed on this low opinion of himself to his children, much to the detriment of their own feelings of self-worth:

> The attack that I hear is that I'm not friendly:
>
> "You're just a quiet creep; you drive people crazy. You're second-class. You're just worthless. You should really try to hide it.

You should just be quiet and stay in the background because when people get to know you, they'll know that you're just a shit person. *And your kids are shit, everything about you . . ."*

So if anybody says anything about my children, I put it in the same attack:

"See, you're shit, your family's shit. You're just like us. What makes you think you're different from your family? You're just a crazy, scummy person."

In some terrible way—(cries deeply)—it totally changes the way I feel. I feel like I can't look people in the face, and it feels like if I could just hide, just create a demeanor that hides this.

I really started feeling a lot when I thought about my children, that they get woven into it in that sense. I strongly felt that I didn't want them to have this feeling. The way I believe this voice about myself and the way I live my life has given that to them in many ways. I felt so bad when I put words to that feeling—that they were shit because I was shit.

CIRCUMSTANCES THAT PROVOKE PARENTAL RAGE

Mom: He'd come to the table like any typical kid and he'd
           spill his milk. Well, I'd take him and hit him about ten
           or fifteen times.
[Another
Mom]:   And it's senseless. When you've abused a kid it's like
           extended self-destruction. Get that rottenness in me.
           60 Minutes: "Mommy, Why Me?"
                   (O'Brien, Schneider & Traviesas, p. 234–235)

The author, conducting in-depth interviews and group discussions with parents where a high level of rapport was established, found that many parents told about hidden thoughts and desires to get rid of their children. Others revealed sadistic feelings toward them that they were afraid they might act upon. Several admitted impulses to "throw the child off a balcony," "strangle it when it kept on crying," or other thoughts of physically harming their children. In the majority of instances, these were only passing thoughts that frightened the parents, but it is reasonable to assume that in extreme cases where these feelings are more intense, they lead to actual physical child abuse.

Other clinicians have reported similar parental responses, among them John Bowlby and Joseph C. Rheingold. In *Separation: Anger and Anxiety,* Bowlby (1973) quotes a personal communication from a colleague (Robert Weiss) stating that a large proportion of mothers raising children "without a partner to help them . . . admit that, at times when they are more than usually anxious or depressed, they entertain ideas of getting rid of their children" (p. 280).

In *The Mother, Anxiety, and Death,* Rheingold (1967) asserts that in postpartum emotional disturbances, indeed:

> In all the postpartum mental complications—confusional states, anxiety, depression, schizophrenia—the wish, the impulse, the obsession, or the feeling of being under compulsion to destroy the child is at the core of the illness. (p. 127)
>
> Many women hate the unborn baby because they feel it has maliciously trapped them in an insufferable situation. Such feeling is frequently dissembled, but it is also expressed frankly and vindictively—to other women, not men, except to a sympathetic physician. (p. 127)

There are a number of typical circumstances that tend to provoke parental hostility and catalyze abusive responses. For example, several parents revealed that they were profoundly disturbed by their infant's prolonged crying and that they sometimes had urges to smother their baby with a blanket or pillow at these times. The wants and needs of their infants were often perceived by these parents as demands or unwanted intrusions into their lives. To illustrate, in one parents' group, a mother of two children described intense feelings of anger that she had attempted to suppress following the birth of each of her children. In this excerpt, she reveals a degrading, derisive voice she sensed on these occasions:

> When I had children, I made all sorts of vows that I was going to give the child the things that I felt were lacking in my childhood. When my first baby was born, I felt the same rage toward

him that I had felt directed toward me, and I was terrified and confused by that feeling.

He had colic, and around 5 o'clock in the afternoon, he would just start crying and crying, and I would just feel like I would want to drown him, or I would want to just choke him, or I'd want to put a pillow over his head or just something to stop him from crying.

If he wanted to be fed, that would bring up a rage in me. Any need that he had, any time he wanted anything, that would bring up that rage. And I would always be trying to suppress it, because I didn't understand it.

Then much later, I had a daughter, and I had the same reaction to her. I was horrified, and I would get glazed over, blank, and I wouldn't even hear her cry. I wouldn't even know that she needed anything. She would be crying and crying and needing a bottle—and I wouldn't even know it. But I had a feeling behind this that she was just a little creep—a voice that said about her:

"You little creep. What do you need *that* for? Why don't you just shut up? Just shut up!"

And that's the same feeling I have about myself, if I want anything. Like if I want to make friends with someone, I think:

"You little creep! What are you doing? What do you need a friend for? You're always needing something. You're always groveling."

I would want to kill that person who grovels. I want to kill that groveling need for food. It's like a little dog who turns over, you know, you want to kick it. *That was the rage that I felt toward my children, but I know that was the rage toward me, toward needing just the simplest thing.*

This mother had been unable to cope with the basic needs of her children as well as her own feelings of rage and inadequacy. She perceived her children as pathetic, needy creatures to be despised, much as she had been rejected by her mother. After she uncovered the source of her internalized rage in the session, she recognized that she heard many voices that attempted to justify the anger she felt toward her children.

A number of parents who had grown up under a regime of cleanliness found themselves reacting with rage to such minor incidents as their child spilling milk or dirtying his clothes. Others were very disturbed by indications of incompetence in their children.

Perceiving their children as vulnerable or fragile can arouse anxiety and anger in some parents. Many noticed that they tended to cut off feelings or blank out whenever their child was in physical pain, especially when the child was seriously ill or in the hospital. They speculated that this emotional numbness resulted from the suppression of the deep fear and sadness or even rage which they felt in relation to seeing their child as vulnerable to pain.

Children who are accident-prone tend to arouse feelings of anger and guilt in their parents. When a child injures himself, parents may blame themselves or accuse themselves of being neglectful but often take it out on the child. In many instances, children are punished or continually lectured "for their own good."

Several parents revealed that they often overreacted to negative feedback about their children, either in the form of bad reports from school or complaints from neighbors or friends. One mother reported severely reprimanding and spanking her ten-year-old son when a neighbor accused him of being among a gang of youngsters who had destroyed her newly seeded front lawn. The boy insisted that he had not been involved. In her rage, the mother refused to listen to her son's side of story. Later, she discovered the boy had been innocent, as he claimed. She was appalled at the impulsiveness of her behavior and the intensity of her anger in the situation, and felt considerable remorse over the incident.

Many of our subjects admitted being provoked by the simple innocence and helplessness of their children. They appeared to be afraid of their own power in relation to the child's powerlessness. In order to preserve a calm facade and to prevent dreaded outbursts of anger, some parents were overly permissive and avoided disciplining their children. Still others manifested patterns of severe discipline inappropriate to the nature of the child's misbehavior.

Children's natural enthusiasm, noise levels, excited exclamations, and laughter may intrude on the quiet, inward state in which some people choose to live. Many parents remembered times they had lost their temper and punished their children severely for disturbing this "peaceful" atmosphere in their home. Some children are victims of an angry diatribe for disturbing a family member's sleep or rest. People who are emotionally deadened tend to overreact with hostility and aggression to the spontaneous, lively expressions of exuberance in their children.

It should be noted here that children who have been damaged psychologically are no longer the innocent, pure beings they once were. Many times they attempt to provoke their parents in order to get negative attention or punishment. At times they may need to prove that they are "bad" to account for why they are not loved or accepted by their parents. Defiance, rebelliousness, and other forms of provocation often lead to severe punitive responses on the part of parents.

Surprisingly, many parents react negatively to positive expressions or characteristics of their children because these responses arouse painful, repressed feelings of sadness in the parents. Children's vulnerability, sweetness, and lovability may reawaken deep emotional pain in parents who were deprived or abused as children. From our work with individuals in Feeling Release Therapy, we concluded that most people are well defended against repressed pain from childhood trauma. They attempt to regulate their lives to avoid activating these "primal" feelings. However, when people attempt to protect themselves from this anxiety, pain, and sadness—emotions that are inherent in any close relationship—they necessarily push away or punish those persons who love and value them the most. This damage may be minimized in casual social contacts; however, it is frequently acted out in a person's intimate relationships, and especially in interactions with children. In that sense, parents preserve their defense system at the expense of their child's emotional well-being. We found that the more immature and defended the parents were, the more likely they were to feel hostility toward their child because of the child's intrusion on their defense system.

We have consistently found that parents tend to remain insensitive to their children in the areas where they (the parents) are the most defended. As noted earlier, a woman who cannot tolerate an image of herself as an attractive, lovable woman will punish a man who offers her love. Similarly, she will avoid contact with or even punish her child at those times when the child is most loving or affectionate toward her. When a child's love and emotional response to the parent become threatening to the parent's defense system, the child comes to believe that his or her feelings are unacceptable. These children eventually learn to hold back their loving responses, thereby completing the cycle of inwardness, defensive withholding, and hostility, and insuring its perpetuation into future generations.

In conclusion, there is a considerable amount of righteous indignation, even hysteria, in relation to the subject of physical child abuse, to the point that the legal profession is very concerned with the problem of insuring the provision of a fair trial for suspected offenders. The dramatic focus on this issue and the comparative disregard for cases of emotional abuse are an attempt on people's part to disown their covert hostility and destructive feelings toward their offspring. Only with the recognition of the internal voice, the self-hatred towards one's child self, and its later extension to one's children, can we develop a truly humane approach to child-rearing.

NOTES

[1]Estimates of the incidence of physical child abuse vary:

> Helfer estimates that the number of reports [of child abuse] are increasing at the rate of 30 per cent a year and that between 1973 and 1982 there will be 1.5 million reports, 50,000 deaths, 300,000 permanent injuries, and one million potential abusers. . . . Kempe's estimate . . . amounts to 49 to 63 per 100,000 children. (Gil placed the figure at 8.4 to 9.3.) (Justice & Justice, undated, p. 88)

The sources quoted by Justice and Justice are: Helfer (1974), Kempe (1971), and Gil (1970).

[2]The reader may find documentation for the prevalence of emotional child abuse, deprivation, and neglect in such works as: *For Your Own Good* (Alice Miller, 1980/1984); *Prisoners of Childhood* (Alice Miller, 1979/1981); *Child Care and the Growth of Love* (John Bowlby, 1965); and *Child Abuse: An Agenda for Action* (Gerbner, Ross, & Zigler, 1980). Although precise statistics are lacking, class and economic groupings do not appear to differentiate between rates of incidence.

[3]"[Child] abuse is sometimes defined as one broad problem category encompassing several subcategories of problems (physical abuse, sexual abuse, emotional deprivation, negligent or inadequate care) . . . with physical abuse defined as only one aspect of the problem, albeit the most severe and most visible" (Gerbner, Ross, & Zigler, 1980, p. 121-122).

See also Korbin, J. E. (Ed.) (1981), *Child Abuse and Neglect: Cross-Cultural Perspectives,* for other definitions and standards for defining child abuse and neglect.

[4]Our work with Feeling Release Therapy was primarily a treatment procedure characterized by the cathartic ventilating of deep seated feelings. It consisted of 1½-hour sessions, several times a week, that took place over a period of many weeks, followed by an extended period of once- or twice-a-week sessions. Group psychotherapy augmented the individual sessions in most cases.

[5]Excerpted from *The Inner Voice in Child Abuse,* videotape, The Glendon Association (Parr, 1986).

6

The Fantasy Bond and "The Divided Self"

No one ever becomes completely emancipated from the state of
infantile dependence . . . and there is no one who has completely
escaped the necessity of incorporating his early objects.

W.R.D. Fairbairn (1941/1952, p. 56)

This *identification of the self with the fantasy of the person by
whom one is seen* may contribute decisively to the characteristics of
the observing self. . . . This observing self often kills and withers
anything that is under its scrutiny. The individual has now a *perse-
cuting observer in the very core of his being* [italics added].

R.D. Laing (1960/1965, p. 117)

Resistance to challenging or changing the negative conception of self is centered in the pattern of thoughts and behaviors
that act to preserve a core psychological defense. This basic defense consists of the process of parenting oneself, both internally by utilizing the introjected parent or voice, and externally
by utilizing objects in the interpersonal environment. The child
develops a fantasy bond or imagined connection to the parent,
thereby maintaining the illusion that he can take care of and parent himself.

The self-parenting process originates in response to emotional deprivation and separation trauma in early childhood. As such, it is an attempt on the child's part to reduce his anxiety and sense of helplessness in the face of overwhelming frustration. That is why he or she is so stubborn and resistant to changing this defensive posture in later life. It is as though, if that defense breaks down, the person will face anguish beyond his tolerance level.

Within the infant's psyche, *negative parental introjects tend to develop in conjunction with the evolving "child-self."* In other words, the internal guiding and parenting aspect of the personality is inextricably tied to a corresponding perception of oneself as a helpless child. This image is made up of the all-encompassing physical and emotional pain, the fear, the sense of loss, anger, and even rage, that characterized the child's original response to frustration and helplessness. By introjecting the negative, hostile, or defensive parental attitudes and at the same time retaining painful "primal" feelings, an individual develops the fantasy of *being at once the good, strong parent and the weak, bad child.* It is this illusion of total self-care and self-nourishment that we refer to as the *self-parenting process.* In other words, the parental voice tape administers to the hurt or victimized child-self, giving the impression of pseudo-independence and maintaining one's psychological equilibrium.

PSEUDO-INDEPENDENCE AND THE PROCESS OF INTROJECTION

Very early in its life, the infant takes in or "swallows" the image of the "good and powerful mother." As previously described, *this image also includes the mother's covert rejecting attitudes toward the infant.* The infant now has a sense of needing nothing from the outside world; that is, he has an illusion of being completely self-sufficient. He develops a posture of pseudo-independence—"I don't need anyone; I can take care of myself"—to protect himself from really experiencing his mother's rejection. Although she may attempt to hide her fears and anxieties from her infant, the mother's true emotional state is transmitted on an unconscious level.

The introjected parent takes on the significance of a survival mechanism in the child's mind. The illusion of being connected to or merged with the mother provides partial gratification of the infant's needs. In other writings, the author (1984) has described the formation of this imaginary connection or fantasy bond through the process of introjecting the mother's image. The "primary fantasy bond" is "an illusion of connection, originally an imaginary fusion or joining with the mother's body, most particularly the breast" (p. 218). It is a *core defense* and is protected by other patterns of thoughts and behaviors (secondary fantasies).

Internal manifestations of the fantasy bond, represented by childish feelings and self-parenting responses, are preserved intact in the adult personality. *External manifestations* of the fantasized connection can be observed in behaviors that lend support to an illusion of belonging to another person or that they belong to you. Paradoxically, while imagining himself to be at one with the internalized parental figure, the individual actually becomes increasingly divided within himself.

In his work, Hellmuth Kaiser wrote extensively about the universal neurotic need for connecting with another through the process of incorporating the other person into the self. Kaiser's (1955/1965) formulations to some extent parallel the author's thinking in relation to the defensive function served by the fantasy of fusion:

> He [the neurotic patient] wants either to incorporate himself into the other person and lose his personality, or to incorporate the other person and destroy the other person's personality. When an opportunity for such fusion or identification seems to be offered, every function is drawn into the service of the desire for closeness, in the *regressive* [italics added] sense. (p. 4)

Object-relation theorists have also formulated this process of imaginary merging with the maternal figure in terms of internalizing the agent of his frustration.

> As Melanie Klein has shown, the infant *internalizes his objects* [italics added] and builds up an inner world of object-relations. Fairbairn regards the infant as internalizing his unsatisfying ob-

jects in an effort to master them in inner reality because he cannot master them in the outer world. (Guntrip, 1969, p. 71)

The formation of the fantasy bond creates profound distortions of reality. *As a by-product of introjecting the parental figure, the child needs to idealize the real parent at his own expense*; at the same time, he or she projects the parent's negative traits onto the environment at large. The image of the parent must be positive, because it would be impossible for the child to feel safe or secure with an internalized parent perceived as inadequate or destructive. In spite of the fact that many people criticize their parents outwardly, on an *internal* level they maintain the idealization as a defense.

In summary, the core defense or primary fantasy bond originates in early childhood to fill a gap where there is environmental deprivation; it "nourishes" the self, and it becomes the motivating force behind the voice and consequent neurotic or self-destructive behavior. No child has an ideal environment; thus all people depend to varying degrees on internal gratification from an imagined connection with the introjected parent. However, the greater the frustration and the greater the degree of reliance on self-parenting, the more maladaptive the person is in his interpersonal relations. Indeed, the more dependent on the fantasy of fusion, the less the child will accept real gratification in his personal life. In other words, the stronger the defense system, the greater the degree of distrust of other persons and the more distortion of reality.

THE ADDICTIVE NATURE OF THE FANTASY BOND

The fantasy bond is highly effective as a core defense because man's capacity for imagination provides partial gratification of needs and reduces tension arising from physical or emotional deprivation. The infant, in experiencing separation and deprivation as a threat of annihilation (Winnicott, 1958), draws upon its imagination for relief from emotional pain and anxiety. Sucking its thumb and other self-nourishing habits are also attempts to cope with deprivation. Satisfactions achieved by the child in fantasy and through various self-parenting behaviors eventually come to be preferred over real gratification because they are under the child's control. In actuality, real gratification disturbs the fantasy process of self-gratification. Therefore, once the fantasized connection is formed and the parental introjects well established, people have strong resistance to investing emotionally in genuine, satisfying associations with others. Their principal goal then is to maintain the imagined safety and security of the illusory connection with the internal parent.

The more pain and suffering a child experiences in his developing years, the more that child will need to introject the mother and maintain the self-parenting process. Similarly, the more the person depends on an illusion of pseudo-independence, the more *dependent* in reality he becomes. This is best exemplified in psychotic patients who have omnipotent delusions and, at the same time, are unable to take care of themselves, requiring full-time institutional care from others.

REPRESSED TRAUMA

Our work with patients in Feeling Release Therapy revealed that virtually all of our subjects had incorporated and retained the frustrating and painful events of their childhood on some level. Dramatic memories and traumatic events surfaced during deep emotional expressions, indicating trauma that had been partially or completely repressed. The most remarkable phenomenon we noted here was that patients tended to repeat this process over and over again in what Janov (1970) termed an attempt to drain the pool of "primal pain." In our experience, we found that once they overcame their initial resistance to painful emotions, our subjects were not only willing to undergo these painful relivings repeatedly, but that there was something compelling about the process. Later, we interpreted our results to indicate that (1) patients were somehow anxious to hold on to their child selves and their painful childhood experiences; (2) the "pool of primal pain" did not exhaust itself; and (3) holding on to "the child self" caused people to maintain a childish or immature aspect of their personalities, even in otherwise adjusted individuals. It appeared that the child-self remained fixated on a regressive developmental level and was preserved intact, much as the parental aspects of the personality were retained. Indeed, the good parent/bad child dyad appeared to persist into adulthood and insured the repetition of painful and unsatisfying relationships comparable to the experiences in the nuclear family.

RECAPITULATION OF THE PAST

Once an individual relies on fantasy gratification, there is a tendency to avoid real gratification, because it disrupts the fantasy of pseudo-independence and causes anxiety. Secondary fantasies of rejection, negative anticipations, and cynical views of others in the form of the voice are self-perpetuating and function to protect the core defense. Most people retain the specific patterns of hostile, self-critical thoughts and distorted stereotyped attitudes toward other people that they used in childhood to protect the self-parenting process.

When people have been hurt in early family interactions, they are reluctant to take a chance again and really trust another relationship. Their voices predict rejection and create anxiety in personal associations, predisposing behavior that leads to actual rejection. The end result is that earlier rejections by the parents are recapitulated in the present. Thus, people become strengthened in the conviction that they are the only one who can take care of or love themselves (Firestone, 1985). Finally, they tend to act out either childish or parental responses on other persons. Generally one style of behavior or another may become predominant and polarize in relation to the new object.

In the course of the developmental sequence, psychological equilibrium is achieved when a person arrives at a particular solution to the basic conflict between relying on internal fantasy processes for gratification and seeking real satisfaction in the external world. This equilibrium may be attained at the expense of satisfying object relations and may be actually threatened by warm or constructive events that contradict early childhood experiences. To protect the fantasy process from these "positive" intrusions, most people tend to recreate the original conditions within their family through the defense mechanisms of selection, distortion, and provocation. (1) They tend to choose and marry a person who is similar to a parent or family member, because this is the type of individual to whom their defenses are appropriate. (2) Their perceptions of new objects are distorted in a direction that corresponds more closely to the members of the original family. (3) If these maneuvers fail to protect them, they tend to behave in ways that provoke similar parental reactions in their loved ones. Utilizing these methods, people are able to *externalize the self-parenting process through acting out either the "good parent" or "bad child" image with new attachments*. In this manner, they recreate the negative aspects of their family life in present-day interactions.

THE BASIC SPLIT IN SCHIZOPHRENIA

In the regressed world of the schizophrenic, the introjected, idealized parent is personified to an extreme degree by delusions of omnipotence and grandiosity. These patients have the fantasy of simultaneously being the highest and lowest members of mankind. In some way they have identified with their omnipotent mothers, and at the same time regard themselves as the dirty, evil, unlovable child. In the schizophrenic regression, these patients have become at one with the idealized mother and see her negative rejecting characteristics in other persons. The end product of this regression is a form of psychological equilibrium at the expense of object relationships. Schizophrenics literally shut people out of their lives and become their own mothers, psychologically. The omnipotent "good" mother and weak "bad" child are both part of the *self-nourishing system,* and the split between these two parts of self leads to the thought disorganization that is an important feature of the illness. Aspects of each system are combined, and there is much confusion and fragmentation in the regressed patient.

For example, the patient might describe himself as God or "the infinite being"; however, at another point in the conversation he might refer to himself as worthless and insignificant (Firestone, 1957).

Hannah Green's (1964/1967) dramatic account of a schizophrenic girl, *I Never Promised You a Rose Garden,* graphically depicts the role of the voice in protecting the psychotic self-parenting system made up of the internalized good parent and bad child dyad. In one instance, the patient, sixteen-year-old Deborah, revealed a pertinent fact of her personal history and, in so doing, was able to make *real* contact (symbolizing *external* gratification) with her therapist for a few moments. Immediately, however, there was retaliation from the girl's "voices," threatening in "an acid, mocking tone":

> *You are not of them! . . . Walk out of this with that famous doctor of yours! . . . Do you think you can go telling secrets and be safe forever? There are other deaths than death—worse ones.*
> (p. 69)

Time and again, the fragile contact with her therapist was lost. Whenever there was progress, there were repeated virulent attacks by Deborah's "voices," striving at all costs to "protect" her from the so-called dangers of the real world.

THREE MODES OF EXPERIENCE: THE PARENT, THE CHILD, AND THE ADULT

In neurotic or less disturbed patients, the various parts of the self are less fragmented than in the psychotic patient. The functioning adult ego is more integrated, yet "normal" or neurotic individuals tend to move in and out of states of being childish or parental in their personal relationships.

In the following pages, we will attempt to delineate behaviors that typify these *three modes of experience*: the parental, the childish or regressive, and the adult mode. These modes of experience refer to *internal* ego states as well as to behaviors and feelings expressed *outwardly*. Each person is in transition between these modes, but he or she may become stabilized in one mode or another in relation to other people.

The Parental Mode

A person who is primarily in the parental mode is generally judgmental, critical, and condescending toward other people. These same parental attitudes are applied to oneself in the form of voices.

Manifestations of the parental mode. Throughout this work, we have described various aspects of the parental mode: the punitive, hostile, self-limiting, restrictive voices introjected during traumatic experiences in early childhood. We have noted the self-protective thoughts or warnings perpetuated by the voice. It would be valuable here to call attention to those seemingly *positive* voices that reflect another parental function, one that reveals the fundamental ambivalence of many parents toward their children, that is, their indulgent, "coddling," and overprotective attitudes. These attitudes originate in an inaccurate or distorted perception of children. For example, many parents perceive children as more helpless than they actually are. Misperceptions that overdramatize the child's innocence and susceptibility to pain can lead to overprotective parental responses that are as damaging as hostile or abusive attitudes.

Self-indulgent attitudes and voices that attempt to cope with anxiety and painful emotions by influencing an individual to relieve tension through self-nourishing habits are the result of this form of parental abuse. If a person complies with these parental voices, he or she may regress to a childish mode and become very self-protective. Indeed, soothing or nurturing voices mediate a wide range of maladaptive behaviors that are prominent in all forms of substance abuse. Alcoholism, drug addiction, eating disturbances, etc., are examples of behaviors controlled by the indulgent voice that, carried to the extreme, may be detrimental or injurious to one's physical health and well-being.

Offering a buildup, unnecessary support, or exaggerated praise are related examples of destructive or indulgent parenting. As noted earlier, when incorporated as voices that inflate or distort a person's positive traits, talents, and abilities, they are a setup for subsequent self-attacks. A person whose vanity has been built up tends to become overexcited by positive events but later becomes easily demoralized and self-critical.

Excessive praise or flattery are often utilized by parents as substitutes when genuine feelings of caring are absent. Later, one's vanity represents an internal connection with one's family. Interpersonally, when people demand special treatment or buildup from their mates, they are, in effect, attempting to reconnect with the parent who originally praised them and made them feel special. They have a strong need to hold on to an exaggerated, fantasized image of themselves and seek the kind of relationships that tend to confirm this image.

Behaviors characteristic of the parental mode. When parental voices are acted out toward others, they have a toxic effect on personal relations. Critical, judgmental, and abusive behavior damages both the parental person and the recipient. People who typically act out parental responses tend to have a superior, evaluative, or self-righteous quality to their tone of voice, as well as in their pronouncements. They can be dominant, controlling, and intrusive in social situations. Parental behaviors should not be confused with honest leadership and personal power.

When people are parental, they are, in effect, "pseudo" adults in the sense that they are acting out of weakness, not strength. They revert to a parental or authoritarian facade or role whenever they are afraid or unsure of themselves. They demand to be taken care of by others and often tyrannize over their subordinates and employees. Rather than relating to other people on an equal basis, they shift to an overbearing, domineering, or condescending approach.

Thus, parental, authoritarian individuals are destructive because they support destructive voices in other people and capitalize on their dependency needs. Career choices may reflect underlying parental needs or present a platform for acting out parental behavior. Businessmen, politicians, doctors, nurses, and teachers often operate from the parental mode, without being aware that they treat employees, patients, clients, or students as inferiors. Many ministers castigate their congregations for their sins, urging them to seek redemption, much as the internal voice maligns the individual for his errors, faults, and weaknesses.

Judgmental or domineering behaviors and communications are not the only responses manifested in the parental mode;

overly sympathetic, reassuring, or so-called helpful responses are also common. The authors believe that sympathetic responses to people who are playing a victimized, misunderstood, or childish role can be extremely detrimental, yet this type of response may be supported by cultural norms. Expressions of sympathy (not empathy) validate or support passive or paranoid attitudes and therefore are damaging to the "childlike" recipient, as well as maladaptive for the "parental" individual.

Transactional Analysts view the parent state as manifesting itself in two forms. Their formulations are somewhat analogous to our descriptions of the punitive and indulgent aspects of the parental mode.

> The Parent is typically exhibited in one of two forms. The *prejudicial* Parent is manifested as a set of seemingly arbitrary non-rational attitudes or parameters, usually prohibitive in nature, which may be either syntonic or dystonic with the local culture. . . . The *nurturing* Parent is often manifested as *sympathy for* another individual, which again may be either culturally syntonic or culturally dystonic (Berne, 1961, p. 76)

In conclusion, when a person is operating in the parental mode, he is not himself. He is acting out or manifesting signs of the internal parent. He is not representing his true point of view and loses compassion for himself and others. Many times his actions are provoked by persons acting out of the child mode. These childish individuals draw out parental responses from others that are a mechanical repetition of the behavior of their own parents.

The Child Mode

When an individual is in the child mode, he or she generally feels powerless, self-depreciating, and victimized by others. Childish or regressive behaviors are regulated by the voice process. Indulgent parental voices administer to or protect the child self, while critical voices punish and chastise. People preserve in their imagination a mental image of themselves as a small child. They alternate between feeling sorry for themselves and feeling harsh and self-attacking.

Manifestations of the child mode. The *child mode* is characterized by responses that are immature and more appropriate to earlier stages of an individual's development. Melodramatic reactions, exaggerated feelings of fear, and a sense of helplessness are common. People act as though the frustration and pain in their adult lives has the same significance to them as when they were dependent and powerless children.

As noted earlier, we observed that not only were many of the participants in Feeling Release Therapy willing to repeat painful early experiences in their sessions, but they seemed willing to recapitulate these trauma in their personal lives as well. This phenomenon raised an important theoretical question: what is so compelling about reliving unpleasant, even painful, experiences that people would repeatedly immerse themselves in these regressive states? From a broader perspective, why would they continue to overreact melodramatically and childishly to minor upsets in their current lives, despite insight? On a behavioral level, what is so compelling about this regressed, childish state that would cause many adults to persist in objectionable, immature actions and habit patterns which their friends, associates, and mates find unpleasant and abrasive?

Why would an adult man, for example, provoke anger in his superior by defiant, passive-aggressive attitudes and actions? Why would an intelligent, competent woman revert to helpless attention-getting behaviors in certain situations? From observing the pervasiveness of these tendencies in our subjects, we concluded that most people have a *strong stake in preserving the child-self,* because it is an important aspect of the core defense or fantasy bond.

Individuals who are in the child mode frequently feel misunderstood and victimized. Distorted views of other people influenced by the voice contribute to their feelings of being the innocent victim. For example, a number of our subjects reported "listening" to a series of negative thoughts or voices about friends, marital partners, and acquaintances whenever they were feeling especially childish or inadequate. These voices supported the "noble child" feeling, thoughts such as:

"Nobody understands how hard you try."

"Look at all you've done, the least they could do is. . . ."
"You don't matter to him. Look at all the friends he already has!
What do *you* have to offer?"
"Why bother working hard? Nobody notices your work."

Interestingly enough, when the subjects identified the voices underlying their feelings of helplessness and hopelessness ("It's no use; you'll never get what you want, etc.") and their feelings of being victimized or exploited ("They're just using you, etc."), they found that they were better able to achieve an adult perspective and approach to their problems. In other words, *after* isolating and identifying specific voices associated with victimized feelings, they were able to move from the child mode into a more realistic posture.

Attitudes of paranoia and distrust emanate from the child mode of experience. Often, people's voices warn them about other people and their motives. These voice attacks represent incorporated family attitudes toward the outside world and are closely related to the defense system of the parents. Suspicion and cynicism exemplify this point of view, thoughts such as:

"Women are unreliable."
"You can't trust men."
"The world is a dangerous place."
"Never trust a stranger."
"All politicians are corrupt."
"Doctors and lawyers are only out to get your money."

A passive orientation toward life, exaggerated feelings of dependency, and a sense of feeling weak and inadequate are dominant ego-states for these individuals. Passive individuals view their experiences as happening to them rather than seeing themselves in control. From this vantage point, they view life as passive victims and become essentially paranoid in their approach. Serious paranoid states ("People are plotting against you; they're about to harm you") are exaggerations of the distortions manifested by "normal" or neurotic individuals in a childish or regressed state.

The immature person tends to be egocentric and narcissistic and appears to lack genuine interest in others. In seriously disturbed patients, this inward, self-centered focus culminates in actual delusions of reference.

People who spend the major part of their lives in the child mode do not develop the strong *internal* value system characteristic of a healthy conscience. Their feelings of self-hatred and self-punitive attitudes, indeed, their basic feelings of self-esteem, are generally regulated by submission to, or in some cases, a stubborn defiance of, *external* standards of behavior and moral codes.

When people are in a regressed or childish state, they tend to block out genuine feeling reactions appropriate to the present; at the same time, they have intense primal feelings of being hurt or dramatic outbursts of emotionality. For example, a childish or immature person may react in an indifferent manner to important events in his life and have strong emotional reactions to what would seem to be relatively unimportant, or "pseudo," events to the outside observer.

The evidence that many people overreact to the "pseudo" issues in their lives when listening to voices can be seen in the example of the patient who comes to a therapy session distraught and emotionally overreactive to an unpleasant event. During the session, when the event is seen in perspective, dealt with matter-of-factly, or treated with humor, he or she often leaves in a completely different frame of mind. The actual external situation had not changed, yet the patient's orientation shifted considerably. In fact, almost any experience dealt with from an adult perspective will assume proportions that are acceptable and manageable. The painful effects of rejection or negative circumstances are due more to the voice's distorted interpretation of the situation than to the actual loss.

Incidentally, the feelings of fraudulence reported by a large number of high-achieving individuals in Clance and Imes' (1978) study of the Impostor Phenomenon indicated the persistence of an underlying childlike posture. Achieving an important milestone in one's career or being acknowledged for one's *adult* accomplishments frequently arouses feelings of being a fraud because one senses that underneath he or she still feels like a child. These childish feelings and responses are perceived as being incongruent with one's adult achievements; therefore the person experiences voices that suggest that the success is not valid or appropriate.

People do not exist exclusively in a childish or regressed state. They tend to vacillate between the parental mode and the child mode. Consequently, they may spend only a small proportion of their time in the adult mode. Many of the machinations and interactions in families, close relationships, and the business world reflect parental or childlike states, rather than adult functional responses.

Behaviors characteristic of the child mode. As previously noted, many people exhibit behavior that can be defined as childish or immature. Sulking, whining, complaining, manipulating to get sympathy, repeatedly seeking direction, being disorganized and irresponsible, procrastinating, being habitually late, driving carelessly or recklessly, misplacing important possessions, carelessness and slovenliness, neglect of personal hygiene or one's health are all symptomatic of the child mode of experience. Further, people's physical appearance, demeanor, and tone of voice often change dramatically when they retreat into the child mode. Their voices may tremble or become halting and hesitant; they may use words, phrases, and expressions more appropriate to earlier states of development; or they may turn to certain regressive habits such as nail-biting or daydreaming. They tend to become incompetent, inept, or irresponsible around people whom they identify as authority figures: with employers in their place of employment, with teachers in learning situations, and in their marital relationships.

People who feel inferior assume submissive roles in relation to authority figures and abdicate their rights in intimate relationships. By acquiescing to other people's wants and needs, they hope to be able to earn love, or at least approval, from parents or parental substitutes. On some level, they continue to idealize their parents, because their hope is based on the premise that their parents were loving and adequate and that it was only because *they* (the children) were "bad" that they were not loved. Their voices remind them of their faults and validate their sense of being bad or worthless. Provoking angry, punitive, parental responses from authority figures through subservient or childish behavior satisfies their need for punishment, reduces their guilt, and temporarily diminishes the intensity of their voice attacks.

Defiant, rebellious behavior is also characteristic of the child mode. Both submission and defiance are outer-directed and of a different character from independent responses. Both elicit parental responses of either approval or disapproval. For example, rebellious adolescents do not outwardly idealize their parents; to the contrary, they are usually very critical of them and seem to take pleasure in defying traditional values. However, their disruptive behavior proves that their parents were *right* in defining them as unlovable or incorrigible.

Delinquent behaviors, such as truancy, running away, shoplifting, and petty theft are more extreme examples of defiant childish responses that confirm negative parental attitudes. These acts provoke negative attention and punishment from authority figures. Paradoxically, antisocial responses give the delinquent, and later the adult criminal, a certain sense of security through an ongoing involvement with police, judges, and probation officers (parent substitutes). Indeed, the high rate of recidivism in "rehabilitated" criminals may indicate their desire, albeit unconscious, to return to the security of prison where they are ordered about, taken care of, and strictly controlled, like children in the family situation.

Behaviors That Elicit Parental Responses in a Bond

> Some people undoubtedly have a remarkable aptitude for keeping the other tied in knots. There are those who excel in tying knots and those who excel in being tied in knots. Tyer and tied are often both unconscious of how it is done, or even that it is being done at all.
>
> R.D. Laing (1961/1971, p. 158)

Whenever one person in a marital relationship characteristically responds to the other from a childish, immature posture or from a parental, controlling posture, the relationship inevitably deteriorates into a destructive bond. By regressing to childish modes of relating, an individual can manipulate another person into taking care of him. In this way, he preserves the imagined security of the original fantasy bond with his parents. Behaviors that elicit or provoke negative reactions—worry, fear, anger, and even punishment—act to cement the fantasy of being connected to another person and relieve the anxiety of feeling separate and alone. As long as these manipulations and the corresponding reactions are in operation, both partners feel inextricably bound to each other.

Childish individuals tend to imagine or even provoke rejection. Overreactions to slights, pleas for reassurances of love, withholding of personal responses and affection, and overly dependent behavior all may provoke rejection and concern. Destructive behavior or responses that are primarily self-destructive act as a powerful distraction and demand the attention of one's marital partner.

Where does the tendency to act out childish and immature responses with one's mate originate? Why is there such an overriding, compelling need for couples to polarize in this way, with either one or the other playing the child role? First, as children they learned at an early age how to maintain the connection with their parents through attention-getting maneuvers and displays of helplessness. Second, *early in life, they learned to imitate their parents' style of interacting with each other from parent/child modes*. Indeed, children *rarely* see examples of their parents relating to each other as two equal adults. Therefore, they lack role models for their own interactions in marriage.

Our analysis of marital relationships has shown that the partners generally act out "complementary" parent/child modes in their couple relationships, thereby externalizing their voices. People often elicit the exact voice attacks that they experience internally, frequently word for word. Tansey and Burke (1985) define this unconscious process of projective identification as follows:

> Projective identification, although having intrapsychic characteristics, represents an interactional phenomenon in which the projector unconsciously attempts to *elicit thoughts, feelings, and experiences within another individual which in some way resemble his own* [italics added]. (p. 46)

To complete this polarity, one person acts childish and the other partner disowns his child self, denies his feelings of fear and helplessness, and acts out an authoritarian, parental role. This type of interaction tends to dominate the marital relationship with occasional role reversals. Consequently, it is rare that *both* parties are relating from an adult ego-state.

Jurg Willi (1975/1984) describes this polarity in his book, *Couples in Collusion*:

> *In the disturbed partner relationship we often observe that one partner has a need for over-compensatory progression while the other seeks satisfaction in regression. They reinforce this one-sided behavior in each other because they need each other as complements.* (p. 24)
>
> *This progressive and regressive behavior is a major reason for the mutual attraction and the resulting bond.* (p. 56)

On some level, both partners feel guilty for participating in this destructive collusion. However, they find it difficult to disengage, because the polarized patterns in the relationship give the illusion of safety and protection.

Man vs. Woman.   When a woman identifies her husband as the parent or authority figure, which is more typically (though not exclusively) the case than the reverse, she will tend to act out childish, dependent behaviors in the relationship. Although there have been significant changes in the roles of men and women in our society, there are still residuals of stereotypic views that see men as powerful and competent and women as helpless and incompetent. These stereotypic attitudes exert a form of unconscious social pressure on women to act out childish responses toward men and on men to act out corresponding punitive or caretaking parental reactions.

Wherever a power structure exists and these modes of experience are polarized, aggressive aspects of the childish ego-state are expressed through withholding responses, which in turn provoke angry parental responses in others. For example, by holding back qualities and responses that are most admired or desired by the mate, one can turn a partner's feeling of love and respect into anger or even hatred.

A significant characteristic of the withholding defense is a lack of independence or a strong point of view. For example, many married women display a passive, resentful acquiescence to their husband's opinions. Some women break down in tears or simply threaten to break down. Many play the martyr and make other family members feel guilty about their self-sacrifice; others are self-indulgent and compete with their children for their husband's attention. Needless to say, many men also exhibit withholding characteristics and manipulate through weakness. However, prevailing cultural norms predispose these responses more in female marital partners.

The child mode is exemplified in the style of sexual relating that characterizes many couple relationships. Typical symptoms that develop in this type of sexual relationship have been observed to follow this sequence: (1) One partner or the other generally becomes less responsive sexually, indicating a regression to the child mode. Most often it is the woman who tends to become sexually withholding. (2) The man reacts to his mate's withholding in a manner similar to the way he initially responded to his mother's rejection, that is, with intense feelings of emotional hunger, rage, and/or self-hatred. (3) A pattern of immature sexual relating develops, and the sex act itself is characterized by a greater degree of inwardness and takes on a more impersonal, masturbatory quality. The focus turns more to self-gratification and dependence on fantasy in order to intensify excitement, with a concomitant decrease in genuine emotional contact and an increase in the voice attacks of each partner.

The Adult Mode

A person who exists in an adult ego-state has feelings, attitudes, and behaviors that are generally adaptive. Accordingly, he is neither melodramatic nor obsessed by the voice. He actively pursues personal and professional goals, responding appropriately to the frustration or fulfillment of these goals. An adult individual exhibits greater tolerance for frustration, ambivalence, and conflict. He feels an enthusiasm for living, a spontaneous enjoyment of the moment; however, he also is capable of feeling and reacting appropriately to negative events and the tragic aspects of life.

A person who is primarily in the adult mode is neither defiant nor submissive, but has his own point of view. Having a strong, individualistic attitude may subject him to feelings of anxiety if his opinions differ from prevailing social mores. Incidentally, creative people probably have a higher tolerance for feeling different or separate, which permits them to develop a unique outlook.

The adult mode is characterized by independence and self-assertion. It implies acceptance of a unique identity that may differ from the way one was defined in the family. Interpersonally, adult individuals make choices and pursue goals in a direction *away* from repeating the patterns they observed in their families, particularly if these patterns represented an acting out of the parent/child polarities. Acts of independence and unconventionality (personal responses that are not role-determined) disrupt the bond with the family. They challenge or sever the illusory connection to others based on dependency and conformity. The adult acts out of choice and a personal sense of responsibility rather than from a position of guilt or obligation.

The individual who is truly adult is nonmanipulative in pursuing his own goals. He recognizes the distinction between exploitative, manipulative power and the personal power that emanates from his own natural expression. Because he has developed a strong internal value system, he is capable of achieving his goals without intruding on the rights of others. Less mature individuals attempt to achieve *their* goals through negative power, self-denial, and childish maneuvers, whereas the adult values honest selfishness over dishonest selflessness. An adult individual has a strong sense of self, a realistic self-concept unencumbered by vanity and unrealistic expectations, and a nonwithholding style of accomplishing his goals. He or she does not assume a false parental or childlike posture by disowning one side of his or her personality. Therefore, because they are less divided within themselves, people in the adult mode exhibit an inner harmony and a self-affirming approach to life.

In the adult state, a person remains relatively free of destructive voices and experiences a liking of the self on a feeling level. Everyone has had a taste of this, but often this phenomenon is short-lived because feeling a separate sense of self and a state of happiness often precipitates anxiety states. Feeling adult increases one's sense of vulnerability, because in finding oneself and liking oneself, one has a self to lose.

Manifestations of the adult mode in an equal relationship. People whose actions are based primarily on the adult mode relate to each other as independent individuals with considerable give and take in terms of reciprocal need gratification. In this sense, real friendship where each person recognizes the uniqueness of the other as a separate human being exemplifies this type of adult relationship. There is a conspicuous lack of judgmental, parental role-playing and childlike responses, and each party respects the other's point of view.

In contrast to a dependency bond, a genuine friendship between two mature adults is characterized by a lack of possessiveness. Couples who are *not* in a bond refrain from imposing rules and obligations on the relationship; consequently, each person is left alone, in the best sense of the word, to pursue his or her own goals.

People who relate to each other from the adult mode have a sense of vitality and energy that contributes considerably to their physical attractiveness. Indeed, these individuals have what I refer to as the "look of self," that is, their facial expressions are open, vibrant, and natural. These people look natural, in contrast to many people whose defensive postures are etched into their faces and bodies. Finally, both individuals see their commitment as providing an opportunity to experience real companionship *and* a gratifying sexual relationship, an ideal combination.

Resistance to maintaining the adult mode of experience. Transactional Analysts state that "the Adult is still the *least* understood of the three types of ego states" (Berne, 1961, p. 76). They believe that the Adult can be best conceptualized as the residual state "left after the segregation of all detectable Parent and Child elements" (p. 76). Perhaps the "Adult state" is the "least understood" because of the fact that even mature, well-adjusted individuals find it difficult to remain in the adult mode for extended periods of time.

Negative circumstances and threats of symbolic or actual separation and loss can at times precipitate intense anxiety states in an individual who is in the adult mode. Indeed, any interaction that symbolizes individuation or lack of fusion can arouse tension in interpersonal relationships and lead to subsequent regression to childish or parental modes of interacting.

Both positive and negative events can throw us off balance, and we frequently find ourselves suddenly responding from another mode of experience. Many of us tend to take a positive experience and run with it, so to speak, and feel that we're the "greatest," or overexaggerate its significance, only to feel depressed and self-depreciating later on. Many times, we become polarized in relation to feeling great and small, or powerful and insignificant. These polarizations represent remnants of the parental/child dichotomy that we retain in our personalities. To a great extent, we *don't* experience our lives in the adult state, pursuing adult goals and having appropriate emotional reactions, but slip easily into other modes.

It is apparent that the adult mode represents an ideal state of adjustment that individuals achieve to varying degrees. As such, it represents an important goal of psychotherapy.

CONCLUSION

In conclusion, it appears that most individuals spend the major part of their lives in either the parental or child mode, repeating patterns they observed in early family interactions. They feel compelled to reenact these modes of experience because (1) they lacked role models for adult behavior patterns; (2) they are desperate to hold on to the internal parent manifested in the form of the voice; and (3) they act out a core defense that externalizes either parental or childlike aspects of an internalized, self-parenting mechanism.

The three modes of experience depicted here parallel the descriptions of clinicians who analyze data in relation to transactional analysis. T.A. phenomenological studies of the Parent, Child, and Adult ego states, including a structural analysis of internal states, games, and life-scripts, are similar in many respects to our own analysis of these modes. However, our analysis differs from the formulations of the transactional analysts in terms of emphasis. We tend to stress the underlying defensive processes determining the movement between the ego states, whereas T.A. clinicians generally concentrate more on phenomenological aspects.

Our interpretation of the patient's need to repeat past experiences in his present-day relationships also differs from T.A. interpretations. Eric Berne (1961), writing in *Transactional Analysis in Psychotherapy,* states:

> The motivation for the patient's behavior is his need to recapture or augment the gains of the original experience. He may seek to bring about a repetition of the original catastrophe, as in the classical repetition compulsion; or he may try to attain a happier ending. Since the object of script analysis is to "close the show and put a better one on the road," it is not too important to determine which of these alternatives applies or to sort out the conflicts in this area. (p. 118)

Berne basically agrees with Freud's conception of repetition compulsion, which states that people's tendencies to repeat the past are manifestations of their attempts to achieve the gratification that was originally missing from the early environment, whereas we believe that the person repeats the past in order *to protect the defense system.* Once an individual relies on fantasy gratification and fantasies of connection, he prefers to seek satisfaction in imagination and to minimize constructive experiences in reality. He tends to repeat patterns of behavior and defenses that he was familiar with in his family situation in order to control his life experiences and avoid separation anxiety.

Regarding the patient's need to relive the past, we agree with the position taken by the transactional analyst and the Freudian psychoanalyst in one respect: that people *do* repeat these patterns compulsively and unconsciously. We also share the belief that these machinations inevitably lead to frustration in terms of genuine goal-directed activity and have a damaging effect on the patient's adjustment.

The author feels that speculations as to the *reasons* people repeat these patterns are not as important as understanding and expressing how the mechanism functions. However, we suggest that when a strong defense system is activated, there is an overriding need to protect that system, i.e., once a fantasy bond is formed, one is reluctant to take a chance again on gratification from others. Ultimately, people's anxieties drive them to form illusory connections that invariably lead to a reenactment of their parents' defensive styles of interacting. The process of reverting to outmoded defense patterns interferes with the establishment of secure and satisfying adult relationships characterized by feelings of humanity, compassion, and equality.

4/17/88

II

Self-Destructive Manifestations of the Voice

7

The Dual Nature of Guilt Reactions*

> The unconscious force which drives people to deny themselves enjoyment and success, to spoil their chances in life or not to make use of them, may be more accurately defined as the need for punishment. . . . Unconsciously . . . people inflict punishments on themselves to which an inner court has sentenced them. A hidden authority within the ego takes over the judgment originally expected of the parents. . . .
>
> The origin and the essential features of moral masochism are strange indeed, but anyone can perceive a faint echo in himself if he listens to the melody. We are surprised that the feeling of guilt or the corresponding wish to be punished can remain completely unconscious.
>
> Theodore Reik (1941, p. 10–11)

Human beings spend their lives in a restricted range of personal relationships and experiences. Their freedom and initiative are constricted by a self-destructive process. Furthermore, their internal conflict is primarily unconscious, and they are generally unaware of the circle of guilt that limits them.

Guilt reactions are mediated by the voice. The form and substance of experience that people permit themselves is limited by this system of self-accusatory thoughts and injunctions. To

*The substance of this chapter is taken primarily from an article entitled "The 'Voice': The Dual Nature of Guilt Reactions," *American Journal of Psychoanalysis*, Vol. 47, No. 3, 1987.

whatever degree these self-critical thoughts remain unconscious, they cause considerable damage, and the individual is unable to break the cycle.

The concept of guilt refers to an insidious process of self-limitation and self-hatred that seriously restricts people's lives. Out of a sense of guilt, people become self-denying, self-defeating, self-destructive, and even suicidal. The voice represents the thought process underlying the behavior noted above.

NEUROTIC AND EXISTENTIAL GUILT

There are two distinguishable forms of guilt that create a basic conflict in each individual: neurotic guilt and existential guilt. It is useful for purposes of delineation to conceptualize them as follows: the first, termed *neurotic guilt,* may be defined as feelings of remorse, shame, or self-attack for seeking gratification, for moving toward one's goals, and for pursuing one's wants. The person essentially characterizes himself as "selfish." This form of guilt reaction appears to be related to emotional deprivation, parental prohibitions, and faulty training procedures in childhood.

Becker (1964) defined neurotic guilt as "the action-bind that reaches out of the past to limit new experiences, to block the possibility of broader choices" (p. 186). He attributed the cause of this constriction of life to the "early indoctrination" of the child.

In his essay, *The Ego and the Id,* Freud (1923/1961) delineated two kinds of neurotic guilt: (1) conscious guilt (conscience) "based on the tension between the ego and the ego ideal . . . the expression of a condemnation of the ego by its critical agency" (p. 51); and (2) an unconscious sense of guilt that Freud believed to be the basis of the patient's "negative therapeutic reaction" (p. 49) to progress or to praise from the therapist. The reappearance of symptoms signified an underlying, *unconscious guilt* ["as far as the patient is concerned this sense of guilt is dumb; it does not tell him he is guilty; he does not feel guilty, he feels ill" (pp. 49-50)]. This guilt "expresses itself only as a resistance to recovery which . . . is extremely difficult to overcome" (p. 50). Freud was confounded by the punitive aspects of this unconscious guilt reaction:

> How is it that the super-ego manifests itself essentially as a sense of guilt (or rather, as criticism—for the sense of guilt is the perception in the ego answering to this criticism) and moreover develops such extraordinary harshness and severity towards the ego? (p. 53)

Freud and Becker see neurotic guilt as preventing an individual from achieving satisfaction or fulfillment in life, as well as interfering with his progress in psychotherapy. The author's (1985) views concerning neurotic guilt are similar to Becker's and Freud's formulations:

> [Neurotic guilt reactions arise] when a person chooses self-actualization. . . . If we choose to go against our inhibitions and spontaneously embrace life, we would then have to deal with the fear and guilt aroused by our affirmation of individuality and personal power. We would experience anxiety from having separated ourselves from our bonds with others and would be vulnerable to guilt for surpassing our parents and contemporaries. (p. 260)

The second type of guilt, termed *existential* or *ontological guilt,* is triggered by holding back or withholding one's natural inclinations. It is generally experienced by individuals when they turn their backs on their goals, retreat from life, or seek gratification in fantasy. Rollo May (1958) has described this form of guilt as:

> . . . rooted in the fact of self-awareness. Ontological guilt does not consist of I-am-guilty-because-I-violate-parental-prohibitions, but arises from the fact that I can see myself as the one who can choose or fail to choose. (p. 55)
>
> When the person denies these potentialities, fails to fulfill them, his condition is *guilt.* (p. 52)

Yalom (1980) discusses existential guilt in terms of responsibility and states:

Most simply put: one is guilty not only through transgressions against another or against some moral or social code, but *one may be guilty of transgression against oneself.* (p. 277)

Yalom quotes Paul Tillich in further elaborating the concept of existential guilt and shows its relationship to ontological anxiety:

Man's being is not only given to him but also demanded of him. He is responsible for it; literally, he is required to answer, if he is asked, *what he has made of himself.* He who asks him is his judge, namely he himself. The situation produces the anxiety which in relative terms is the anxiety of guilt, in absolute terms the anxiety of self-rejection or condemnation. Man is asked to make of himself what he is supposed to become, to fulfill his destiny. [Tillich, P. (1952), *The Courage to Be,* New Haven: Yale University Press, p. 52] (p. 278)

Yalom (1980) concludes that "there is a general consensus among . . . [Heidegger, Tillich, Maslow, and May] that existential guilt is a positive constructive force, a guide calling oneself back to oneself" (p. 280). According to Yalom, the failure to acknowledge one's existential guilt inevitably leads to confusion, despair, and alienation such as was experienced by Joseph K. in Kafka's (1937/1969) novel, *The Trial.* Constricted by neurotic guilt, leading a banal existence, yet stubbornly unaware of his acts of omission, Joseph K. was imprisoned (symbolically) within the narrow boundaries defined by neurotic guilt and existential guilt.

Abraham Maslow (1968) has also pointed out the sense of loathing one experiences when one moves toward security and stasis rather than striving for personal growth or self-actualization:

If this essential core of the person is denied or suppressed, he gets sick sometimes in obvious ways, sometimes in subtle ways. . . . Every falling away . . . [from our core], every crime against one's own nature . . . *records itself* in our unconscious and makes us despise ourselves. (p. 4-5)

Guilt feelings and anxiety reactions are aroused by positive as well as negative circumstances. For example, if people achieve more than their parents did, if they seek gratification of wants denied them in their families, they experience painful feelings of self-recrimination. If, however, they submit to this guilt and regress to an inward posture of passivity and fantasy, they become progressively more demoralized and self-hating. In a certain sense, each individual is suspended between these polarities of guilt, and they form the boundaries of his life experience.

In the following pages, we will elucidate the basic relationship between guilt, separation, regression, self-destructive behavior, and the voice. If we are to interrupt regressive trends and modify self-destructive behaviors, we must first be able to identify the patterns of thought at the core of these phenomena. It is important to understand that the same mechanism that operates in psychotic states of regression and self-destructive acting out in the schizophrenic patient is operating, to a lesser degree, in the neurotic or "normal" individual, fostering guilt reactions and depression.

GUILT AND SEPARATION

The inordinate force of moral authority derives from the conditions of the first psychological birth, when an infant's physical and psychological survival depended entirely on the protection and approval of her parents. Dread of loss [of the parents] . . . can make cowardly, submissive infants of us all—which is why the human conscience is so largely an instrument of the status quo. It is ruthless in its opposition to change. It preserves the past.

Kaplan (1984, p. 110)

Both guilt feelings and fear arise when there is a threat of separation—separation from the mother, from parents and parental substitutes, and the ultimate separation from self and loved ones in death. There is considerable guilt as an individual moves toward independence and self-realization, thereby separating from the bond or imaginary connection with the family. On the other hand, there is guilt if one attempts to maintain one's fantasy of connection with one's family for purposes of security. The failure to differentiate oneself from the mother or other family members inevitably leads to regressive behavior that sets up a pattern of guilt reactions.

R.D. Laing (1961/1971) has portrayed the dualistic nature of guilt relating to destructive bonds in his discussion of collusion:

> The one person does not use the other merely as a hook to hang projections on. He strives to find in the other, or to induce the other to become, the very *embodiment* of projection. The other person's collusion is required to 'complement' the identity self feels impelled to sustain. One can experience a peculiar form of guilt, specific, I think, to this disjunction. If one refuses collusion, one feels guilt for not being or not becoming the embodiment of the complement demanded by the other for his identity. However if one *does* succumb, if one is seduced, one becomes estranged from one's self and is guilty thereby of self-betrayal. (p. 111)

Laing, in effect, is describing both types of guilt: the guilty feelings aroused when one separates from a bond and, by contrast, the existential guilt that arises when a person surrenders his individuality for the security connection. Being original, nonconformist, separate, and independent creates anxiety and guilt and can lead to regressive behavior and increased dependency, whereas submitting to the attachment, remaining fused or linked to the family and later to one's mate for imagined safety, also generates feelings of guilt and self-castigation.

Otto Rank was well aware of the contradictory sources of guilt and its dualistic structure. He wrote extensively about guilt reactions in relation to the problem of the "will" and parental prohibitions. However, he perceived that guilt feelings were also reactions to separation experiences. The author's understanding of the role that neurotic guilt plays in causing a constriction of life-affirming activities is in accord with Rank's thinking. In his essay on *Separation and Guilt,* Rank (1936/1972) writes:

> The problem of the neurosis itself is a separation problem and as such a blocking of the human life principle, the conscious ability to endure release and separation, first from the *biological power represented by parents,* and *finally from the lived out parts of the self which this power represents,* [italics added] and which obstruct the development of the individual personality. It is at this point that the neurotic comes to grief, where, instead of living, of overcoming the past through the present, he becomes conscious that he dare not, cannot, loose himself because he is bound by guilt. (p. 73-74)

Rank's reference to the "biological power represented by the parents" calls attention to a special transcendental quality that parents transmit to their children, that is, the possibility of triumphing over death by merging with the parents. However, the illusory merger is costly; the individual is too guilty to "loose himself" from his bonds.

In his brilliant synthesis of Rank's work, Becker (1973) writes of children's identification with their parents as being a "special case of the urge for immortality."

> The child merges himself with the representatives of the cosmic process. . . . When one merges with the self-transcending parents . . . he is, in some real sense, trying to live in some larger expansiveness of meaning. (p. 152)

Both parents and child imagine their merger as somehow imbuing them with immortality. In this sense, the family symbolizes immortality; it is the link in an unending chain of persons passing on unique traits from one generation to the next.

Many parents, in believing that their children "belong" to them, have strong feelings of exclusivity and possessiveness in relation to their offspring. This sense of ownership stems partly from parents' deeply held, unconscious belief that through their children, they can achieve immortality. After all, their children are the products of the parents' bodies and extensions of themselves. To the extent that children resemble their parents in appearance, characteristics, and behavior, they are the parents' legacy to be left in the world after the parents' death as evidence that their lives were meaningful and made a difference. On the other hand, the more the child is differentiated from the parent in looks, in character traits, in behavior, or in significant career choices, the more guilt he feels about breaking the continuous chain symbolically linking the generations. By disrupting this continuity, the developing child becomes acutely aware of his vulnerability to death. He also becomes aware that his movement toward individuality and independence challenges his parents' immortality.

Therefore, in moving away from the family, the child experiences considerable guilt in relation to the pain and anxiety that he believes he is causing his parents. To avoid this guilt, the child tends to cling to the bond with his parents by maintaining a sameness with them rather than "living out the parts" of himself that would cause him to stand out from family patterns and traditions.

In other writings, the author (1985) has referred to the guilt and anger associated with separation experiences:

> Each successive stage of maturity confronts the child and later, the adult, with the basic facts of personal existence—aloneness and separateness, as well as the vulnerability to death. . . . Each phase is also marked by guilt at leaving the mother [parents] behind, and by anger and resentment at having to face the world alone. (p. 173-174)

A number of other theorists have written about guilt reactions associated with separation and death anxiety (Guntrip, 1961). For example, in his book, *Death Anxiety,* James B. McCarthy (1980) notes that a "psychological inquiry into the meaning of anxiety about going to school . . . very often discloses fears that either the child will be hurt or killed or that his parents will be hurt or killed" (p. 65). In more serious cases of school phobias, McCarthy writes:

> In severe phobias, the young child's fear of death arises not just out of a need for punishment or guilt but because he or she depends on and identifies with the parent. To this extent, the child may view himself or herself as a psychological extension of the parent. (p. 65)

Many adults retain strong feelings of being connected to the parent; consequently "independence for either partner threatens the self with the loss of a part of the shared inner psychic structure" (p. 67). In other words, independence and individuation disrupt the fantasy bond with one's parents and arouse strong feelings of guilt and anxiety.

McCarthy recounts the case of a mother who, in the process of admitting her twenty-year-old daughter to a psychiatric hospital, attempted to give her daughter the jewelry she was wearing:

Noting the girl's reluctance, the mother said repeatedly, "If you stay in the hospital, I'll never see you again." . . . These reactions coincided with the mother's depression, and they would be likely to induce feelings of guilt, helplessness and anxiety in the daughter. . . . The hidden message contained in the mother's interaction with the daughter could be oversimplified to read: "I'm furious at you for thinking of leaving me. You'll be sorry; I'll die without you" or, "You won't be able to live without me." (p. 67)

Threats of desertion or warnings to the child that he or she will be sent away because of "bad behavior," together with subtle or direct threats of parental illness or an emotional breakdown, occur in families more often than is commonly thought (Bowlby, 1973). Overprotectiveness toward children is also symptomatic of a strong fantasy bond in the family.

For example, a seven-year-old boy asked his parents if he could travel with his grandparents to their home in the country. Initially, the youngster was very happy and enjoyed the drive, but later became very agitated and wanted to return home. When questioned about his change of mind, the boy responded with: "Mommy said she would die if something happened to me. I want to go back so she won't die, so she can see I'm not hurt." His mother's unintentionally destructive statement about her concern for his safety had aroused the boy's guilt about being away from her for an extended period of time.

Children's guilt about their hostile fantasies of destroying the parental figure has been assumed by some clinicians to be a principal cause of the guilt and depression that they experience during actual separation (Klein, 1930/1964). However, other explanations are also relevant and may be more parsimonious. For example, many parents experience considerable distress at their child's growing freedom and independence and openly indicate their displeasure. The child senses the parents' pain or grief over the anticipated loss and responds with guilt. If the parents are immature and dependent, these feelings are even more exaggerated, and the child comes to feel that movement toward adulthood and his own goals is mean or destructive. As noted earlier, bonds or fantasies of connection between parents and children are powerful agents of security, often far more significant than the realistic security in the actual relationship. Breaking a bond is analogous to letting the other person die, because an individual has difficulty maintaining the illusory connection without the cooperation of the other.

Patients have reported numerous experiences where their parents, mates, or family members responded with episodes of physical illness when they (the patients) moved toward independence. For example, one young man was successfully manipulated by his mother's illness when he was eighteen years old and striking out on his own. On the morning of the young man's departure on an extended automobile trip with a friend, his mother developed severe chest pains. She was convinced that she was having a heart attack. The young man's father prevailed upon him not to leave at this time because his departure would make his mother feel worse, and her condition might become critical as a result. Out of a deep sense of guilt, he cancelled his trip. Doctors placed his mother under observation, but released her 3 days later without discovering the cause of her symptoms.

This event was not an isolated incident and significantly affected the young man's approach to life. His guilt generalized to other situations, causing him to be fearful and nonassertive. It played a part in the formation of his basic character defenses of self-denial and passivity.

According to Freud (1915/1957), the guilt associated with our illusion of immortality, together with our "daily and hourly" death wishes toward strangers and loved ones alike, engenders a deep sense of guilt about surviving where others die, about enjoying our fortune where others suffer misfortune.

> For strangers and for enemies we do acknowledge death, and consign them to it quite as readily and unhesitatingly as did primaeval man. . . . In our unconscious impulses we daily and hourly get rid of anyone who stands in our way, of anyone who has offended or injured us. (p. 297)

Real and symbolic separation from parents toward whom one has held ambivalent feelings arouses deep feelings of guilt, as though one were leaving them to die, while one lives and flourishes. To illustrate, a woman who at twenty-five had never gone out with a man, but who had a homosexual relationship, became freer and more assertive in other areas of her life as she progressed in her psychotherapy. Gradually she overcame her extreme shyness and began to express an interest in men. Soon afterward, she met a man whom she liked and admired and entered into a sexual relationship. The relationship progressed, and the couple began to talk seriously about the possibility of marriage. After several months of struggle and internal conflict, she attempted to give up the relationship with her girlfriend. That same evening, the woman had a terrifying nightmare that left her extremely anxious. She dreamed that she was walking through a bombed-out city when suddenly she saw her mother, ill and pathetic, beckoning her to come back. Her mother appeared so weak and helpless that the patient could not bear to leave her there among the ruins. Superimposed upon her mother's face were the features of the girlfriend. She returned to her mother's side and picked her up and began carrying her through the empty city. She awoke still feeling the weight of this phantom of her nightmare around her shoulders. In the weeks that followed, the patient became disillusioned with her boyfriend, eventually broke off their relationship completely, and returned to her former homosexual relationship.

In reality, the patient's mother had been weak and self-sacrificing, selflessly devoting herself to her husband and daughter. The call of the self-denying mother had been too compelling for this young woman to resist. She healed the fracture with her mother symbolically by reconnecting with her girlfriend and renouncing the relationship with her boyfriend that was both happy and satisfying. The nightmare was representative of her guilt and fear of separation.

SELF-HATRED AND GUILT

There is a strong relationship between feelings of guilt and one's feeling of self-hatred. Theodore Rubin was well aware of the major importance of guilt in man's propensity for self-destruction. In his book, *Compassion and Self-Hate*, Rubin (1975) writes with an acute sensitivity of the methods that people use to destroy themselves.

We "murder" ourselves when we invoke self-hating devices and when we annihilate our potential for enjoying life's realistic good offerings. . . . These self-hating activities often have the special characteristics of being passed off as virtues. The victim rationalizes . . . guilt as a high sense of responsibility and morality. . . . [But guilt has] a depleting, fatiguing, constricting effect and . . . [is] ultimately destructive to self-esteem and to one's actual person. (p. 72-73)

In a similar vein, the author (1985) has described the purpose of the "voice" in instilling guilt in the individual:

Withholding and self-denial are regulated by the destructive thought processes of the voice. . . . The effect of chronic patterns of withholding is an ultimate shutting down, a paralysis, of that part of the individual that strives for emotional health and growth—the part that contributes to feelings of self-esteem. (p. 153-154)

Clinicians are familiar with the primary guilt reactions experienced by patients when they attempt to overcome inhibitions of the past and actively pursue a more fulfilling life. They understand the relationship of this form of guilt to early parental training and prohibitions. Similarly, they recognize that many patients feel a sense of guilt when they indulge in self-nourishing habits, e.g., masturbating, overeating, drinking to excess, smoking, or drug abuse. Less is understood of the existential guilt aroused by surrendering one's independent point of view and submitting to sameness and conformity. We are not cognizant of the full extent to which people feel guilty when they retreat from life and act out a self-destructive, self-limiting process. In fact, a person's most stubborn or oppositional behavior centers around this form of guilt.

Individuals go to great lengths to cover up or hide their propensity for self-destruction. Patients in therapy are often the most defensive, disagreeable, and hostile toward the therapist when they are defending the acting out of self-destructive impulses or when they are attempting to deny their self-destructiveness. These urges are humiliating and shameful facets of the personality. To complicate matters, regressive behavior, unhappiness, even depression, often follow success and achievement and therefore appear illogical and inappropriate. Negative reactions to positive events seem perverse without a deeper understanding of man's basic fear of independence and separateness.

Both patients and psychotherapists fail to appreciate the full significance of the self-destructive process that is set into motion when one adopts an inward life-style characterized by self-denial, role-playing, fantasy, and retreat. We recognize the dangers inherent in substituting fantasy gratification for actual satisfactions in the real world when they reach monumental proportions as in the psychoses, yet we remain largely unaware of the extent of micro-suicidal behavior manifest by so-called normal individuals as they move through the life process.

THE VOICE AND NEUROTIC GUILT

Guilt reactions represent the internalization of parental rejecting attitudes in relation to simple body needs, as well as the need for affectionate contact and love. Frustration of infantile urges and primitive hunger caused by emotional deprivation are at the core of guilt feelings and negative feelings and attitudes toward self. When parents are unable sensitively to care for and love their children because of their own inadequacies or dependency needs, the child begins to feel guilty for expressing or even having natural wants and needs. As adults, people rationalize their habit of rationing or limiting themselves in an ever widening range of situations and, as a result, become increasingly alienated from themselves as vital, feeling human beings.

Guilt About Being Alive

As described earlier, the voice represents an external point of view toward the self initially derived from the parents' overt or covert hostile feelings toward the child. If, for example, a child was unwanted or was born at an inopportune time, he might grow up believing that he is a *burden* to his parents or might entertain fantasies of having been adopted, of not really belonging to his family. Later, such individuals would feel undeserving, believing that they had no rights, or might, on a deeper level, feel guilty for even being alive. In this case, the voice would attack them derisively: "People don't really want you around," or, "You don't belong here—you're a misfit." "People don't want to listen to you." "You would never be chosen."

For example, one subject, a very reticent, inward young woman, had been raised in a family that she described as dominated by her mother's chronic alcoholism and subsequent neglect of her children. As a result, the subject was painfully shy, quiet, and extremely self-conscious. In a Voice Therapy session, she revealed a voice that directed her to be unobtrusive and to remain in the background. In a subsequent session, she said she had been able to identify this voice as representing her mother's rejecting attitudes toward her:

> I have never been aware of how she felt towards me as I was growing up, but I think as the result of that, that I'm quiet. I constantly act on the feelings that I have. I even thought that *I felt guilty for just being alive*. I thought it would be interesting to say more of that feeling. The feeling is:
> "Just don't say anything! Look, just leave me alone! I don't care about you. (Angrily) Just stay away! Little Miss Priss! Just stay out of my life. I don't want you around. Who do you think you are? *I'm* Daddy's little girl, not you! Just stay out of my way! Just don't come around me trying to act cute. There's nothing cute about you. There's nothing pretty about you . . . (cries)

The young woman's symptoms had inhibited her natural expression and significantly constricted her life. Following the sessions where she verbalized her self-attacks and identified their origins, she experienced a sense of relief from guilt and became more outspoken and assertive. She also reported feeling a strong sense of identity for the first time in her life.

Another subject, an associate, recalled being told by his parents that he had nearly died during a long childhood illness. The boy's mother had confided to him that at one point his father had said he would kill himself if the boy died. According to an uncle, his parents were thrilled when the boy lived; however, the weeks of constant fear had evidently taken their toll. The threat of loss had damaged their emotional involvement with their son, and they became more distant from the youngster. His parents' unconscious rejection of him affirmed his sense of being "bad" for being sick and causing his parents suffering. Later, as an adult, whenever he became ill or sensed weakness in himself, he felt guilty and "bad." In some sense, the feelings of self-recrimination he felt for inadvertently causing his parents grief were extended and generalized to a guilty feeling for enjoying life. It was difficult for this man to maintain a sense of legitimacy, in spite of unusual achievement and dedication.

Guilt About Being Different From Family

Guilt about moving in a direction that is different from or more fulfilling than one's family is often expressed by the voice in the following terms: "Who do you think you are?" "You always want your own way!" "You only think of yourself."

In one case, a man verbalized a series of self-attacks representing guilty reactions he experienced relating to important new friendships he was developing. As he talked, his voice assumed a snide, parental tone, which he identified as sounding like his father's.

> What are you doing here with these people? What do you need these friends for? You don't need friends! All you need is us, your family. You always were a weird person. When you were a kid, you were so strange. You never wanted to be like us. You always wanted to be different. Who do you think you are?

The key dynamic in this case concerned the subject's guilt about his movement away from the family and its problems. Achieving more financial success, developing friendships, and choosing to live life more fully than the members of his family gave rise to a considerable amount of anxiety and led to feelings of remorse and self-reproach.

Many people suffer intense feelings of guilt about leaving others behind and succeeding where others close to them have failed, and these successes arouse strong voice attacks.

Often, contact with a family member will serve to remind the person that he has stepped out of line or broken the family tradition. I am pained to be reminded of a patient with a borderline personality disorder, who had progressed significantly during 3 years of therapy, changing her hostile, suspicious views of men and integrating fragments of a disorganized ego. She had overcome serious paranoid attitudes, was in the process of forming closer relationships, and in general felt cheerful and well. She was in an optimistic state when her sister (also seriously disturbed psychologically) called her on the phone. After the patient told her about her progress and her sense of hopefulness, she asked her sister how she was feeling. Her sister responded bitterly and sarcastically with: "You want to know how I'm feeling? Well, I'll tell you how I'm feeling. I feel like killing myself!" Tragically, the patient, torn by unbearable guilt feelings about her sister's unhappiness, turned against herself and soon afterwards impulsively discontinued her sessions. Subsequently, she resumed the isolated life-style in which she had existed prior to the psychotherapy. Although this is a dramatic example of regression following renewed contact with a family member, it is not a singular or isolated phenomenon.

In reviewing the patient's case material, several factors became evident. In her sessions, the patient's feelings of deep remorse and culpability had come to light. For instance, early on she had reported feeling guilty about revealing details of her family life to the therapist. In one session, she verbalized her voice as follows:

> You don't even know what you're going to say! You have nothing to say! This man doesn't want to hear what you have to say. You'd better keep your mouth shut if you know what's good for you!
> You think you feel good from this session? Well, wait until morning. You'll wake up feeling so rotten you won't know what to do. You can't talk to this man and then expect to feel good. You're going to feel terrible if you talk about the family.

In working through the negative transference, the patient developed positive regard for her therapist and had overcome her paranoid expectations of mistreatment and exploitation at the hands of men. Toward the end of therapy, she approached issues that lay at the core of her illness. In one session, she expressed the rage she had internalized early in childhood, representing her mother's death wishes toward her as well as her mother's obvious preference for her sister. The introjected anger and hostile attitudes of her mother contributed to the patient's generalized guilt reactions, specifically about being different from her sister:

> Why can't you be like your sister? She's beautiful, and look at you! You have the ugliest face. Why don't you just die? Why weren't you one of the ones who died? [The patient's mother had had several miscarriages.] Just get out of here! Just leave me alone!

Soon after this session, the patient had received the call from her sister. Guilt about her attempt to separate herself symbolically from her mother's and sister's wretched outlook on life made it impossible for her to tolerate the difference between her own state of happiness and her sister's depression and misery. Follow-up revealed that the woman's brief contact with her sister, even through the medium of a long-distance phone call, was a key factor in disrupting her adjustment.

THE VOICE AND EXISTENTIAL GUILT

> A person may feel consciously guilty for not pleasing authorities, while unconsciously he feels guilty for not living up to his own expectations of himself.
>
> Erich Fromm (1947, p. 169)

We have consistently found that whenever our subjects submitted to guilt reactions and regressed, they generally "heard" voices telling them that they were no different from their family. For example, one man became deeply concerned that his five-year-old daughter might feel rejected or deprived of his affection and interest. Whenever he noticed her unhappiness or felt distant from her, he tortured himself with thoughts such as:

> See, you thought you were going to be different. Well, look at your kids. There's the proof! You're no different! What made you think you could be different? You can't change it. You're a failure. You're rotten all the way through.

Rather than serving as a "constructive guide," this man's guilt and remorse, as expressed in the form of the voice, only served further to demoralize him and actually *prevented* him from feeling compassionate toward himself and his children. Self-critical thoughts reminding people that they are no different from their parents have been reported by many individuals as significant factors in their acting against their own interests.

People feel strong guilt feelings when they act in a manner that goes against their stated goals and real preferences. They are basically depriving of themselves when they are opposed to their own point of view, but in addition, they feel bad about hurting others who depend upon their love. A number of subjects reported increased feelings of self-hatred and guilt reactions whenever they withheld affection and became alienated from close friends or marriage partners. They not only castigated themselves for losing the relationship or damaging it ("See, now you have *no* friends;" or, "He/she will never want you back"); but also felt remorseful and self-hating about hurting the other person ("You really made him/her feel terrible; you have such a bad effect on people"). This form of voice attack is characteristic of people who are self-denying or who limit their involvement in close relationships by holding back positive emotional responses. On some level, they are troubled by deep-seated guilt feelings and frequently try to compensate for their cutting off of genuine feeling by substituting role-determined responses.

In an earlier work (1985), I have referred to a patient, Joanne, who wrote a letter to friends in her therapy group describing the guilt and self-hatred that revolved around her self-destructive pattern of living. The following excerpts from her letter demonstrate an unusual understanding of the part played by her voice in preserving her isolated, inward life-style and her self-hatred:

> Self-loathing has become so firmly entrenched in my being, it feels like the very core of me—in some crazy way, self-hatred feels like my "life-force."
> I can't hang on to self-hatred around you any more—even with briefest contact of groups and weekly sessions. *No matter how I "insure" the feeling by acts of self-destructiveness during the week—the eating, picking at myself, calling up my mother's voice to ridicule and denounce myself*—you just have to see me, I mean

really see and address the person that's real in me, to strip away the self-hate, even for just a second or two. . . .

In my case, self-hatred was formed very early, to protect myself from the certain total insanity that rejection would have led me into. From there, keeping a layer of fat surrounding me, twisting my face into ugly expressions, kept that basic or primal defense alive in me. (I just remembered that I began being fat at the age of five, when a friend of the family began showing an interest in me. It was also a time during which I first acted out self-destructiveness, inflicting a concussion on myself, sitting on a live battery and burning my legs. He was the first to threaten that primary defense . . . by being nice to me.)

This letter was written over 11 years ago, about the same time that my conceptualization and understanding of the voice process were unfolding. This patient, who described herself so honestly, showed insight that was partially ahead of my knowledge at that time. For example, Joanne writes of "calling up her mother's voice" to denounce her during the week for her self-destructive habits. Prior to therapy, this woman had become progressively demoralized by powerful feelings of self-hatred, guilt, and a chronic sense of despair and futility. As she improved, she became more intolerant of her life of self-loathing and guilt and, at the time she wrote the letter, was making concerted efforts to change behaviors that caused her to despise herself.

The tragedy is that this woman, who was so painfully intolerant of nice treatment as a child that she deliberately burned her legs when someone took a friendly personal interest in her, could not bring herself to give up her basic defense. She eventually left therapy and her friends, and today is living the isolated, guilt-ridden life of which she so poignantly wrote (Firestone, 1985).

MANIFESTATIONS OF GUILT IN SCHIZOPHRENIA

The end result of a pathological process of regression and self-destructive behavior, followed by remorse, existential guilt, and increased self-hatred, can be observed in the auditory hallucinations of schizophrenic patients. In these cases, the voices continually direct, reprimand, and punish the patient in the form of parental injunctions. Furthermore, the voices attack the patients for giving in to self-destructive impulses, thereby compounding the problem.

Manifestations of guilt in schizophrenic patients reach significant proportions whenever there is progress in therapy. Paradoxically, guilt reactions are also severe when there is regression and acting out of self-destructive behavior. M. Sechehaye's (1951) classic analysis of Renée, a regressed schizophrenic girl, clearly illustrates both types of guilt. We are indebted to Sechehaye for her appreciation of the regressed patient's inability to accept gratification in reality and her recognition of Renée's need for substitute or alternative gratification in the form of symbolic realization.

Because of early childhood deprivation, Renée had turned to fantasy for gratification. The rationale underlying Sechehaye's method of feeding her patient apples (Renée's personal symbol for maternal milk) is pertinent to our discussion:

> While Renée had returned to the oral phase, she would have been angry to receive real milk, and that would have made her more ill. It was necessary for her to receive a symbol and not a reality. Why? *Because guilt feelings make it necessary to camouflage the repressed desire* [italics added]. Once the guilt feelings have been calmed (in this case, by having appeased the legitimate desire), one can accept reality. (p. 52)

By offering only symbolic or fantasy gratification, Sechehaye was able to counter the patient's profound feelings of guilt. She was able to "wean" Renée gradually to actual satisfactions and the simple pleasures of reality.

Both M. Sechehaye and Renée herself, in writing about her illness (*Autobiography of a Schizophrenic Girl*, 1951/1970), pointed out that the "flight into madness" was torturous, because tremendous feelings of guilt and self-destructive impulses were aroused when regression took place. In the course of treatment, when Renée submitted to self-destructive impulses or retreated further into autism, there were strong guilt reactions. The voices instructed Renée over and over again to hurt herself, and it required all her strength to resist. Yet when she gave in to these voices and acted out physical abuse on herself, they became even more intense and derisive.

As she retreated into autism, Renée's guilty reactions focused on three principal themes: (1) the existential guilt of self-betrayal; (2) betrayal of the people who loved her and wished her well, most particularly the therapist who was attempting to help her; and (3) guilt about becoming progressively less functional and thereby presenting a burden to others. Her voices played a part in all of the above reactions of guilt.

The analogy to neurotic behavior and the seemingly perverse actions of many normal individuals is clear. People far less disturbed than Renée also feel guilty about pursuing goals directly. Like Renée, they appear to prefer fantasy gratification to fulfilling their wants in reality. Yet as they choose fantasy, passivity, and self-nourishing life-styles, they feel existential guilt. For example, people who give up genuine caring and real interest in their mates for role-playing and a fantasy of love (a bond) experience considerable suffering and remorse.

As individuals retreat from pursuing life fully, they feel guilty of self-betrayal and, incidentally, betrayal of their loved ones as well. Indeed, many couples' disputes are triggered by concern about the self-destructive impulses and actions of the marital partner. Fear and worry about the other unfortunately lead to intrusive behavior and aggressive interference, which further damages the relationship. As is the case in more serious pathology, whenever people become withholding and less adaptive in their overall functioning, they feel guilty about their failures. Any behavior that leads to unnecessary withdrawal and increased dependency intensifies this process. Furthermore, in their attempts to cover up their withdrawal and withholding toward a love object, most people act as if they are still pursuing satisfying relationships and personal goals, and, as a result, their communications become duplicitous. This lack of integrity further intensifies their guilt.

GUILT AND DEATH ANXIETY

In a deep sense, people feel afraid to live fully in the face of their ultimate fate or to give value to a life that they know they eventually must lose. They are reluctant to become too attached to other people or to allow others to become close to them because of the pain and grief involved in potential separation. They often feel guilty about enjoying physical pleasure because they wish to remain unaware of being connected to or trapped in a body that will someday die. In that sense, their guilt may be an attempt to disown their physical nature because of its obvious impermanence.

A form of guilt closely related to separation and death anxiety is "death guilt," described by Robert Lifton and Eric Olson (1976) in their paper, *The Human Meaning of Total Disaster.* They define death guilt as "the survivor's sense of painful self-condemnation over having lived while others died" (p. 3). Interviewing survivors from the Buffalo Creek Flood of 1972, Lifton and Olson determined that:

> People who have gone through this kind of experience are never quite able to forgive themselves for having survived. Another side of them, however, experiences relief and gratitude that it was *they* who had the good fortune to survive in contrast to the fate of those [many of whom were close relatives] who died—a universal and all-too-human survivor reaction that in turn intensifies their guilt. (p. 5)

Lifton and Olson's concept of "death guilt" coincides with the descriptions of "survival guilt" related by those individuals who were incarcerated in concentration camps and survived the trauma. In other writings, Lifton and Olson (1974/1976) relate survivor guilt indirectly to death anxiety and the individual's attempt to cope with the kinds of experiences where this anxiety is aroused. Lifton and Olson (1976) believe that when an individual suppresses these painful feelings of guilt, the result is a kind of *"psychic numbing*—a diminished capacity for feeling of all kinds—in the form of various manifestations of apathy, withdrawal, depression, and overall constriction in living" (p. 5).

In our terms, the survivor in this situation undoubtedly possesses a questioning, sneering, accusatory voice—"Why did *you* survive while others died?" or, "Did you *really* deserve to live?"—as part of an unrelenting guilt reaction.

William Styron's (1979) novel, *Sophie's Choice,* graphically portrays this form of self-blame and the painful self-accusations associated with "survivor guilt." After choosing to save her son by sacrificing her daughter in order to avert death for both her children at the hands of the SS guards, Sophie was tormented by guilt for surviving her ordeal. Basically her terrible choice involved choosing life for herself, for which she was never able to forgive herself. Later, her lover, Nathan, became a tool in her own self-destruction. His accusations and questions about the methods she employed that allowed her to survive—"How did *you* escape?"—echoed Sophie's own self-condemnations. In a sense, she projected her voice onto Nathan and used him to punish herself. In her own eyes, the punishment was not severe enough to equal her crime—that of being alive, and Sophie ended her life by submitting to Nathan's psychotic plan for them to die together.

To feel one's guilt about surviving, simply living, or valuing one's life is painful. For this reason, it typically is repressed, surfacing at times as feelings of self-consciousness or in apologetic gestures toward others who are less fortunate (Firestone, 1985). People who restrict their lives experience boredom, a sense of emptiness, and feelings of existential guilt; however, they *do* minimize or avoid painful feelings associated with death anxiety that would follow from investing in a full life. Many individuals are willing to pay the price of living a defended, self-hating existence (as in the case of Joanne) and choose an emotionally deadened, self-limiting life-style.

Indeed, a common response to "survival guilt" and death anxiety is to renounce the very activities and relationships that give one's life the most value. The author (1985) has described this form of progressive self-denial as an accommodation to death and a defense against death anxiety:

> We *attempt to gain control over death through a process of progressive self-denial*; that is, we deny ourselves experiences that would enhance our lives and give them value. . . . In withdrawing feeling or affect from personal pursuits and goal-directed activity, [we reduce our] vulnerability to hurt, rejection or loss. (p. 256)

This process, which is suicidal in nature, diminishes the guilt about choosing life, yet it inevitably leads to the second type of guilt, existential guilt, of which Becker (1973) has written: "Guilt results from unused life, from 'the unlived in us'." (p. 180). This guilt, in turn, is responsible for people's acting out destructive impulses in a desperate attempt to atone for acts of *omission*—in effect, to punish themselves for their withdrawal from life.

The verbalization of guilt reactions through the procedures of Voice Therapy evokes feelings of compassion and support for the self and for one's personal point of view. In contrast, when the process of voice attacks is *not* interrupted, a person increasingly submits to the injunctions of the voice and progressively abandons his/her real self and unique point of view.

CONCLUSION

It is not an accident that the three principal cases described in this chapter had negative outcomes. Guilt reactions can predispose serious consequences and regressions based on these feelings and can be very detrimental to a person's development over extended periods of time. Indeed, the range of an individual's experience is defined by the boundaries imposed by neurotic guilt on the one hand and existential guilt on the other—and by the thought process that mediates guilt, the voice. However, by identifying this voice and making it conscious, people can progress and cope more successfully with their self-limiting and self-destructive tendencies. In our present state of knowledge, we feel that this technique helps patients isolate and become conscious of the dual nature of their guilt feelings. It is our opinion that Voice Therapy is a valuable research tool for understanding the relationship and structure of *neurotic* and *existential* guilt. Furthermore, in systematically challenging the voice, the patient becomes freer to pursue his life, thereby minimizing regressive trends and the complicated guilt feelings associated with self-betrayal.

8

*Micro-Suicide and Suicidal Threats of Everyday Life**

The prisoner on death row who ends his life prematurely in an overt suicide is not unlike the average person who limits and denies himself life in the face of separation anxiety and death anxiety. Suicidal behavior does not always entail such direct and overt means as putting a gun to your head. Indeed, it includes a whole range of behaviors not always thought of as suicidal. "Micro-suicide," as referred to here, encompasses those behaviors, communications, attitudes, or life-styles that are self-induced and threatening, limiting, or antithetical to an individual's physical health, emotional well-being, or personal goals.

All self-destructive behaviors are related; that is, they differ only in quantity, nature, and degree. While the great majority of suicide attempters will not proceed to kill themselves, a few will. Suicide attempts are approximately three times as common as completed suicides. Verbal threats of suicide are more frequent still, and the fantasy of suicide is so common that it is regarded as a prevailing fact of normal adolescence (Seiden, 1984b). In the words of the philosopher, Nietzsche (1886/1966): "The thought

*The bulk of the material and substance of this chapter closely parallels an article with the same title published in *Psychotherapy,* Vol. 24, No. 1, 1987.

of suicide is a powerful comfort: it helps one through many a dreadful night" (p. 91).

In this chapter, we will focus upon those behaviors that are not actually life threatening but that are so widely disseminated in the general population that we have named them the "*micro- suicides of everyday life*." It has long been acknowledged that there are self-damaging life-styles or behavior patterns that are not necessarily undertaken with the ultimate aim of self-destruc- tion. Such behavior has been referred to by a variety of names including: indirect suicide, partial suicide, installment-plan sui- cide, slow suicide, inimical patterns of behavior, embryonic sui- cide, masked suicide, hidden suicide, para-suicide, and chronic suicide. While there are minor distinctions between these terms, they all describe life-styles of gradual self-destruction.

Durkheim, the great French sociologist, was one of the first writers to recognize an essential continuity of self-destructive behaviors. In his pioneering text, *Le Suicide,* written at the close of the nineteenth century, Durkheim (1897/1951) declares:

> Suicides do not form, as might be thought, a wholly distinctive group, an isolated class of monstrous phenomena, unrelated to other forms of conduct, but rather are related to them by a con- tinuous series of intermediate cases. *They are merely the exag- gerated form of common practices* [italics added]. (p. 45)

Durkheim illustrates his remarks with examples of certain forms of "embryonic suicide": the daredevil who toys with death, the man who imperils his health by neglecting it, the "workaholic" scholar who dies from the excess of his own labors.

The eminent suicidologist, Edwin Shneidman (1966), pre- sents a similar conceptual scheme in the analysis of what he calls "inimical patterns of living." He defines these (literally) "un- friendly" behavioral responses as the "multitudinous ways in which an individual can reduce, truncate, demean, narrow or shorten his own life" (p. 199). Such responses, he cautions, are not necessarily a "substitute suicide" but a range of behaviors in which completed suicide is but one, albeit the most extreme, example.

In recent years, the Finnish psychiatrist, Kalle Achté, and the American psychologist, Norman Farberow, have published studies in the area of indirect self-destructive behaviors. Achté (1980) discusses the case of persons who characteristically sabotage their own successes preferring instead to play the role of miserable, unhappy sufferers.

Nelson and Farberow (1982) note that chronically ill hospitalized patients frequently exhibit "behaviours involving noncompliance with the treatment programme, and conflicts with the medical staff" (p. 5). They evolved a scale to measure *indirect self-destructive behavior* (ISDB), one that measures noncompliant acting-out behaviors and more direct forms of self-injury. They found a correlation between high levels on the ISDB and actual suicide potential. Incidentally, the researchers also linked incidents of "micro-suicide" or indirect self-destructive behavior to the patients' desperate attempts at control:

> At some perceived or unconscious level of psychodynamic choice, a patient may feel compelled to risk his health or welfare through ISDB in an effort *to gain some sense of mastery* [italics added] over a relatively powerless life situation. (p. 13)

In *The Many Faces of Suicide,* Farberow (1980) enumerates specific self-destructive behaviors which:

> . . . by their very familiarity and frequency of occurrence . . . must merge into the normal, acceptable end of the continuum of behavior. On the other hand, if they can be so self-destructive or self-injurious, they must merge into the pathological end of the continuum represented by overt suicidal activity." (p. 2)

From their description of these slow, often unconscious, self-destructive processes, Achté, Nelson, and Farberow have expanded upon the concepts and examples developed by Karl Menninger (1938) in his classic book, *Man Against Himself.*

Menninger used the term "partial suicide" to signify a variety of self-destructive life-styles that amount to suicide on a continuing, attenuated basis. The psycho-dynamic frame of reference is established early in the book's preface when Menninger declares: "In the end each man kills himself in his own selected way, fast or slow, soon or late" (p. vii). He then proceeds to enumerate and develop the many, often perversely ingenious, ways that people manage to accomplish their self-defeating objectives, such as ascetic denial, repetitive accidents, alcohol addiction, unwise financial speculation, failure to follow medical advice.

In the following pages, we will examine the myriad self-destructive behaviors that are so ubiquitous that we can fail to appreciate their diagnostic importance or the profound negative effect they exert on people. Further, we will analyze the underlying thought process that mediates or influences these actions and life-styles.

THE DYNAMICS OF MICRO-SUICIDE

Self-denying and self-destructive behaviors derive from strong feelings of self-hatred and negative attitudes toward the self that are incorporated by the child at an early stage in his development. Feelings of worthlessness, self-critical thoughts, and the erratic mood swings that characterize certain types of depressive states are controlled or strongly influenced by the voice. Our studies show that self-attacks of the voice vary along a continuum of intensity from mild self-reproach to strong self-accusations and suicidal thoughts. Similarly, micro-suicidal behavior exists on a continuum ranging from self-denial to accident-proneness, drug abuse, and other self-defeating behaviors, culminating in actual bodily harm. The core of the voice is directed toward unnecessary self-denial and ultimately toward the self-destruction of the individual. As such, it becomes the mechanism that regulates and dictates a person's self-denying, micro-suicidal behavior.

Micro-Suicide as an Accommodation to Death Anxiety

Statistics show that suicide rates are high in prisoners awaiting execution on death row. Thinking about this paradox leads inevitably to other conclusions about human self-destructiveness. The situation faced by a convicted killer is analogous to the circumstances faced by all men. Like the convict, people are aware of an inescapable sentence of death as a function of life itself. On an intellectual level at least, we acknowledge our limitations in time. The prisoner, faced with the knowledge of the exact hour of his execution, takes life and death in his own hands, while the "normal" individual commits "micro" suicide in an attempt to accommodate to death anxiety. In both instances, suicide, actual or partial, is a desperate attempt to avoid primitive feelings of dread and anxiety surrounding the existential awareness of separation and death. As individuals give up their lives through progressive self-denial and self-destructive habit patterns, they are able to maintain a false sense of omnipotence, as if they retained some power over life and death.

In this sense, we can say that all people are suicidal; it is only the individual style and strength of the movement toward self-destruction that varies from one individual to the next. Man does not want to die; yet he does want to protect himself when faced with the specter of death. Through the process of progressive self-denial, the terror of death is transformed into a fear of living or of becoming too attached to life.

The Manipulative Aspect of Micro-Suicidal Behavior

Micro-suicidal behavior is manipulative in that it is capable of eliciting fear, anger, guilt, or alarm in other persons. No one can neglect a self-destructive person whom one cares about; therefore, all self-denying and inimical behavior toward self has a pulling component. Most people are highly susceptible and responsive to unspoken suicide threats, even though the manifest behavior may not be overtly suicidal.

Very often, observers tend to *overestimate* the manipulative intention of suicidal acts because they confuse manipulative effects with manipulative motives. Micro-suicidal behavior *is* coercive, but this effect generally takes second place to the more basic motive to withhold commitment to a life process that is temporal and limited in nature. Obviously, the closer one comes to overt suicide, the greater the hostility or malice toward oneself, whatever the cause.

Considerable stress and emotional turmoil are experienced by a friend or family member who is closely involved with a person persistently engaged in self-destructive behavior. Intense feelings of guilt stem from a fear of being implicated in the destruction of another human being. It is obvious that a family is dysfunctional when one parent is an alcoholic or a drug abuser or is severely self-destructive; however, any family with a self-denying, self-sacrificing parent is dysfunctional in the same sense, only to a lesser degree. Manipulations on the part of self-denying parents restrict the flow of communication in the family and limit the development of independence and self-reliance in the children. Individuals growing up in families dominated by a self-denying parent feel guilty about surpassing the parent of the same sex personally or professionally. Thus, the self-denying behavior and attitudes induced in children by a self-sacrificing mother or father are repeated in the next generation, perpetuating a neurotic cycle of intimidation through guilt.

MICRO-SUICIDES OF EVERYDAY LIFE

Several basic divisions of micro-suicidal behavior can be delineated. These behaviors are not discrete, but can be categorized for purposes of clarity and elucidation:

1. Progressive self-denial.
2. Increased involvement in an inward life-style.
3. Behaviors that adversely affect physical health.
4. The formation of restrictive bonds.
5. Withholding—renunciation of personal and vocational goals.

1. Progressive Self-Denial—Giving Up Interest in Life-Affirming Activities

In our society, it is often considered a sign of "maturity" to withdraw from specific activities as one grows older. However, the tendency to give up interest in and excitement about life is built into an individual's defensive posture and may manifest itself much earlier in life. In fact, many people prematurely constrict their lives or put limits on their experiences; they tend to become self-denying as soon as they develop guilt feelings about having so-called selfish wants or needs. The process of gradual self-denial is supported by consensually validated attitudes on the part of most members of society about age-appropriate roles and behaviors.

Examples of this disengagement from life can be found in every area of human endeavor: early retirement, a premature giving up of participation in sports and physical activities, a diminished interest in sex and reduction in sexual activity, a loss of contact with old friends, and a decline in social life. Concomitantly there may be an increase in sedentary or self-nourishing occupations, and people frequently become plagued with a sense of boredom and stagnation.

As people become progressively conscious of middle age, many become fearful and apprehensive. During this stage of life, the internalized parental image takes increasing precedence over other facets of the personality. Thus, the voice becomes more dominant, exerting increasing influence by instigating and rationalizing self-denying behaviors. As individuals follow the dictates of the voice, they tend to reduce their activity levels, but they generally remain unaware that they are acting against their own best interests. Very few people question their loss of enthusiasm for pursuits they enjoyed when they were younger. They rationalize the loss with well-known clichés, e.g., "Act your age," or "Grow old gracefully."

An analysis of this destructive thought process indicates that the majority of the voice's injunctions and rationalizations are attempts to limit life by persuading the individual gradually to eliminate exciting and spontaneous pursuits. Physical life is thus maintained, yet emotional suicide is being committed on an everyday basis, as people gradually narrow their world and trivialize their experiences.

2. Withdrawal from Relationships and Increased Involvement in an Inward Life-Style

An unprecipitated breakup of a close relationship for no appropriate reason can be considered a self-destructive act. Therapists are rightly concerned when patients decide to give up an apparently satisfactory relationship over some minor problem, particularly when they are not moving on to something better. Continually changing relationships, jobs, or careers, as well as frequent moves to new physical surroundings, are often indicative of a self-destructive life-style.

Incidents of adolescent running away as well as mysterious disappearances of adults also can be symptomatic of serious pathology. People frequently run away or suddenly leave relationships in order to isolate themselves, to maintain an inward posture, and to more freely act out self-destructive habits. The self-destructive aspect of running away or sudden disappearances is often more alarming than the object loss itself. People sense that the runaway is acting on self-destructive impulses, which arouses considerable fear and concern.

A gradual withdrawal into isolation and fantasy, loss of feeling for the self, obsessional ruminations, unusual reserve and quietness, withdrawal of affect, and a forsaking of responsibilities are other signs or symptoms of regression to an inward posture. Similarly, people who increase their acting out of behavior that is degrading and demoralizing to them over an extended period of time are expressing micro-suicidal tendencies. These actions, in turn, give rise to increased feelings of self-condemnation and self-hatred. Guilt about acting out behavior that is beneath one's standards contributes to a feeling of inwardness, withdrawal, and paranoid feelings toward others.

When a person allows his or her environment to become dirty, unduly cluttered, or lacking in basic amenities, there is an indication of pathology. A total lack of concern with one's living circumstances is symptomatic of underlying self-destructive tendencies. When an inward person appears impervious to suggestions, everyday advice, or therapeutic procedures that could provide solutions to his problems, it is an indication of the strength of his resistance. People who characteristically hang on to a problem and who will not accept solutions, or who are resistant to logic or reason that would improve their situation, are exhibiting a self-destructive, inward life-style.

A recent study by Gove and Hughes (1980) indicates that inwardness is related to self-destructive behavior. They demonstrated that alcoholism and suicide were two forms of pathology related to social isolation, operationally defined as living alone. These self-destructive behaviors were much more prevalent in those living alone than in those who lived with others. This study agrees with the results found in studies of student suicide (Seiden, 1966) and in research relating high suicide rates to areas of low population density with its resultant physical and social isolation (Seiden, 1984a).

By promoting a state of passivity and feelings of self-hatred, destructive voices contribute significantly to an individual's defensiveness and withdrawal. To complicate matters, an inward person frequently projects his angry, self-critical thoughts onto other people and sees *them* as critical or hostile. Thoughts that predict rejection are common in people who are inward and secretive. For example, they tell themselves: "This relationship will never last"; or "Don't get too involved." In effect, *the voice persuades men and women to avoid the risks of close attachments which, in turn, contributes to their tendencies toward isolation and a defended posture.*

Many individuals "listen" to a voice telling them that privacy and isolation are necessary. These thoughts are difficult to counter because they appear reasonable on the surface. Obviously one does need some degree of isolation for creative or concentrated work and for time away from the stresses of daily living. However, as noted in the studies cited above, extended periods of isolation from social contacts can be detrimental to mental health.

3. Behaviors That Adversely Affect Physical Health

Accident-proneness, working compulsively to the point of exhaustion, and psychosomatic illnesses are obvious manifestations of self-destructive tendencies that have long been recognized. These and a number of other behaviors including drinking to excess, drug abuse, and obesity and eating disorders represent direct assaults against the individual's physical health and emotional well-being, leading to gradual deterioration. For example, cases of anorexia nervosa have been, until the 1970's, potentially life threatening in 15 percent of the cases. (The death rate is currently at 2 percent.)[1]

In her penetrating look at pathological syndromes, including anorexia, resulting from the adolescent's struggle to individuate, Louise Kaplan (1984) writes:

> With the anorectic, asceticism takes over. She is unrelenting in her war on bodily pleasure. . . . She is totally uncompromising in her thinking and attitudes. Rules, obedience, duty are all that count. . . . She *listens only to the voices of infancy and childhood* [italics added], which demand a narrowing of roles, renunciation, sacrifice. (p. 263-264)

Kaplan's analysis of the origins of the anorectic's drive toward starvation and eventual death shows her understanding of the internal thought process that provides the impetus for the patient's extreme self-destructive tendencies:

> The words she speaks are a parody of her parents' values, of their great pretense at moral perfection. Her emaciated body is a caricature of the mirroring baby her mother needed her to be—a baby without desire, in absolute control of her bodily functions. (p. 265)
>
> One of the major complaints of the anorectic is that she cannot rid herself of the sense that she always acts on the commands of others. "There is another self, a dictator who dominates me. . . . A little man screams at me when I think of eating." (p. 269)

Kaplan's conceptualization of the dynamics of anorexia nervosa parallels the author's theoretical approach to the psychodynamics of many other forms of micro-suicidal behavior. For example, Kaplan writes that:

> [In her particular family constellation] a child is deprived of the opportunity to own her conscience. She is ruled by a conscience of weaning, absence, toilet training, controlling bodily functions. The parental prohibitions and commandments then will continue to be experienced as coming from outside the self, or as *alien inner voices* [italics added]. (p. 269)

This particular form of micro-suicidal behavior occurs in "about one out of every 250 teenage girls" (p. 257). In these cases the voice process appears to act as a self-protection, in some sense, a defense against the adolescent girl's emerging sexual desires. The patient's asceticism, however, is applied at the infantile oral level, and either death or a life of chronic anorexia and self-denial can be the eventual outcome.

The manipulative element in behaviors that threaten physical health is clear. Consider the woman whose doctor orders her to stop smoking due to a dangerous lung condition, yet who continues to smoke. Her friends and family will necessarily react with stress. They register her self-destructive habit for what it is—an implicit suicide threat. Individuals who eat or drink to excess or who are addicted to drugs are generally using these habits to nourish themselves and relieve emotional pain and tension. Although these compulsive habits are satisfying and ego-syntonic, they act to weaken one's adaptation and capability of coping with the environment. In this sense, they exert a pulling effect, forcing one's mate or associate into taking over the parental caretaking role in the relationship.

see p. 38

4. The Formation of Restrictive Bonds

The fantasy bond or illusion of connection that exists within many couples serves as a defense against the anxiety of being separate and vulnerable to death. As the relationship deteriorates in actuality, the couple or family members become increasingly involved in a fantasy of love and connection. The process is circular in that this pretense leads to a neurotic life-style that is antithetical to the survival of an ongoing relationship based on genuine affection, intimacy, and companionship. Indeed, *the process of forming such a bond or fantasized connection with another person leads to a steady declination in personal relating*. Both partners tend to give up broad areas of independent functioning in order to cling to an *illusion* that offers them a false sense of security and immortality. A progressive loss of identity and individuality is symptomatic of the mutual self-destructiveness inherent in a fantasy bond. In some cases, there is observable physical deterioration or illness directly attributable to the dysfunctional style of interacting that characterizes marital bonds.

In substituting form, i.e., routines, roles, and role-determined behaviors, for substance, i.e., the genuine love and affection in the relationship, people in a fantasy bond necessarily dull their real experiences. They learn to rely on repetitive, habitual contact without much feeling. *In such a bond, people essentially give up their real lives for an illusion of connection and find life increasingly hollow and empty.* Thus, the fantasy bond, as manifested in many marital relationships, is a form of micro-suicide. Further, society's conventions support the myth of enduring love in couples and families. Conventional responses based on form and role-playing act to cover up the truth and prevent people from becoming aware of or understanding the basic source of their personal problems in relationships.

5. *Withholding—A Renunciation of Personal and Vocational Goals*

Withholding refers to a holding back of positive responses, talents, and capabilities as a form of micro-suicide or retreat from life. Whenever an individual withholds behaviors or qualities that were once an important expression of his personal motivation, he is no longer goal-directed and becomes more oriented toward failure. Withholding or negativistic behavior can become habitual with a subsequent reduction in one's ability to function adequately in the real world. Acting in opposition to one's basic wants has serious consequences; it implies a withdrawal of affect and interest from external objects, which is a movement toward emotional or social suicide.

In a fantasy bond, patterns of withholding practiced by one partner can effectively change the other's positive feelings of love to those of hostility and anger. For example, men and women often hold back qualities that originally attracted their mates, such as their general appearance and sexual involvement. They may refuse to help create a pleasant home environment or withhold companionship, financial support, and personal communication from their partners.

Withholding, as an ongoing defensive posture, is symptomatic of a pervasive tendency to renounce life. In retreating from an adult posture and an equal relationship, a withholding person recreates the situation of his childhood in present-day interactions. The end result of withholding is a shutting down, a paralysis, of that part of the individual that strives for emotional health and growth. The process of withholding involves a progressive elimination of the self as a feeling person.

Paradoxically, achievement, an unusual success, or personal fulfillment in a relationship often lead to anxiety states that precipitate withholding responses. In these cases, an individual gives up or holds back the adult, competent behavior which led to success or accomplishments. This corroborates previous research which indicated that positive life events can trigger stressful reactions (Paykel, 1974). Although positive events have been accorded some recognition as causative factors in the appearance of self-destructive behavior, many psychotherapists still characteristically tend toward conventional explanations; that is, they stress negative circumstances as being the more logical antecedents.

MICRO-SUICIDAL BEHAVIOR FOLLOWING POSITIVE RECOGNITION—A CASE REPORT[2]

The following interview documents the progressive retreat of a young woman from close relationships into an isolated, self-destructive life-style. Following a particularly happy period in her life, Beth, twenty-nine, suddenly and inexplicably left her husband and sought an inward and withdrawn way of life. After some time had passed, she returned to her husband, and the couple decided to seek professional help. Excerpts from this videotaped interview reveal how Beth's self-critical, self-hating thoughts regulated her behavior and directed her toward an unfeeling, self-destructive state.

The interview begins with Beth relating how she felt during her childhood. (The negative thoughts which Beth expressed in terms of a voice are underlined.)

BETH: As a child growing up, I didn't feel a whole lot. Looking back, it was like an empty existence.

Then I met Richard and slowly, over a period of time, I started to feel him caring for me in a way that I don't think I've ever felt anyone care for me before.

I also started having relationships with children, because a lot of Richard's friends had children. In particular, I took care of one little girl, and I could tell she started to like me, and I think that threw me for a loop. I wasn't ready for that.

T: What did you feel, when you say it threw you for a loop?

BETH: I think that it stirred up feelings of wanting to have a baby myself. I felt like it was a possibility of something I had never thought of before. But then there was a whole process of undermining that feeling. I started thinking things about Richard, like that he wouldn't make a good father, that he couldn't support a child. I had a voice that I wouldn't be a good mother, that I would be hurtful to a child.

Later in the interview, Beth had an important insight regarding the pathological direction her life had taken due to the influence of this derisive, self-accusatory "voice." She realized that she had become withholding in her relationship with Richard and the small child and had given up activities and experiences in which she had previously taken pleasure. Here she articulates the specific negative thoughts underlying her unconscious pattern of withholding. Her destructive voice led to the ascendance of an alien point of view that transformed her perception so that behavior that was gratifying originally was now perceived as obligatory and imprisoning.

BETH: I started thinking: *"This is too hard. It's a pain in the neck to watch kids. It's a hassle; you always have to get up. You can't do what you want."*

        I wanted to get rid of Richard, too. I thought: *"It's a bother having a husband, you always have to worry about him, what he wants, and he always is worried about you. It would be such a relief not to have him worrying about you."*

        In my mind, I twisted it into that everything is taking me away from what *I* want to do—God!—that's such a reversal, because everything *was* what I wanted to do! [sad]

T: Like two different points of view. One point of view that you really felt loving of that child, enjoyed being with her. You felt warm toward your husband. You really liked him. And another point of view where he was a terrible person, pushing you, looking after you. And the same thing with the child. She became an annoyance. What was originally a free choice was now a burden.

BETH: Right, right. An obligation.

As Beth went on to explore her motives for running away, she recalled that at a certain point, she had become acutely aware that the positive circumstances of her present-day life were very different from her childhood situation. In this segment, she recognized that, in particular, she had found it difficult to tolerate loving feelings being directed toward her. Her subsequent withdrawal and the actions she had taken to alienate her husband had been directed toward changing his positive feelings.

BETH: I became conscious that I was different than how I had always thought of myself. Something to do with somebody loving me [sad]. And then I started acting in ways to undermine Richard's feeling for me, to make him start feeling differently toward me, to protect that way of seeing myself as bad.

T: And when you reach a point where you're loved, it doesn't fit in with that. It makes you uncomfortable.

BETH: It makes me totally uncomfortable.

In describing the self-destructive, isolated life she had planned to lead after leaving her husband, Beth realized the profound meaning of her running away; it signified commitment to a life-style of stillness and self-annihilation. This insight caused her pain and led her to a deeper understanding of the self-denying and self-destructive urges which had been operating in her since childhood.

BETH: When I thought about living my life away from Richard, it wasn't a happy picture, but a part of me craved *not* being happy.
I can almost picture myself just curling up. I picture

just getting almost in a womb—like going back to something dark and curled up and not feeling.

I pictured going back to my parents. I wanted something from them, something secure. It wasn't something happy. It was almost like it was a secure feeling of *dying* [cries deeply].

Over the course of the interview, Beth's ambivalence became evident as she talked of her intense and painful reactions to being loved and to seeing herself as lovable. Her new, positive self-image threatened an image that she was a "bad" person, a deep-seated feeling about herself that was very familiar. This change in self-image, in turn, aroused anxiety and feelings of deep sadness. In turning against her new identity, she became progressively more self-denying, and her actions came more under the control of her "voice." She became distant and alienated from her husband and developed a pattern of negative thoughts and attitudes about him and about herself.

Beth's need to defend herself against these painful reactions and against an awareness of being unloved in her family caused her to perceive her husband as mean, demanding, and controlling. Her hostile, secretive thoughts about him contributed to her inwardness and her subsequent leaving. Seen from the alien point of view to which she had submitted, Beth had believed that it would be a relief to her husband if she left. However, in the days that followed, she was also tortured by painful self-recriminations about the ordeal to which she was subjecting her husband by her desertion.

Beth's behavior represented a symbolic suicide in that she was running away from everything in her life that she had valued and cherished. In general, this type of running away has been called "the substitute suicide," indicating its equivalency with actual suicide attempts. Rather than killing oneself, one renounces all aspects of one's life that give it meaning and significance.

In later sessions, Beth became more cognizant of her own point of view about having a child. She was able to articulate an answer to the specific voice attacks predicting that she would be harmful to a child. In one session, Beth directed her statements symbolically to her mother and answered back to her voice:

You wanted to hurt me, that's the truth. You couldn't stand having me around. I was a bother to you. *You* couldn't stand me. You really missed out. [Sad] . . . You missed out on a lot. It would have felt good. . . . I like holding a baby, it feels good. You couldn't stand it. You can't stand anyone getting near you. You can't stand anyone touching you nicely . . . *You're* sick! Not me.

By affirming her natural desires about having children, Beth strengthened the healthy, adult side of her personality. Gradually she was able to make constructive behavioral changes that weakened the power of her voice and disrupted the cycle of demoralization and self-punishment.

This particular interview portrays the symptomatology of regressive trends that, in certain circumstances, eventually lead to suicide. The clinical material uncovered in the course of the interview revealed the content of Beth's voice attacks that had furthered a self-destructive cycle of alienation, self-hatred, and increased withdrawal from life. During the interview, it became evident that Beth felt deeply about the people she had turned against during the period of her regression. She recognized that she had changed her own point of view about her husband, friends, and children to an alien point of view. As she regained compassion for herself, she felt genuine remorse and sadness about the hurt she had caused the people closest to her.

This case, typified by a retreat from life and subsequent micro-suicidal behavior, is indicative of a broader pattern. Often, as people progress in their personal lives, they reach a stage where they experience a strong sense of self, of being a separate individual, of being a valuable person, of being lovable. Subsequently, as they become aware of reaching this stage, they tend to turn against themselves, to renounce the gratifications, to give up the relationships where they felt especially valued and loved, or to sabotage the successes they had achieved. The author has seen many cases where this phenomenon of adverse reactions to positive events was the precipitating factor in suicidal crises and serious depressive disorders. Furthermore, Beth's fundamental ambivalence and differential points of view about her situation are not unique. As noted previously, every individual lives in conflict between two points of view: a defensive, alien, self-critical attitude toward self and others; and a positive view that is personal and goal-directed.

CONCLUSION

Suicidal behavior in all its manifestations is not restricted to actual suicide, the pathology of depression, various addictions, or self-destructive fantasies; unfortunately, it is generally representative of the norm in conventional life. Inimical behaviors toward self and self-denial are not isolated phenomena; they interfere in close interpersonal relationships, causing much of the ongoing dissension in family life. Threats implied by these habitual patterns of behavior act as a manipulation and coercion of others.

The therapist, in being aware of the pervasiveness of micro-suicidal behavior in "normal" and neurotic patients, can diagnose these patterns early in treatment and prevent these behaviors from progressing to more pathological forms of self-destructiveness. Because defensive, self-denying modes of behavior are severely restrictive of the life process and experience of the individual, it is important for the therapist to identify the contents of the underlying negative thought process that regulates micro-suicidal behavior in his patients.

Micro-suicidal behavior forms the fundamental core of resistance in psychotherapy. Patients are reluctant to change because therapeutic progress or movement in a positive sense always leads to increased vulnerability. Just as they cut off personal relationships to avoid the prospect of potential rejection, most individuals restrict their personal freedom to varying degrees by refusing to commit fully to a life they must certainly lose. Ultimately, all of us live in conflict between emotionally investing in life and protecting or defending ourselves by withdrawing affect and involvement.

NOTES

[1]Primary sources (quoted from Kaplan, 1984) are: Center for the Study of Anorexia and Bulimia (1982), *The Eating Disorder Bulimia* and *Anorexia Nervosa*

(New York: Institute for Contemporary Psychotherapy); and John Sours (1980), *Starving to Death in a Sea of Objects* (New York: Jason Aronson).

²For clinical material that supports this thesis, see *Micro-Suicide: A Case Study,* 29-minute video produced by The Glendon Association (Parr, 1985).

3/23/88

9

*The Voice in Depression and Suicide**

It is always so shocking when you learn that someone you have seen in your periphery for years has committed suicide. . . .

That's the dark side of it—the idea that unseen demons haunt the men and women who populate your everyday world, and that you discover the existence of those demons only when it is too late.

Bob Greene (1984/1985, p. 71)

It is more pragmatic to conceptualize mental illness as a form of suicide than to represent suicide and suicidal ideation as a subclass of mental illness. Self-destructive thought patterns alter and distort an individual's perceptions and behavior. They are an attempt to escape primal pain originally related to emotional deprivation, separation anxiety, and later connected to death anxiety (eternal separation). Neurotic symptomatology is reflected in a person's choice of a defended, repetitive life-style and in the acting out of micro-suicidal behavior in the face of death anxiety.

All giving up of self, one's sense of reality, one's feelings,

*The substance of this chapter is taken primarily from an article entitled "The 'Inner Voice' and Suicide," *Psychotherapy,* Vol. 23, No. 3, 1986.

one's personal responses, represents a defensive, self-destructive posture toward life that leads inevitably to neurotic or psychotic symptom formation. Suicide is the ultimate abrogation of self—as such, it represents the extreme end of the continuum of self-destructive mental processes. Because it represents the extreme, we may well study this phenomenon as it sheds light on the entire gamut of mental illness in all of its varieties. Furthermore, the incidence of suicide being of epidemic proportion, together with the importance of sparing even a single life or spirit, compels us to search for the underlying dynamics.

THE PROBLEM OF THE RISING INCIDENCE OF SUICIDE

We are currently in the throes of a suicide epidemic that has become alarming in its proportions. The incidence of suicide among young people has been rising steadily for the past 30 years. The 1980 figures show that there were 5,000 deaths by suicide in the fifteen to twenty-four-year-old age group. This represents a *173 percent increase* over the rate reported in 1950. Yet this figure does not tell the whole story. Anywhere from 7 to 50 attempts are made for every actual suicide during adolescence, bringing the number of youthful suicide attempts to somewhere between 35,000 and a quarter of a million annually.

"Suicide is a special kind of guilt-provoking tragedy which has been aptly described as the *number one* cause of *unnecessary* and *stigmatizing* death" (Seiden, 1971, p. 243). Regardless of the actual statistics, every suicide attempt—and certainly every death by suicide—has profound effects on the survivors.

While the topic of suicide, especially the tragedy of adolescent suicide, is of great concern to all of us, the specific causes of suicide remain elusive. Demographers have compiled statistics comparing suicide rates in various countries, between occupational groups, and among different age groupings. Researchers have initiated any number of programs and studies related to suicide prevention; however, the findings have generally proven to be inconclusive.

Despite the difficulty of predicting suicide attempts, the authors believe that there are certain recognizable signs or clues of suicidal intent embedded in the thought processes of suicidal individuals. We have been able to document clinical evidence that the majority of these people are tortured by a subliminal "voice" or systematic pattern of thought that is degrading and derisive to the self. These hostile attitudes toward self are generally accompanied by depressed states and lowered self-esteem. Under certain conditions, this system of negative thought and accompanying feelings of intense self-hatred become progressively ascendant until they finally take precedence over thought processes of rational self-interest.

As noted previously, the voice process exists on a continuum of intensity, ranging from mild self-criticism to extremely angry, self-abusive thoughts. In suicidal individuals, these thoughts have been observed to change, at some point, from guilty self-recriminations to vicious self-attacks and injunctions to mutilate the self. We believe that *suicide is the ultimate conclusion of acting upon this negative thought process*.

If we are to more effectively identify potential suicide victims, we need to recognize the profoundly self-destructive intent of the voice that underlies inimical life-styles. The voice, which operates to arouse self-hatred in "normal" or neurotic individuals, is essentially the same mechanism that leads to severe depressive states and self-destructive behavior. In the interests of prevention, we need more vigorous research to explore and analyze this destructive thought process.

THE VOICE IN DEPRESSION

The literature on depression is far too voluminous to survey in depth in this chapter. Furthermore, there are complex predisposing factors. Biological components should be considered in determining the etiology of depression, particularly in Bipolar Disorders and Major Depressive Episodes. In our studies, however, we have focused on the psychodynamics of depression and will review only a few theoretical works relevant to our findings about the thought processes manifest in depressive disorders.

Most theorists categorize depression as an affective state that "may occur in any pathological condition as well as in normal persons" (Beres, 1966, p. 480). Freud (1923/1957) described the symptoms of melancholia (or depressive illness) as:

> . . . a profoundly painful dejection, cessation of interest in the outside world, loss of the capacity to love, inhibition of all inactivity, and a lowering of the self-regarding feelings to a degree that finds utterance in self-reproaches and self-revilings, and culminates in a delusional expectation of punishment. (p. 244)

David Beres (1966) makes a distinction between childhood grief, sadness, and feelings of disappointment and adult states of depression. Together with a number of other theorists (Rochlin, 1959, and Mahler, 1961/1979)[1], Beres believes that young children are not capable of developing depression *before* the superego has been formed. He postulates that feelings of guilt, resulting from the internalization of parental prohibitions, are a necessary element in depression.

According to Beres, until a child has introjected the parental images and formed his own *internal judge*, he is incapable of experiencing the affect of depression. In other words, a necessary prerequisite for depression is a structured superego formed through the internalization of external regulations, or, as Hartmann and Loewenstein (1962) describe it: "We would speak of *internalization* when regulations that have taken place in interaction with the outside world are replaced with *inner regulations*" (p. 48). Beres describes the psychological processes leading up to internalization of one's external authorities in the form of an alien point of view:

> We cannot see internalization. We can only see the end results of the entire process, the manifest derivatives in the thought processes, actions, and affective responses of the individual. (p. 490)

John Bowlby (1980) disagrees with Beres about the ability of a young child to mourn and/or to develop a depressive disorder. Bowlby believes, with Melanie Klein (1935/1964, 1940/1964)[2] that:

> Infants and young children mourn and go through phases of depression, she maintains, and their modes of responding at such

times are determinants of the way that in later life they will respond to further loss. (p. 36)

Cognitive Processes in Severe Depressive States

In a paper summarizing a 20-year study of 40 depressed patients, Arieti and Bemporad (1980) elaborate the particular types
of early childhood experiences that inevitably lead to the patient's developing "beliefs about himself and others that are, to
a large extent, unconscious but that determine much of his behavior" (p. 1364). They go on to say that these distortions are
maintained in the adult's cognitive processes and are the basis of
the "depressive personality."

> The depressive adult still rigidly adheres to his unconscious
> cognitive system for structuring his social and inner world. It is
> this continuation of childhood *social-cognitive patterns* [italics
> added] which ultimately predisposes one for depressive illness and
> forms the basis of depressive personality organization. (p. 1364)
> The depressive adult still rigidly adheres to his unconscious
> cognitive system for structuring his social and inner world. It is
> this continuation of childhood *social-cognitive patterns* [italics
> added] which ultimately predisposes one for depressive illness and
> forms the basis of depressive personality organization. (p. 1364)
> Furthermore, he suffers from a paucity of cognitive alternatives
> that would keep him from progressing into further despair follow-
> ing a loss of meaning from the environment. (p. 1365)

John Bowlby (1980), in his definitive work, *Loss: Sadness
and Depression,* also discusses childhood experiences that are
most likely to contribute to serious depressive disorders in
adulthood and the particular beliefs engendered in the child by
these experiences:

> In most forms of depressive disorder . . . the principal issue
> about which a person feels helpless is his ability to make and to
> maintain affectional relationships. The feeling of being helpless in
> these particular regards can be attributed, I believe, to the expe-
> riences he has had in his family of origin. . . .
> (a) He is likely to have had the bitter experience of never hav-

ing attained a stable and secure relationship with his parents despite having made repeated efforts to do so. . . . [Later he may develop] a *strong bias to interpret any loss . . . as yet another of his failures*. . . . [Italics added]

(b) He may have been told repeatedly how unlovable, and/or how inadequate and/or how incompetent he is. . . . [This] would result in *his developing a model of himself as unlovable and unwanted* [italics added]. . . .

(c) He is more likely than others to have experienced actual loss of a parent during childhood. (p. 247–248)

Arieti and Bemporad (1980) differentiate between mild or neurotic depression and severe or psychotic depression. They conceptualize depressed states as existing on a continuum in terms of the extent to which the individual actually *believes* or accepts his distorted pathological conceptions "of himself, of others, of his future, and of his current environment" (p. 1365). Their descriptions of the continuum of neurotic and psychotic depressive disorders parallel our own formulations about the continuum of intensity and severity of the voice process. At a certain point, the patient's cognitive misconceptions of himself as being bad or worthless become a basic part of his identity. Thereafter, the severely depressed patient may completely accept the distortions of the voice as being accurate descriptions of reality. As Arieti and Bemporad observe:

> In milder forms, the individual suffers from the distortions that form the *cognitive aspect* [italics added] of depression, but he does not accept this world view. He sees it as a *painful, ego-alien state* [italics added] that he wishes to be rid of, although he does not know how to extricate himself from his situation. In the more severe forms, the depressive patient's distortions are wholeheartedly accepted, and the individual believes his erroneous world view. As such, the depression crosses the line into psychosis. (p. 1365)

This view of the cognitive aspect of depression is similar to Aaron Beck's model. Beck's (Beck, et al., 1979) term "cognitive triad" describes significant components of the depressed patient's thinking, that is, his "negative view of the outside world, the self, and the future" (p. 188).

Consider also Beck's statements about the particular world-view of the depressed patient. Beck and his colleagues have found that the "specific content of the cognitive distortions and the underlying assumptions are different from those found in other disorders" (p. 24). Studies conducted by this group of researchers resulted in the construction of a new *scientific* model of depressed states:

> The *personal* paradigm of the patient when he is in a depressed state produces a distorted view of himself and his world. His negative ideas and beliefs appear to be a veridical representation of reality to him even though they appear farfetched to other people and also to himself when he is not depressed. His observations and interpretations of events are molded by his conceptual framework—equivalent to Kuhn's[3] description of a scientific paradigm. *The gross changes in his cognitive organization lead to incorrect information processing* [italics added], as a result of which he suffers a wide variety of painful symptoms. (p. 21)

The author's conceptualizations about the thought process in depressed states are generally in accord with Beck's cognitive therapy of depression. In *our* estimation, the depressed patient reaches a stage where the balance shifts in such a way that the *alien* point of view represented by the voice actually becomes the patient's own point of view. In other words, the depressed person adopts the voice—its constrictions, commands, and directives—as his own. He perceives the negative, hostile view as part of himself and no longer moves between his own viewpoint and that of the voice's. For whatever reason, whether because of overwhelming frustration, a deep sense of loss, or a positive event beyond his level of tolerance, the depressed patient is now more *against* himself than *for* himself. In other words, he wholeheartedly *believes* the negative hostile statements of the voice about himself *and* about other people. Consequently, to a great extent, he no longer has contact with his real self and feels hopelessly estranged from the people closest to him as well. As he increasingly submits to the alien voice or personality of the introjected parental image, he now reacts to the self as if he were the incorporated other. If that person wished him dead, he may well oblige by killing himself.

Cognitive Constriction in Suicidal States

At this point in a depressive episode, the patient is at high risk for suicide. By now, his way of thinking is almost completely "possessed" by his voice, and he finds his alternatives narrowed down to the two options described by Shneidman (1985), i.e., that of "either having some magical resolution or being dead" (p. 140).

As the voice asserts complete control over the depressed individual's thinking process, there is a constriction of thought and diminution of genuine affect. The operations of the voice, which are primarily cerebral, act more and more as an anti-feeling agent. The patient becomes totally focused on his own inner ruminations and, as a result, eventually becomes completely cut off from compassionate feelings for himself and others. Shneidman (1985) recognizes the severity of this constriction of rational thought and affect characteristic of the suicidal patient. In writing about the common *cognitive* state in suicide, Shneidman says:

> I believe that it [suicide] is much more accurately seen as a more or less transient psychological *constriction of affect and intellect* [italics added]. Synonyms for constriction are a tunneling or focusing or narrowing of the range of options usually available to *that* individual's consciousness *when the mind is not panicked into dichotomous thinking* [italics added]: either some specific (almost magical) total solution *or* cessation. . . . The range of choices has narrowed to two—not very much of a range. The usual life-sustaining images of loved ones are not disregarded; worse, they are not even within the range of what is in the mind. (p. 138-139)

As we will presently see in the material excerpted from interviews with suicidal patients, specific voice attacks (which the individual in a suicidal crisis more or less completely accepts) are at the root of this type of polarized thinking.

The most important characteristic of severe depression *and* suicidal ideation appears to be the individual's profound feeling of being cut off or isolated from himself, or, in Freudian terms, from the ego. Litman (1967) describes Freud's graphic metaphor of the hated ego manifest in depressive disorders.

In melancholia the ego gives itself up because it feels itself hated and persecuted by the superego instead of loved. To the ego, therefore, living means the same as being loved by the superego, so that the death by suicide symbolizes or reenacts a sort of abandonment of the ego by the superego. It is a situation similar to separation from the protecting mother. (p. 337)

According to Litman's interpretation of Freud's view: ". . . each individual must incorporate controlling, coercing, and punishment components into his superego" (p. 337) because of his lack of control over need gratification and destructive instincts in infancy and early childhood. The result is that:

In civilized man, extra aggression is channeled into the superego and turned against the ego. It is now felt as unconscious guilt, masochism, a need to be punished, or an obscure *malaise* and discontent. (p. 337)

In summary, most psychoanalytic theorists postulate that feelings of hostility, guilt, and a need for self-punishment become attached to internalized parental prohibitions and directives, and these dynamics play a strong role in depression and suicide. The author feels that whether or not these feelings and cognitions are contained within the boundaries of a hypothesized superego or a split ego is not as important as the fact that they are *retained in the form of destructive voices* within the adult personality. The voice process, in turn, plays a major role in precipitating and maintaining the patient's depressive state.

OTHER COGNITIVE APPROACHES TO SUICIDAL IDEATION

A number of clinicians have described various aspects of an internal negative thought process, including Aaron Beck (1976), Victor Raimy (1975), Albert Ellis and Robert Harper (1961/1975), Gershen Kaufman and Lev Raphael (1984), and Gershen Kaufman (1985), among others. Beck's Cognitive Therapy and Ellis' Rational-Emotive Therapy are perhaps the most well-known. Beck (1976) contends that:

Irrationality can be understood in terms of inadequacies in organizing and interpreting reality. (p. 19)

The basis of Beck's therapy is that of restructuring the depressed patient's distorted view of himself, his world, and the future. Beck's descriptions of "automatic thoughts" as "specific, discrete, relatively autonomous" thoughts that "occurred in a kind of shorthand" closely correspond to our observations of the hostile thought patterns elicited through the procedures of Voice Therapy. For example, Beck (1976) depicts the depressed patient's negative view of self as follows:

> The ultimate of his self-condemnation is total self-rejection—just as though he were discarding another person.
>   Consider the effects of self-criticism, self-condemnation, and self-rejection. *The patient reacts to his own onslaughts as if they were directed at him by another person* [italics added]: he feels hurt, sad, humiliated. (p. 115)

In *Misunderstandings of the Self,* Victor Raimy (1975) discusses his misconception theory and defines the *neurotic paradox* in cognitive terms:

> We can say that conceptions that have been persistently disproved by experience may still be retained as untrustworthy guides for action. The paradox lies in the disconcerting discovery that adequate evidence may not dispel a mistaken belief. (p. 12)

Albert Ellis (Ellis & Harper, 1961/1975) views the patient as having entrenched "irrational beliefs" that need to be actively countered by the therapist. His formulations have certain commonalities with the author's thinking, although there are important differences between Rational-Emotive Therapy procedures and Voice Therapy.[4] Ellis, like Raimy and Beck, believes that irrational thought patterns can be reduced to basic underlying false assumptions about the self, others, and the world.

Bach and Torbet (1983) describe a variety of self-reproaching inner dialogues that reflect aggression turned inward upon the self. Butler (1981) has also described two selves within the personality: the Intrinsic Self and the Imposed Self:

> This internal figure has many names: superego, conscience, inner custodian, top dog, parent-part, witch-mother, value sys-

tem. But whatever the name, you experience this inner self as a distinct person speaking to you. (p. xvii)

In describing the child's reactions to "contemptuous, blaming parents," Gershen Kaufman (1985) states:

> The internal image of the contemptuous, fault-finding, brutally critical parent becomes the model for the self's engaging in like action. Here is a likely dialogue within the self: "Oh God, there's something wrong with me. So disgusting. I can't stand myself. Look how fat *you* are. *You're* ridiculous." A part of the self identifies with the parent and begins to treat other parts of the self with contempt. Such an individual reacts with spontaneous self-contempt as well whenever shame is aroused. (pp. 113-114)

It is apparent that Kaufman is reporting phenomena very similar to the self-attacks identified by our subjects. Voice Therapy procedures are particularly effective in bringing this material to the surface.

BIPOLAR CAUSALITY OF SUICIDAL IDEATION AND BEHAVIOR

As previously noted, Menninger (1938), Shneidman (1966), and Farberow (1980) conceive of suicidal behavior as existing on a continuum from micro-suicide or "partial" suicidal behavior to actual suicide. Suicides are not always triggered by negative circumstances; they are also affected by positive events. The statistics of suicide indicate that the favored segments of the population paradoxically have the highest rates of self-destruction: the suicide rate for whites is several times that for non-whites; the rates for men are triple those for women; white-collar workers commit suicide in relatively greater numbers than their blue-collar counterparts; and the 1970-1980 epidemic of youthful suicide is being forged by young white males from affluent backgrounds (Seiden, 1984a). Among college students, it is *the academically superior student who kills himself.* Those who teach and counsel students are impressed with their observations that it is the better students who are the most self-critical, the most critical of others, and the most relentless at self-attack (Clance & Imes, 1978; Harvey, 1984; Munter, 1966; Seiden, 1966).

Similarly, an unusual or atypical success or public acknowledgment of achievement is often followed by regressive trends, depressive states, and an increase in self-destructive thinking. However, these adverse reactions are often blamed on other negative factors. Regarding this phenomenon, Stricker (1983) has noted that role transitions in which "we have difficulty accommodating to a new position in life" (p. 214) are often precipitating factors in depression. Completed suicides have also been found to correspond to an individual's *upward* mobility as well as to his downward social mobility. Thus, a *bipolar causality*—both negative and positive factors affecting suicidal behavior—must be taken into account. Furthermore, we must establish the relationship between these positive events and the ensuing anxiety that precipitates regressive moods and accentuates self-attacks. Lastly, it is important to research and comprehend the dynamics and possible sources of this hostile thought process and further to elucidate its causal relationship to actual suicide.

OPERATING LEVELS

In our investigations of the voice process, we were able to delineate three levels of intensity of the voice in terms of affect: (1) At the first level, we found that each individual could identify an internal running commentary that criticized and derided him, one that was capable of producing a mild state of agitation or a depressed mood. (2) When the volunteers formulated these self-attacks and verbalized them in a more dramatic manner, they frequently launched into an angry diatribe against themselves that was startling in its intensity. At this second level, these expressions were accompanied by strong affect, powerful emotions that customarily remain repressed. (3) On an even deeper level, we observed an intense rage toward the self, manifested by suicidal urges or by injunctions to mutilate or otherwise injure themselves. We also found that the unexpected thoughts or brief suicidal impulses that sometimes erupt into the conscious mind of "normal" individuals are indications of the presence of this underlying system of negative thoughts. The emergence of these self-destructive thoughts and impulses are, at the very least, disconcerting and can at times be terrifying.

Our clinical material indicated that a process of actual self-denial on a behavioral level parallels the voice attacks and that this self-denial can lead to a cycle of serious pathology. As a person gradually retreats from seeking gratification of self in the real world of object relations, he becomes progressively indifferent to life. He tends to give up more and more areas of experience that were once found pleasurable and worthwhile. Actual self-harm is much more likely to be acted out *after* the individual has withdrawn his interest and affect from the external world and from an active pursuit of personal goals, a form of "social suicide."

At the extreme end of the continuum, severely depressed patients become exhausted and listless in struggling against self-destructive urges and self-abusive thoughts. Furthermore, they lack the means of determining an accurate view of self and cannot differentiate an objective assessment from the habitual negative view of themselves that they have accepted since childhood.

CASE HISTORY

Susan was thirty when she made the decision to end her life. She was an exceptionally attractive, active young woman, highly successful in her career. However, she had become very unhappy in a relationship that had been very meaningful to her. A slow deterioration in feelings had taken place over a period of 2 years from the time when the couple had first been very close.

At 5:00 p.m. on an autumn afternoon in 1976, Susan registered in a hotel, went to her room, and once there swallowed a lethal dose of Miltown, Seconal, and Valium. At the last moment, she called a nearby university hospital in an effort to save herself. Paramedics arrived and rushed her to the emergency room, where she remained on the critical list in the intensive care unit for the next 18 hours. She managed to survive, and some time after the incident was interviewed by the author about events leading up to the serious attempt at ending her life.

It has been acknowledged by suicidologists that individuals who have attempted suicide are generally not open to being interviewed. There is a dearth of direct, personal communication with these people that might offer insights into their motives and thoughts prior to suicidal actions (Hubert & Addis, undated). Therefore, the material in this interview is unique because it offers a comprehensive exposure of Susan's thought process in the months and weeks preceding her attempted suicide.

The interview in its entirety is available in the form of a documentary videotape entitled *The Inner Voice in Suicide* (Parr, 1985). As the interview begins, Susan experiences feelings of sadness in relation to talking about her attempted suicide. She indicates that thoughts about suicide had been familiar to her as a child.

SUSAN: I feel sad thinking about this subject—sad and shaky. The first thing that I thought of was that it wasn't only at the time when I actually tried to kill myself that I thought this way—but even as a young child, I thought about suicide a lot when I felt really bad, which I did a lot of the time. I thought that if things really got that bad that I couldn't stand it, that I could kill myself, but it never really got anywhere near taking action until the time when I really tried to kill myself.

As the story unfolds, Susan refers to a pattern of thoughts that almost completely dominated her thinking during the period of her life preceding her suicide attempt. She tells of trying to act cheerful for fear that her friends would become aware of her depressed state.

T: What were you thinking when you were building up to that?

SUSAN: I tried to cut myself off from any feelings—I didn't want anybody to get to me.

T: What did you tell youself, in effect?

SUSAN: *"Don't let anybody see what's going on. Look okay. Smile—look normal."*

T: What thoughts did you think about yourself?

SUSAN: I hated myself—I felt that I was bad—like there was something really bad that I couldn't fix. I couldn't stand myself; that's what I couldn't live with.

T: What did you hate about yourself? What things?

SUSAN: I never liked the way I looked. I couldn't look at myself. The way I felt took the form of: *"You're so ugly. You're so ugly. Who would choose you?"*

The voice injured Susan's relationship by criticizing her lover and belittling her.

SUSAN: *"You don't really like him—he doesn't matter that much to you. There are other people that he likes— there are other people important to his life."*

Later she generalized her distorted views to include everyone in the interpersonal environment.

T: What kind of actual thoughts did you have about suicide?

SUSAN: That I wanted to kill myself. And I tried to get myself to the point where I didn't care enough about anything so that I could do it. Like: *"Don't be stupid, you're not that important. You don't matter to anybody. Who would care if you weren't around? People would miss you a little at the beginning, but who would really care?"*

T: So, basically, were you frustrated in a love relationship at the time?

SUSAN: No, I wasn't rejected, but I thought I was.

T: How do you mean?

SUSAN: Just that the relationship began to change from one that was a really nice relationship, where I was easy with my feelings and where I accepted loving feelings being directed toward me, to one in which I got scared of losing the relationship. And then I started wanting to try to *make* him love me instead of letting him love me. And then the relationship began to change. For the worse. That was on my mind.

Susan began to have thoughts that urged her to seek isolation. Once alone, she found the opportunity to think self-hating thoughts, which further incapacitated her and made her vulnerable to increasingly vicious attacks. Soon she was experiencing snide, vicious commands to actually commit suicide.

SUSAN: I tried to get alone—because this process occurred when I was alone. The voice was weak when I was around other people, so the voice got me to be alone—

saying, *"Get alone. Look, don't you need some time
for yourself? Get alone so you can think—"*
    I started to think things like, *"If you don't matter,
what does matter? Nothing matters. What are you
waking up for? You know you hate waking up every
morning. Why bother? It's so agonizing to wake up in
the morning, why bother doing it? Just end it. Just end
it. Stop it!"*

Just prior to her suicide attempt, Susan progressively isolated herself from others and began to plan the details of her self-
destructive act. Susan confided that thinking about these plans
began to give her pleasure. She was puzzled by the perversity of
enjoying the rehearsal of her strategy for self-destruction.

SUSAN: At first just thinking about the details was enough but
    soon I had to actually make real plans. At the very end,
    close to the time where I really did start to kill my-
    self—I would drive around and think, *"Well, where are
    you going to do it? How are you going to do it? Where
    can you go? You have to go to a hotel—"*

T: Did you hear this voice as an hallucination—as if it
    were coming from outside yourself?

SUSAN: No. They weren't hallucinations. I didn't actually hear
    voices. These were thoughts I had, in my head. But
    clear thoughts.
        I would think *"When are you going to do it? Go
    ahead and do it, you coward! You're so cowardly, you
    can't even do this, can you?"*

During the course of the interview, Susan had a vivid rec-
ollection of an incident in which her mother had hit her until she
began to bleed, overtly expressing her anger and hatred toward
her child. She became aware that she felt the same hatred toward herself and that it had taken the form of a voice. She recognized that she had been "listening" to this voice immediately
prior to her suicidal action.

SUSAN: The voice was vicious. *"You'd better do it. It's the only
    thing you can do. You'd better do it, you'd better do*

it! I hate you! I hate you!" I just had a thought in relation to my mother, remembering feelings directed towards me, when she would get angry at me—(relates incident where mother punished her severely).

I remember the hatred. Her hatred was being directed toward me. *"I hate you. I hate you."* And that was like that voice—my own voice. It turned into my own voice, hating myself. That's when it was vicious.

The voice began to ridicule and taunt Susan for her delay in putting her lethal plan into effect.

SUSAN: *"You thought about it long enough. You've decided you are going to do it. Now do it! Just get it over with. Drop it. Quit fooling around already. Just quit it! Quit fooling around and do it."*

As Susan made preparations for actually taking her life, the voice became progressively dissociated from her own point of view and sounded monotonous and rational. It appeared to assume a personality of its own, taking almost total control over her actions.

T: What was the voice saying as you were going to the hotel?

SUSAN: I was so cut off that it was like rational: *"Here's the hotel. You gotta pull into the driveway. You know, be careful. You don't want to call any attention to yourself. Don't call any attention to yourself. Pull into the driveway. Park your car."*

"Don't act stupid. Don't make this take longer than it has to." But rational, cold, cold talking. *"Do it! You just do it! You set your mind to do this and you're going to do it. Now do it and do it right!"*

"Now here is the key. Go to the elevator, go up to the room and unlock the door," which I did. Then I remember that I wanted to eat. I ordered a big room service, which took some time. It's like a blank—

At the last moment, when Susan delayed taking the pills in order to eat the dinner she had ordered, the voice ridiculed her for procrastinating (an action that may have saved her life).

SUSAN: *"Go ahead, start taking the pills. You've had your meal. Now do it. Coward! Now do it already. You've had your pleasure, now do it."* I don't have much memory for the facts of what happened then—I remember taking the pills . . .

T: Then actually you almost died—you took the pills and you almost died. Is that right?

SUSAN: I know that I took enough pills to kill myself. I also know I called. I called UCLA, the information number at UCLA. I remember that it took every effort that I had to make the call.

T: Something in you wanted to save yourself, obviously.

SUSAN: At some point I realized what was happening, that it was working, because I thought, "Oh my God, this is working! I don't want this to work!" It wasn't a voice any more. That was *me!*

T: You could tell the difference.

[Later]:

T: Do you ever have any recurrences of wanting to kill yourself?

SUSAN: No, never. I'm not scared of that any more. I've gone a whole circle, from looking at suicide as a refuge or a last resort, to feeling that I don't want to die. I want to live. Things matter to me. I want to live my life a lot. I don't have recurrences of wanting to kill myself, ever. I feel bad sometimes, but I never look at suicide as a refuge or a last resort. I don't have last resorts any more.

Several factors in the dynamics and development of Susan's suicidal ideation are important to note. First, the systematic thinking about suicide was experienced by Susan as a pattern of negative thoughts, which she verbalized in the second person during the interview. Near the end, she "heard" the voice as a baiting, harassing command: "Go ahead and do it! You coward, you've *got* to do this." Second, the voice was influencing her to deceive others and was pushing her toward isolating herself. This, in turn, created situations that allowed an increasingly pathological thought process to exert more and more control over her behavior. Regarding this phenomenon, Seiden (1984b) notes that there appears to be a relationship between social isolation and suicides in young people.

Third, thinking torturous thoughts deeply pained Susan, yet paradoxically, the voice would then attack her for being in pain and offer a solution: "What's the point of living if you have this pain?" Fourth, this thought process manifested itself not only in her suicide attempt, but had been present throughout her life until it finally culminated in the self-destructive impulses being acted out. It also appeared that Susan's self-attacks had intensified *after* she had experienced considerable happiness in a personal relationship. Lastly, and most important, at some point in the midst of the suicidal crisis, Susan found her own self-interest again and was able to survive. Forces in her that wanted to live triumphed over the self-destructive process, although she came very close to dying despite her call for help. It was painful for Susan to talk about this material; however, she expressed the hope that others might find her story useful in understanding more about the voice process in suicidal behavior.

OTHER CASE REPORTS

Seiden (personal communication, October 1985) reports the predominance of hostility toward self in the thought patterns of other suicide attempters. He notes that suicidal patients easily related to the concept of a destructive voice, and his studies support the conclusions of our videotaped material. Each subject in Seiden's study had made one or more attempts at suicide (one had made nine attempts) and was involved in a therapy group of suicide attempters. In each case, the subject was not informed of the concept of the voice but was asked near the end of the interview if there was anything else he could think of relevant to the suicide attempt.

In one case, the subject, a thirty-seven-year-old woman, responded to the question, admitting that she had been "hearing" voices for the past 3 years telling her "to kill herself, to get away from *them*; there's no reason to stay here" (to stay alive). Whenever she became severely depressed, she felt as if:

> The voices were coming from the outside, and I had no control over them. I can be talking to somebody, and the voices come in and talk over me, and I can't hear the other person. Also, I've noticed that alcohol stimulates the voices, so I don't drink very much now.

This woman had attempted suicide several times and appears to have been overtly psychotic during certain periods in her life. In one attempt, she tried to jump from the Golden Gate Bridge but became paralyzed and couldn't jump. She stated that she felt completely removed from herself and had profound feelings of dissociation and alienation from both herself and other people.

Another interviewee reported telling herself that she was "hopeless, no-good, a fool and stupid, unable to make it in the world, having nothing to offer." When she attempted suicide by taking pills, she also said that she felt as if she were removed from the experience, "like I was a person outside, watching myself."

In another case, the subject's sister had died of leukemia when she was three. The subject reported intense feelings of guilt and a sensation of being on the outside of every activity and of every human interaction. The voice of this woman echoes the hopelessness common to many suicidal persons:

> When I am badly depressed, I feel: "Well, everybody dies in the end anyway—so what is the point of struggling and hurting and knowing you die anyway, and that it won't matter that you lived."

A male subject who primarily directed hostility toward others rather than against himself reported thinking: "*They* [his supervisors] are watching you." He also held stereotyped views of women, thinking that "they only want our time and money." At the same time, he attacked himself for being unattractive to women: "Nobody finds you attractive." Overcome with hopelessness about the "hatefulness of people in the world," he concluded that he "just couldn't stand living in the world any more," that "God was showing me that the world is an evil place," and attempted suicide by mutilating himself with an electric saw. This patient's voice predisposed him more toward a paranoid orientation and aggression than toward depression; nonetheless, he acted out his hostility in a suicide attempt rather than in homicide.

All of the interviewees were familiar with internal negative thoughts and voices. They tended to verbalize these thoughts spontaneously in much the same form as the participants in our experimental groups.

The subjects interviewed came from extremely disturbed family constellations. There were manifestations of physical and sexual child abuse, inadequate maternal responses, death of a sibling or one parent, and an overt attempt by one parent to get rid of his daughter. ("My father locked me in the garage with the car exhaust going.") Subjects reported sometimes "hearing" voices as if they were coming from the external world, while at other times they identified the voice as a "low opinion" they held of themselves. For example, the woman whose father attempted to harm her described how she experienced her voice at various periods of her life:

> I thought I was stupid, that I was ugly and useless (at age eleven). When I was thirteen, I heard voices which I understood to be God's, who controlled a realm in which I lived that was different from where everybody else lived.
>
> In my recent illness, there was a kind of running commentary: "You're full of evil. You're full of poison. God's looking at you. You're stupid." And always the thought: "If you talk, I'll kill you."

THEORETICAL CONSIDERATIONS

On the basis of data from our preliminary investigations, the following hypotheses were derived: (A) Thoughts antithetical to the self vary along a continuum of intensity from mild self-reproach to strong self-attacks and even suicidal thoughts. (B) Self-destructive behavior exists on a continuum from self-denial and self-limitation to accident-proneness, drug abuse, and other self-defeating behaviors, culminating in actual bodily harm. (C) Both processes, behavioral and cognitive, parallel each other, and actual suicide represents the acting out of the extreme end of the continuum.

Clinical evidence suggested the hypothesis that the voice relates directly to the rejecting thoughts and attitudes of the parents, both overt and covert, that have been incorporated by the child and thereafter taken on as his own thoughts and attitudes (Firestone, 1984). It is important to stress again that this conclusion was arrived at spontaneously by participants in the study. As previously noted, self-criticisms and derogatory attitudes toward self were identified by the majority of the individuals as statements they had either heard stated directly by their parents or as attitudes they had picked up in their parents' behavior. It appeared that these angry parental thoughts and attitudes were internalized at those times when the parent was the most punishing or rejecting, i.e., when the child was under the most stress.

We have further conjectured that the voice may reflect unconscious "death wishes" toward the child. Other clinicians have reached this conclusion based on data from their own studies. Rosenbaum and Richman (1970) found that suicidal patients are often the targets of death wishes directed at them by their families. These researchers introduce their controversial paper by stating: "We believe that the clinician must ask . . . 'Who wished the patient to die, disappear, or go away?' " (p. 1652). Richman, in other studies, has noted that the suicidal person is blamed for all the ills in the family. In contrast to the psychotic person who is labeled as "sick," the suicidal person is singled out as "bad."

In suicidal patients, parental death wishes are incorporated as an internal voice, frequently in a disguised form. For instance, the patient mentioned earlier, whose father had on a number of occasions physically abused her and actually tried to kill her, secretly held a bizarre belief that she was filled with poison. The young woman thought of herself as "bad, evil, and contaminating" and made several attempts to commit suicide. She said she had obeyed a voice that ordered her to "slash your wrists, get rid of the poison!" In this extreme case of pathological acting out, her father's death wishes had been translated into action.

Rosenbaum and Richman (1970) also noted that death wishes toward recovering suicidal patients were "implicit or explicit in many statements made by the relatives and were voiced with unexpected frequency" (p. 1653). "We'd all be better off if you were dead"; "Next time pick a higher bridge"; and other malicious comments were sarcastically voiced to these patients by their parents. The author hypothesizes that parental death wishes are involved in the etiology of the voice and operate to reinforce the drive toward self-destruction.

In relation to causality, the author has found that voice attacks *are activated by unusual positive events as well as by negative events or circumstances*. Failures, financial setbacks, rejection, and other unpleasant experiences tend to trigger voice attacks and feelings of self-hatred; however, it is very important to note that atypical *positive events can also activate the voice, causing regressive trends and self-destructive behavior*. Unusual success, both professional and personal, special acknowledgement, achievement, or attainment of a leadership position often precede periods of self-destructive behavior. Although we all desire success and fulfillment, it makes us feel vulnerable and may create considerable stress. Self-defeating and self-destructive behavior can act to relieve this anxiety. Bela Grunberger (1968/1979), in her essay *Suicide of Melancholics*, states:

> The depressive . . . reacts with extreme sensitivity to the slightest frustration, but he is similarly seized with panic before the least gratification that exceeds the threshold of his powers of narcissistic cathexis, a threshold that is very low. "There is in me," said that great depressive Kafka, "a mortal fatigue and emptiness that overwhelms me every time I am enraptured by something" (Janouch, 1971, p. 99).[5] (p. 245)

The author hypothesizes that the dynamics predisposing the critical voice and self-destructive life-styles are multidetermined but focus on three principal areas: (1) the voice process involves the incorporation of the parental attitudes and defenses; (2) the voice represents an attempt to protect the individual from feeling anxious and vulnerable through a complicated process of predetermining and rehearsing negative outcomes; and (3) the voice has an additional defensive function in that it serves as an accommodation to death anxiety. We feel that people tend to cope with death anxiety by a denial of death and by self-limiting and even self-destructive behavior.

A number of individuals who attempted suicide have reported that their motives for withdrawal could be expressed as taunting questions put in the form of the voice: "Why get involved in a relationship where you might be abandoned or rejected?" "Why become attached to a person you'll lose in the end?" "Why care about a life you're certainly going to lose?" For some individuals, suicide may have been their last response to this voice. For others, asceticism, addiction to drugs, self-imposed limitations, and other micro-suicidal behaviors are attempts to master death anxiety in some sense by prematurely deadening themselves psychologically.

We contend that original trauma is experienced by the child early in life in relation to emotional deprivation, separation, and individuation. Later in the developmental sequence, death anxiety reinforces the original defense system that protected the child against being overwhelmed by the earlier separation anxiety. Thereafter, separations, real or symbolic, arouse death anxiety and set into motion a basic defensive apparatus to cope with the anxiety. The voice may be conceived of as being the language of this core defense.

SUMMARY

In this chapter, the author has described extreme or pathological manifestations of the voice. Our investigations indicate that this subliminal thought process underlies depressive states and is at the core of the negative concept of self. It was noted that varying degrees of angry affect and rage are associated with this cognitive process. Although this thought process has been observed to varying degrees in "normal," neurotic, and psychotic populations, it reaches life-threatening proportions in suicidal acting-out behavior.

Hypotheses about the dynamics and possible origins of the voice were formulated on the basis of clinical material obtained from our preliminary studies of Voice Therapy. Empirical data revealed that the voice, as defined above, is closely related to experiences within the nuclear family. Further, the author concluded that a possible function of this inner voice was to accommodate one to potential loss, separation, and ultimately to death anxiety, as though by rehearsing or preliving negative consequences, one can deaden oneself to these eventualities.

NOTES

[1]Beres quotes Rochlin as speaking "of a 'loss complex' in the deprived child, rather than of a depression," and suggesting that "for the clinical manifestations of pathological mourning and melancholia to take place presupposes that certain phases of psychic development have occurred (p. 314)." (p. 493). (Quoted from Rochlin, 1959)

Mahler (1961/1979) also maintains: "It has been conclusively established that the immature personality structure of the infant or older child is not capable of producing a state of depression such as that seen in the adult'" (p. 271).

[2]The works of Melanie Klein referred to by Bowlby are: *A Contribution of the Psychogenesis of Manic-Depressive States,* and *Mourning and Its Relation to Manic-Depressive States.*

[3]The work referred to is T.S. Kuhn (1962), *The Structure of Scientific Revolutions.*

[4]See discussion in Chapter 11 for comparisons with Ellis' RET and Beck's Cognitive Therapy.

[5]The source quoted by Grunberger is G. Janouch (1971), *Conversations with Kafka.*

III

Therapeutic Approaches

10

Voice Therapy Procedures

Voice Therapy is essentially a laboratory procedure that can be utilized to elicit and identify a person's negative thoughts and attitudes toward self, bringing them more into consciousness. Voice Therapy as a psychotherapeutic methodology is still in its early phases, yet the procedures have thus far proven to be effective in gaining access to patients' core defenses and in facilitating changes in their maladaptive behaviors.

In developing preliminary hypotheses about the voice and procedures to isolate the self-destructive patterns of thought, the author has had many opportunities to observe this process in a wide range of patients and volunteer subjects. As described earlier, my associates and I have been investigating the various dimensions of the voice in group sessions for many years. In addition, Voice Therapy procedures have been utilized as part of a multidimensional approach to individual psychotherapy.

In the following pages, we will describe the techniques of Voice Therapy and discuss clinical material derived from voice therapy sessions. We will analyze significant findings and illustrate the type of resistance encountered in the therapeutic proc-

at 're ak' shun — psy. th, release of psychic tension through verbalizing or acting out an adequate resolution of a represent traumatic experience, upon the appropriate affect

ess. In the next chapter, Voice Therapy as a treatment for emotional and mental illness will be evaluated on its own merits, and we will compare and contrast our technique and theory with important cognitive approaches.

THE ANALYTIC AND ABREACTIVE METHODS OF VOICE THERAPY

The process of identifying the voice can be approached intellectually as a primarily cognitive technique or approached more dramatically using cathartic methods. In the former procedure, the patient attempts to identify and analyze self-criticisms and self-attacks and learns to restate negative thought patterns in the second person as "voices" experienced from the outside. In the latter technique, there is an emphasis on the release of the affect accompanying the voice attacks on the self. In this abreactive method, the patient is asked to amplify his self-attacks and express them more emotionally, with instructions to: "Say it louder," "Really feel that," or "Let go and blurt out anything that comes to mind." In our early studies, patients and subjects frequently adopted this style of expression of their own volition. When asked to formulate their negative thoughts in the second person, they spontaneously began to speak louder and with more intensity of feeling. The participants revealed the patterns of derogatory self-accusations that held special meaning for them. Utilizing this method, much information spilled out, along with a powerful emotional release. For this reason, we began to focus on the cathartic method.

As we described earlier, we were surprised and concerned at the intense anger and sadness expressed by patients and subjects in our initial investigations. Intensely painful feelings were aroused as people learned to articulate their self-attacks and distorted views of self. The powerful feelings of self-loathing and anger against self that quickly emerged during these early sessions gave us an indication of the depth and pervasiveness of the voice process in the personality.

Lastly, in discussing the abreactive method, it is of major

importance to note that as an individual released powerful feelings of sadness and rage, he expressed clear insights into the source of these self-attacks, without assistance or interference from the therapist. The participants became aware of the specific nature of their self-attacks and the extent of their self-destructive consequences.

THE THREE STEPS IN VOICE THERAPY

I.   Identifying the contents of the patient's negative thought process is the first step in a three-step procedure in which patient and therapist collaborate in understanding the patient's distorted ways of thinking. Articulating the self-attacks in the second person facilitates the process of *separating* the patient's own point of view from the hostile thought patterns that make up an alien point of view toward self. Prior to actually articulating the voice, most patients generally accepted their negative thoughts as true evaluations of themselves and implicitly believed them. These critical attitudes had been part of their identity since early childhood. However, with continued participation, our patients and subjects found that they were better able to distinguish their own viewpoints from introjected parental views and distortions. We found this to be evident when utilizing analytic approaches to the voice, as well as abreactive methods.

To illustrate the first step, a twenty-five-year-old male subject verbalized his voice about his relationship to women in a group session:[1]

> You are so disgusting. You are so low. You're beneath a woman. No woman could ever feel anything for you. What makes you think a woman could be attracted to you?
>
> You have no features that could be attractive to a woman. You're ugly. You're short. You're small. You're just not an attractive-looking person.

In this example, note that the subject brought out his hostile self-attacks in the second person. Later in the same session, he expressed considerable anger at being limited by this destructive form of thinking about himself.

II.   In the second step, patients discuss their spontaneous insights and analyze their reactions to verbalizing the voice. Then they attempt to understand the relationship between their voice attacks and their self-destructive behavior patterns. They subsequently develop insight into the limitations that they impose on themselves in everyday life functions. Incidentally, becoming aware of one's self-imposed restrictions reduces paranoid reactions to others and feelings of being victimized.

Here, the same subject discusses his reactions to the self-attacks he had just verbalized:

> Immediately after I finished saying my voice, I had another quick thought, a voice that said:
> "Okay, so now you've said your voice, but what difference is it going to make in your life? It isn't going to change anything."
> I didn't really go with that feeling. I realized what it was—that it was a voice attacking what I'd just said, and I didn't think it was a real point. But I *did* notice how quickly it came up, trying to invalidate everything I'd just said.
> I also realized that since the session last week, I've generally felt better. I felt like taking more positive steps in my life, and it always seems like when I feel that way, positive things tend to happen. I had more to do with girls, and I felt I was making more friends in general. I just felt more alive overall.

III.   Thirdly, the therapist asks the patient to formulate an answer to the voice. In the analytic approach, the patient is asked to respond with a more realistic, objective self-appraisal. In the cathartic method, patients are encouraged to talk back to the voice and challenge it directly as though they were addressing an actual person. Since people tend to identify the voice in relation to parental figures early on, many times they end up talking back directly to their parents in a form of psychodrama.

In the following segment, the same subject articulated his response to the voice attacks concerning his feelings about women. In the course of separating and strengthening his own point of view, he clearly differentiates between his view and that of his parents. It is important to note that the subject responded to his voice with considerable forcefulness, mobilizing deep feelings of anger and sadness as he answered back:

> "I'm not that way. I'm not that person you're talking about. I care a lot for women."
> Another thought that comes to mind, "I'm not like you! [Loud] I've got some feelings. I care! I want something. You never wanted anything. [Mournful] I want something in my life." [Angry]

Responding to one's self-attacks or "answering the voice" is not the same as an actual confrontation with one's parents, with real consequences in interpersonal relationships. It avoids some of the problems, guilt, and responsibilities involved in challenging one's parents directly; however, expressing one's point of view *is* an attack on the *introjected parental images* and, as such, can still cause considerable anxiety and guilt reactions.

In conclusion, when patients utilize the more dramatic style of giving utterance to their voices and answering back, they usually experience strong feelings similar to the emotions experienced by patients in Feeling Release Therapy. The result is a powerful emotional catharsis, with accompanying insight and understanding.

Our subjects tend to "answer back" to their voice attacks spontaneously. They sense the need to reaffirm their own individual points of view after articulating hostile, destructive attitudes and feelings toward themselves. Answering the voice is beneficial for those patients who display sufficient ego strength to cope with the anxiety created by disrupting basic defenses, but is not necessary as part of the overall procedures. Indeed, dramatic methods are specifically contraindicated for patients with weak egos or marginal adjustments, unless applied with considerable care and therapeutic expertise. We will discuss this issue in more depth when we delineate the specific advantages and problems involved in Voice Therapy in the next chapter.

Most patients easily acquire the technique of verbalizing their self-attacks; however, this should not be interpreted to mean that the procedure is necessarily a form of short-term or brief psychotherapy. To the contrary, Voice Therapy is generally, although not exclusively, a long-term dynamic methodology because it attempts to cope with major character defenses. Voice Therapy procedures draw immediate attention to core issues of the patient's personality structure. For this reason, the application of these techniques should be undertaken with sensitivity and considerable attention to patient selection.

The procedures of Voice Therapy elucidate the basic split in patients' thinking and feeling about themselves and their fundamental ambivalence about people and events. The goal of Voice Therapy is effectively to separate out those elements of the personality that are antithetical toward the person, that affect him adversely, and that support the compulsion to repeat deleterious patterns of the past. Voice Therapy increases the patient's awareness of the self-destructive internal dialogue and of the particular events, circumstances, and situations that are likely to activate self-attacks. Most importantly, in exposing these self-attacks, the voice comes more under the patient's control, and he gradually moves toward behavioral choices that are in the direction of his stated goals.

CORRECTIVE SUGGESTIONS

Since the procedures of Voice Therapy challenge core defenses and one's basic self-concept, the process of initiating behavioral changes that expand one's boundaries and expose misconceptions about oneself are a vital part of our overall treatment. Collaborative interventions that effect changes in an individual's behavior in his everyday life functions are a necessary part of any effective therapeutic procedure. The author believes that the potential for therapeutic progress is not merely a function of identifying negative thought patterns and uncovering repressed material; indeed, personal growth ultimately must involve constructive behavioral changes that oppose self-limiting or self-destructive patterns and life-styles.

Our corrective experiences[2] bear a direct relationship to the maladaptive behavior patterns that are influenced and controlled by the patient's negative cognitive processes. In analytic discussions, the therapist and patient identify the specific behaviors regulated by the voice that are self-destructive and constricting, and both participate in formulating ideas about altering routine responses and habitual patterns of behavior. Corrective suggestions are arrived at through a collaborative effort and are in accord with patients' personal goals and ambitions. They specifically apply to those problem areas that the patient wishes to correct or improve.

Initiating changes that help to alter or control the patient's self-nourishing, addictive habit patterns; that disrupt destructive bonds; that attempt to overcome fears; that control provoking, withholding responses; and that lead to a more positive self-image are included in our overall treatment strategy. Until patients learn to take definitive actions that are in opposition to the prohibitions of the voice, they tend to repeat early patterns of maladaptive behavior and continue to live in a narrow range with significant limitations.

Corrective suggestions act as a catalyst to help patients approach new, unfamiliar, or open-ended situations where they will be more vulnerable and less defended. In general, our patients and subjects have shown considerable insight and sensitivity into their resistance about moving toward positive experiences and an expanded world. They recognize their stubbornness about changing habitual responses even when they are known to be maladaptive and self-defeating.

Corrective suggestions, if consistently followed, bring about changes in the emotional atmosphere and often lead to a corrective emotional experience. For example, patients whose style of relating offended their friends, mates, or associates and who characteristically provoked angry responses will make a concerted effort to control their noxious behavior. Once they stop manipulating the interpersonal environment in this manner, they generate a new set of circumstances. This, in turn, creates an unfamiliar, albeit more positive, emotional climate.

Perhaps the most simple and straightforward examples of the use of corrective suggestions are those that are instituted in relation to substance abuse. It is apparent that most self-nourishing habits are directly related to the neurotic process of symbolically gratifying oral needs. Continued substance abuse numbs the patient's feelings of emotional pain and anxiety; however, these addictions also keep him insulated from positive as well as negative experiences. Until patients give up their self-feeding habit patterns, they will continue to maintain a false sense of security and an illusion of self-sufficiency that severely impairs their competency in the interpersonal world. Suggestions to stop addictive behaviors leave patients vulnerable to painful feelings they have been suppressing for years. As they give up a particular habit they have used as a painkiller, they expand their lives and move toward a healthier overall adjustment.

The therapist, in introducing the idea of corrective experiences into the therapeutic alliance, must pay special attention to the proper timing of suggestions. Careful follow-up is needed of the patient's reactions, including the identification of intensified voice attacks, which are generally activated by the patient's move toward expressing his individuality. This is especially evident in marital therapy when, for example, one partner begins to relinquish withholding patterns or excessively dependent or submissive behavior as a result of carrying out therapeutic suggestions. In these cases, the partner who is initiating changes may face increased self-attacks, as well as punitive responses from his mate that support his voice. Corrective suggestions in marital therapy challenge the false security of the fantasy bond. Both partners progressively adapt to a growing independence and sense of separateness and at the same time learn to develop greater tolerance for genuine love and friendship without reverting to parent/child modes of relating.

By disrupting dependency bonds and breaking down defenses that have protected the patient against emotional pain and anxiety, corrective suggestions effectively move patients to a new level of vulnerability and openness. If they are able to withstand the strong voice attacks that are activated by their movement toward positive goals, progress will be maintained. Indeed, patients report that their self-attacks gradually diminish after they have maintained the new behavior over an extended period of time without regressing to old habit patterns.

The importance of "sweating out" important changes in one's style of relating and thereby holding on to the psychological territory gained by patients at each new level cannot be overemphasized. Only through a willingness to risk living without one's customary defenses, routines, deadening habit patterns, and bonds can one learn that survival is possible without these psychological crutches. In this sense, corrective suggestions teach patients, on a deep emotional level, that by using self-discipline, they can gradually increase their freedom of choice without being overwhelmed by primitive fears and anxiety states. They learn that the anticipatory anxiety involved in following through on a corrective suggestion is often more intense than the actual emotional response to the action of changing one's behavior. They learn that if they are persistent about their resolve, they will accommodate to the new circumstances, and there will be therapeutic movement. However, if they submit to their voices and retreat, they tend to remain fixated at a lower level of development, and therapeutic progress is attenuated or may be halted altogether.

Corrective suggestions are very valuable at crucial points in the therapy process and may be applied as follows: (1) the patient formulates his personal goals, thereby establishing his priorities and underscoring his life's purpose and sense of meaning; (2) he plans, with the therapist, corrective experiences that support these goals and that are opposed to the dictates of the voice; (3) there is movement toward risk situations, openness, and a new level of vulnerability; and, finally, (4) the patient learns to tolerate the anxiety of positive change and is able to expand his life space.

In summary, corrective suggestions function to challenge the voice and attempt to alter the patient's self-destructive or nonfunctional behavior outside the office setting. They assist the patient in his initial efforts to develop a greater tolerance for "a better life." Patients learn gradually to accommodate to the anxiety, guilt reactions, and voice attacks aroused by the process of individuating themselves and adopting a strong, goal-directed point of view.

CLINICAL FINDINGS

The first two case studies illustrate the *analytic* method of isolating and identifying hidden patterns of thinking that were related to each patient's presenting problem and symptomatology.

We will describe the development of insights achieved by these individuals over the course of their therapy, as well as the constructive behavioral changes they instituted as a result of these insights. In the course of our case descriptions, we will describe the crucial points at which the patient's resistance came into play and the form that the resistance took.

Case Study—"The Demon on My Shoulder"

Dave was referred to me for therapy by a colleague who had become intimidated by his paranoid ideation and rage. My associate, who had seen the patient's family in family therapy, had told me: "Dave is one of the strangest individuals I've ever met, and his parents are among the most rejecting parents I've ever worked with."

Dave's disturbance consisted of a well developed system of paranoia, an orientation of deep distrust and cynicism toward other people that was extremely difficult to challenge. For example, the patient was particularly paranoid in relation to his boss, obsessively worrying that he would be fired or that his performance would be severely criticized. His negative anticipations created real problems in relating and acted as a self-fulfilling prophecy. His irrational fears also extended to imagining impending assault by strangers; he would cross the street to avoid walking past a group of adolescent boys, because he was afraid they might physically attack him.

Dave lived on two distinct levels: on one level he thought logically and coherently; on another level, he had bizarre thoughts, usually accompanied by intense anger. He spoke in words that painted vivid pictures for his listener, yet his communications were often hopelessly tangled expressions of the two levels on which he thought. Indeed, it was often difficult to determine if Dave's words or his emotions came out the way he had intended. When he spoke, his eyes sometimes teared up, revealing the presence of his regressed child-self, continually under attack from his introjected parental voices.

One of the major reasons Dave sought therapy was because he and his wife were thinking of having a child, and the thought filled him with dread. The couple had no close friends, and Dave was deeply concerned about the effect that his social isolation would have on a child. His Scroogelike tightness and lack of warmth typically caused people to avoid him or dislike him. These factors contributed significantly to his isolation. He complained strenuously about having no memory of his childhood prior to adolescence and expressed a desire to recover these memories through therapy.

Dave not only held paranoid and distrustful attitudes toward others, he also felt extremely self-critical and self-hating. He graphically described his voice as follows: "A demon sits on my shoulder, constantly ridiculing me." Dave was fully aware of what this "demon" was saying to him:

> You little creep, you're too stupid to have a child. Look, you're even too stupid to do a good job at work. Sooner or later, you're going to make a terrible mistake; then all your fancy ideas of success will come crashing down on your head. And you'll deserve everything you get, you miserable shit!

Dave's voice, while not an actual auditory hallucination, nevertheless approached the level of an external sensation in the sense that it interrupted and almost drowned out his rational thoughts.

During the first phase of therapy, Dave's hostility and paranoia focused on his distrust of the therapist. Early in the course of treatment, he developed strong negative transference feelings. Although he had sought my help and trusted me to a certain extent, on another level he was deeply cynical, and his behavior was very unpleasant and provoking in his sessions. His resistance in therapy took the form of guarded, vague ramblings and a seeming unwillingness and fearfulness about bringing out his attacks on me directly. He also refused to verbalize them as "voices." Despite the fact that he readily expressed his self-critical thoughts and feelings, he stubbornly played "dumb" about revealing his external anger. Instead, he tended to blurt out angry questions: "Why are you looking at me like that?" or "What did you mean by that last statement?" Eventually Dave learned to put his suspicions and hostile thoughts in terms of a voice directed against the therapist:

> Look, Davie, this man is going to influence you in the wrong direction. He's going to sit you down and reeducate you and you'll have no opinions of your own after he's through with you. You can't trust him, you'd better listen to *me*, Davie, if you know what's good for you. You were always a gullible, stupid kid.

At other times, Dave's "voice," which he identified as sounding very much like his father, questioned my character and qualifications as a therapist:

> This man is out to get your money. What does he know about people? You think he's read all these books on his shelves? For all you know he's a quack, a fake. If he's so darn good, why isn't he more well-known?

After approximately 2 years of therapy, Dave began to develop positive feelings that intruded on his paranoid distortions. At this point, he became fearful of being separated from me for a 3-week vacation period. His fear was compounded by the fact that he was planning to undergo minor surgery during my absence. In our last session before the vacation, Dave verbalized these fears in the form of a voice:

> See, Davie, now you're hooked. Take that man, for instance. What right does he have to go away? [sad] He's always been around, so now he's going to go away. He knows you're going to have that operation, that's just when you need him.
> What do you mean you're just scared? Of course, you're scared, you need somebody to take care of you. That's what you're paying him for, isn't it?

Much later in therapy, when Dave started his own business, his cynical, judgmental voice about other people was translated into belittling, sarcastic one-liners aimed at his employees. He noticed that by berating others, he sometimes was able to reduce the voice attacks "in his own head"; on the other hand, he hated himself for mistreating the people in his office.

As Dave slowly and painstakingly isolated his distorted attitudes toward other people and controlled his tendency verbally to abuse his employees, he began to break down his fundamental resistance to changing deep-seated character defenses. Both

Dave and I thought it would be valuable at this juncture to challenge his characteristic tightness and lack of generosity, so together we discussed a number of possible corrective suggestions in the form of bonuses to his employees and simple acts of generosity toward his friends.

Initially, Dave was afraid and reported a number of voices telling him that he was a sucker. Later, he found that these actions gave him pleasure and led to friendly responses from others. He discovered that his acts of generosity surprisingly enough acted to dispel his deep-seated fear of being exploited. Dave reported this period as being the "happiest time in my life."

The fact that people responded favorably to the results of Dave's corrective experience, as they often do to corrective suggestions, moved him beyond the limitations he had previously imposed on himself. He then had to cope with the anxiety aroused by disturbing his "psychological equilibrium." He had to adjust to the feeling of closeness and increased sense of vulnerability brought about by these unfamiliar positive experiences.

Dave eventually was able to work through basic paranoid beliefs that had been a fundamental part of his resistance. Much later, when he made the decision actually to have a child, his voice escalated its attacks on him and his wife:

> You won't know what to do with a baby. You certainly won't know how to talk to a kid. What an incompetent, lousy father you're going to be!
> Look at this woman. She's got you where she wants you now. I've always told you that women were tricky, that they'd swallow you up. Once you make a commitment like this, you're going to have to be devoted to her and the kid for the rest of your life.

In summary, it required several years of psychotherapy for Dave to separate out his paranoid distortions from his more rational ways of thinking. Interestingly enough, throughout the long therapy process, Dave did not substantially recover memories of his childhood. However, following the birth of his son, he recalled an incident that had occurred when he was a young teenager, a humiliating experience that he had repressed for years. He remembered his father severely berating and chastising a high-school friend of his in a style very similar to the way he had mistreated Dave. His outraged feeling for his friend prevailed, whereas he could not feel directly for himself.

Late one afternoon, Dave was driving with his year-old son along the same route he had driven with his father many years before. He felt nervous and had the familiar, albeit disturbing, thought that he wouldn't know how to relate to the boy. Immediately recognizing the thought as a voice, Dave then recalled an event from his childhood. He recounted this poignant and painful memory in one of his last sessions:

> I was driving with my father and feeling imprisoned against my will. I wanted desperately to jump out of the car. On that particular afternoon, I had just learned a new song at school. My father asked me to sing the song for him. Then he ridiculed me and made fun of my voice and the fact that I couldn't carry a tune. I had been so proud of learning the song, and I was trying to show my father I could remember all the words. Since then, I've never been able to remember the words to songs.

In his therapy Dave had succeeded in uncovering the hostile, cynical thoughts underlying his overall maladjustment, as well as his fears of having a child. The therapeutic process enabled him to rebuild his trust in other people and in himself.

Case Study—"My Mother's Voice"

In 1969, a woman phoned me early one morning and requested an appointment at my earliest convenience. She said she felt she literally couldn't make it through another night of intense anxiety attacks. It seemed she was tortured by self-hating, sadistic thoughts to such an extent that she had been unable to sleep for several nights.

The patient, Rosie, was a large woman, tall, overweight, asexual in appearance, her face marked by deep scars where for years she had picked and torn at her skin. At the time, she lived almost as a total recluse in a large house with her father and brother.

At our first meeting, Rosie told me that her mother had died when she (Rosie) was thirteen. She clearly recalled her mother's last words to her: "Take care of your brother." Out of guilt, Rosie complied and almost completely raised her brother from the time he was seven years old.

In 3 years of psychoanalytic-oriented psychotherapy, Rosie lost 40 pounds and shed the long black coat she had always worn to cover herself. The scars on her face healed and faded, and she developed into an attractive, sexual woman. She successfully terminated therapy, married, and continued her career as a social worker. Then, some years later, she sought me out once again for professional help. Serious problems had arisen about the time she and her husband started to plan a family. Once again, she allowed her looks to deteriorate and had regained much of the weight she had previously lost. One day, while filling out a credit card application, Rosie was unable to remember her address or phone number. Frightened by this brief lapse in memory, she recognized that she was in serious trouble psychologically.

For approximately a year, I met with Rosie twice weekly as she systematically identified and analyzed the contents of her self-destructive thoughts and impulses. I also encouraged her to talk about her voices to a close friend and to write her self-attacks in a journal. Here, the patient describes, in her own words, the principal voice attacks she identified early in her sessions, degrading views of herself that formed the core of her resistance.

ROSIE: "Before each session, I heard a continuous series of self-attacks that went like this:

> What are you going to bother him for now? You think he wants to talk to *you*? He's got other things to do. Who's interested, anyway, in what you have to say about anything? Why can't you take care of this yourself?
>
> Look at the trouble you caused him years ago when you were first in therapy. You remember what you were like then, don't you? You were disgusting. You bothered him all the time. You called him, wrote him letters. You had fights with him. Do you think he'd want to talk to you after the way you were before? Just forget it—stay in your place!

"I had been so isolated and secretive that this voice went around in circles in my head. It was a constant barrage of 'Who cares?' and 'Don't bother him.' It was difficult for me to think straight. I realized later that the continual barrage of voices had a lot to do with my general confusion and temporary lapses of memory.''

After Rosie revealed the voices behind her resistance to her therapy sessions, other voice attacks surfaced, and she became more aware of the core issues in her life. She was able to expose and identify the hidden thoughts she entertained about becoming pregnant.

Rosie dated her current depression from the occasion of a visit to her obstetrician in order to determine her eligibility for motherhood. The doctor's remarks at the time activated a series of angry self-attacks. Although he mentioned the possibility of amniocentesis as a method for detecting birth defects, he nevertheless advised her against having a baby at her age, forty, and told her that, statistically, a higher percentage of women over thirty-five give birth to babies that are deformed. He offered to show her photographs of some "examples" to prove his point. She refused to look and left his office in a state of agitation and misery.

Rosie related her voice attacks about the potential hazards of having a child at her age:

> So you're going to have a baby? That's a joke. Look at you, you're disgusting-looking anyway. You're fat enough as it is. And look how old you are. You think that doctor was wrong? He was *right*! That's what happens to women like you—they have deformed children.

Later, Rosie identified a succession of self-attacks concerning the sex of her unborn baby. She dramatized the voice as though her mother was talking to her:

> What do you think I felt like when I had a boy? What was I supposed to do with a boy? I didn't know how to take care of a boy. You think I liked it? I didn't like it. I didn't ask for a boy.

ROSIE: "Taking that attack to its ultimate conclusion":—

> And what do you think I felt like when I had *you*? You think I felt any different? I didn't know what to do with you either. I

didn't like babies. I didn't know what to do with a baby. What was I supposed to do with you? I didn't like you any better than I liked him.

Soon after Rosie had identified the voice about having a boy, she began systematically to control her diet and started losing weight rapidly. Prior to isolating this basic fear and the associated thought process, Rosie had been unable to lose weight.

Rosie's most painful memory associated with the voices she identified concerned a traumatic event that had occurred before her mother died, when she was approximately eleven years old. Her mother had told her that her uncle was going to have a suit custom-tailored for her for graduation from elementary school. Rosie remembers:

> I was thrilled, and we went to my uncle's clothing store for the fitting. He brought out a suit for me to try on, but it was a *boy's* suit. I was outraged. I didn't understand my parents or what they were trying to do. I remember ripping off the jacket, saying, "I don't want *any*thing."
>
> Remembering that scene made me feel some compassion for myself, about my sexuality and about my family's negation of me as a girl. Recognizing, on a *feeling* level, that my mother had rejected me for being a girl and that she also had deep feelings of hostility toward my brother, gave me an understanding of why I had been so afraid to have a child of my own, especially a boy. On a deep level, I had been horrified at the thought that I might be like my mother in raising my own child.

For years, Rosie had repressed the memory of this painful event. Interestingly enough, soon afterward, she began to question the role that food had always played in helping her numb herself to painful situations. She recognized that she had been trying to soothe herself from the distress caused by her vicious self-attacks by indulging in eating binges whenever she felt especially self-hating.

Rosie had also projected her voice onto friends who were aware of the couple's plans to start a family. When she took back these projections and verbalized the feelings as a voice, she uncovered deep misgivings about herself as a woman.

I had become extremely paranoid; I remember dreading that someone might ask me if my husband and I were trying to have a baby. My thoughts about what other people might think of me went something like this:

"You think you can be a mother? That shows you how crazy you are. You're not like normal women. Don't you forget for a minute where you came from!"

The process of consistently identifying her self-attacks over an extended time period eventually freed Rosie to be able to make a practical, rational decision about having a child. Maintaining her weight loss was crucial to her progress in therapy. Whenever Rosie neglected her dieting regime, she became demoralized and less responsive sexually. Her resistance obviously centered around her conflict between retreating into an asexual, childish, self-nourishing life-style and developing further into a sexually responsive woman—and mother.

In reviewing these two cases, it is important to note that voice attacks appeared to be at the core of the resistance to therapy. They played a significant part in the intensity and duration of the negative transference reactions that developed relatively early in the therapy of both patients. In both examples, analysis of the voice process revealed a chronic pessimism and deep-seated conviction on the patients' part that they could not really change or develop. Dave strongly believed that people were untrustworthy, while Rosie held a firm conviction that she was doomed to repeat her mother's life. These misconceptions were the basis of Dave's and Rosie's resistance to change and could only be challenged successfully and countered (by the patients themselves) after the appropriate voices were uncovered.

The Abreactive Method—Clinical Studies

In general, our studies have shown that the abreactive method effectively and rapidly uncovers fundamental issues that are central to people's inner conflicts and life-styles. In early sessions, many of our volunteer subjects revealed basic misconceptions that had guided and controlled their behavior since early childhood. For example, one subject, in expressing the negative

thoughts behind his feelings of painful self-consciousness, uncovered a deep inner conviction that he was substandard and
therefore had no right to live—because he was black. Although
not fully conscious of this process, he associated his skin color
with prejudiced stereotypes of racial inferiority.

Another subject revealed a similar feeling that she was a
burden to her family. She was exceptionally quiet, unobtrusive,
and feared close relationships. Prior to her participation in our
investigations, she had not recognized the extent to which she
had been rejected by her parents or how she had carried that past
rejection into her marriage in the form of derogatory self-criticisms.

Another volunteer, a young man, had serious doubts about
his masculinity that made him continually cater to women in a
desperate bid for love, approval, and validation of his manhood.
By verbalizing his voice along with the powerful release of suppressed emotions, the subject gained access to primary process
thinking and painful primal feelings of deprivation that were at
the basis of his confused sexual identity.

Another subject, Stan, had difficulty believing that women
could really be attracted to him because he felt deep feelings of
being physically unappealing, even repulsive to women. The
physical abuse Stan had sustained as a youngster at the hands of
his father connected in his mind to feelings of self-disgust. In a
group session, he explored his anger toward his father after verbalizing the self-attacks related to his feelings of self-loathing.
Here he tells how he dramatically *answered* the voice and, in so
doing, uncovered the source of his self-disgust:

> I remember that we had foster kids at home, and my father
> would beat them. I would put myself in the middle, and he would
> end up beating me. After these beatings, I felt ugly and loathsome
> and ashamed of myself.
> That made me think of an answer to that voice about being dis-
> gusting:
> "*You're* the one that's slimy. You're the one that feels like he's
> slime, not me. I'm not like those things that you showed me, calves
> being born, slimy—and you telling me that's the way *I* was born.
> [sad]
> "*You're* the coward! You're too chicken to stick up for your-

self. I'm not! *Dammit*! [loud, angry sounds] I'm not a failure like you. I'm not a dirt farmer. You're the one who's afraid of women. I'm not. I want a woman to love me. I want to love them."

In almost every example of dramatizing the voice or answering it back, our subjects and patients were able quickly to identify its source in the family scene. Insights were exceptionally clear, appropriate in affect, and generalized to present-day limitations and consequences.

VOICE THERAPY IN MARITAL AND FAMILY THERAPY

The analytic and cathartic approaches to voice therapy can both be utilized effectively in marital and family therapy. Voice Therapy procedures may be applied in a group setting or in sessions with one couple or a family. To illustrate, in a group composed of married couples, partners were asked to reveal their negative perceptions and critical views of themselves and of each other. One couple, who had been married 5 years, had settled into a routine of blaming each other for the slow erosion of genuine love and affectionate feelings that had existed between them at the inception of their relationship. In an in-depth interview,[3] they attempt objectively to trace the causes of this deterioration, examining various aspects of a crucial turning point in their relationship. In the following dialogue, they explore the negative attitudes each had toward the other during that phase of their marriage.

BOB: When I realized that I had fallen in love with you, when I really knew that you meant a lot to me and I told you, I became self-conscious. I began to feel strange around you and around our friends. I thought to myself:
"Now everybody knows. What if she rejects you now? You're a fool! A real sucker!"

ARLENE: I know when you told me you loved me, that it was a turning point for me, too. After that, I didn't feel like doing the same things together that we had always enjoyed doing. I had a feeling that things were

being demanded of me. I remember hearing a voice
that said:

"He's such a demanding person. He expects you
to do all these things for him and be with him all the
time. What about *you*? You need some time for
yourself."

BOB: But it almost appeared that I was demanding because I felt hurt and angry. I became so confused and
had thoughts like:

"See, I warned you. She's acting different, she's
bored with you. She's just like all other women."

I didn't really believe those voices, but still I was
angry and pained by your lack of interest. I tried hard
not to act on my anger, but at times I did pull away
when I became really discouraged about the relationship.

ARLENE: I remember at the time I started thinking things that
would stop my actions like:

"Don't show him you're enthusiastic to see him.
It's not necessary. Just sit there, besides, what's the
big deal. He's not that great. He's kind of an awkward person, lazy, passive. . . ."

I really started picking you apart in my mind. I realize now that I really *did* believe those things I was
thinking. Realistically, what I understand today is
that you haven't changed that much in all the years
we've known each other. But I have.

Looking back, I can see how I've twisted you in
my mind, to protect against seeing myself differently
than I was raised to believe I was. Your feelings for
me made me feel differently about myself—made me
feel like I was really lovable. I couldn't live with that
different identity. . . . By listening to the voice, I
twisted everything, to do away with that new feeling
about myself, and I hurt you in the process.

In this case, it appeared that Arlene had reacted adversely
to being chosen and loved by Bob and implicitly believed her
critical thoughts about him. She tended to act on the directives
of her voice and played out the role of a petulant child, responding inappropriately to imagined obligations and demands. In the

interview, she again began to see her husband from her own point of view and felt deeply about the damage that had occurred in the relationship. During the course of therapy, both individuals were able to reexperience their original feelings of tenderness and love.

As this case demonstrates, the nature of the fantasy bond as it manifests itself in marital relationships is that both individuals, more often than not, are "listening" to the dictates of their respective voices. Their communications are filtered, in a sense, through biased and alien points of view that distort their partner's real image. Both parties ward off loving responses from the other, using rationalizations propagated by the voice to justify their anger and distancing behavior. Often, too, men and women project their own specific self-attacks on one another and respond as though they were being victimized or depreciated by their mates.

Withholding, as a defensive maneuver, is frequently at the core of a couple's problem and causes untold distress to both individuals. These patterns have been found to be regulated by the voice process. For example, Arlene's voice had directed her to hold back an enthusiastic response from her husband. Only in retrospect, however, was she able to identify the particular voice that was operating at the time she first held back her natural excitement and warmth. For his part, Bob had vacillated between acceding to his voice at being a sucker for loving Arlene and sustaining his own point of view.

Incidentally, we have found that voice attacks deriding a person's pursuit of love and satisfaction in long-lasting relationships were among the most common voices reported by our subjects. This almost universal voice warns individuals against investing themselves emotionally in caring for another and emphasizes the possibility of being hurt or victimized in the end. People who ignore the dictates of this seemingly self-protective voice discover that attacks labeling them as foolish for loving and trusting another person are not logical or accurate. The capacity to love someone brings its own reward because it feels good. Besides, caring for and being generous toward another person enhances one's positive feelings for oneself.

We frequently instruct both partners of a couple to reveal the negative voices about themselves and about the other in a frank exchange of views. We encourage them to spend a few minutes a day engaged in this form of communication. Each individual strives to be nonevaluative and empathetic in giving away his or her internal dialogue, and both attempt to not react to this feedback as personal criticism. We found that couples who followed this practice benefited considerably from this type of discussion and progressed significantly in their feelings of friendship and closeness.

The goal of Voice Therapy with couples is to help each individual identify the voice attacks that are creating friction and avoidance behaviors. In identifying specific self-attacks, as well as judgmental, critical thoughts about the other, each partner is able to relate more openly to the other. Patterns of dishonest communication and duplicity can be interrupted by the process of revealing the contents of voice attacks in sessions facilitated by a well trained professional therapist.

It is important to emphasize that in the process of admitting critical, angry thoughts about each other, the marriage partners must be sincere in giving these thoughts away and must not hold on to grudges and personal slights even when their critical views may have some basis in reality. Refusing to relinquish one's animosity and the pent-up anger connected to one's negative view of the mate or family member only leads to disharmony in future interactions.

It goes without saying that men and women have ambivalent views of their marital partners. Their fundamental ambivalence is partially based on an idealized view of the mate, as well as on a destructive internal tape continually running the mate down. The fundamental ambivalence originates in each partner's own defenses but may also be an appropriate response to the changing moods and behaviors of one's mate. In other words, when one's partner is operating from his or her own point of view, the other could potentially respond with love and affection. In contrast, when one's partner is operating on the basis of his or her voice, he or she tends *not* to be lovable and wards off the other's loving responses.

We have concluded that Voice Therapy procedures used in the context of marital therapy can help prevent the reliving and recreation of the same or similar type of negative circumstances that existed in each partner's original family. Therefore, we feel that the procedures of Voice Therapy can be a valuable tool in marital and family psychotherapy.

In conclusion, the author believes that the ultimate goal of psychotherapy is to help individuals achieve a free and independent existence, remain open to experiences and feelings, and to maintain the ability to respond appropriately to both positive and negative events in their lives. To this end, the process of identifying the voice and its associated feelings of self-hatred and rage toward self, combined with corrective suggestions for behavioral change, significantly expand the patient's boundaries and bring about a more positive sense of self.

NOTES

[1]The statements of this subject were excerpted from a 40-minute videotape, *Voice Therapy* (Parr, 1984), presented at the American Psychiatric Association Annual Convention, May 13, 1986, Washington, D.C.

[2]The term "corrective experience" was first suggested by Franz Alexander (cited by Arlow, 1979) to describe procedures applied to cases that had been generally refractory to treatment:

> Alexander (1932) felt that since most patients had been traumatized by parental mismanagement during childhood, it was necessary for the analyst to arrange a "corrective emotional experience" that would counteract the effects of the original trauma. (p. 17)

[3]Excerpted from videotape, *Closeness Without Bonds* (Parr, 1985).

11

Voice Therapy
Evaluation

What I want to do battles the voice. . . . The voice wants to back me into a secure channel. . . . I think my parents installed the voice as a governor to limit myself.

No treatment could do any good until I understood the voice and saw that it was running me, that I was an automaton. . . . It's incredible to know that the voice prevented me from doing this [writing a biography], even took over my real self image. . . . I feel as if I've been reprieved from a lifelong sentence.

From the journal of a borderline patient
(Masterson, 1985, p. 68)

Although Voice Therapy is still relatively new on the psychotherapy scene, there is accumulating evidence demonstrating its effectiveness as a therapeutic procedure. Used in conjunction with corrective suggestions, the method can help patients counteract the directives of the voice, thereby ameliorating neurotic symptoms and achieving greater personal fulfillment. Because its techniques gain access to latent or important unconscious processes in the personality, Voice Therapy has the added potential of becoming a valuable research tool for elucidating the causal relationship between destructive cognitive processes, their associated affect, and neurotic, maladaptive behavior.

In this chapter, we will evaluate the efficiency and effectiveness of the methods we utilized in our preliminary studies of the voice process. We will delineate the crucial points in the treatment process where resistance is likely to be encountered and indicate the forms that this resistance may take. Because Voice Therapy directly challenges deeply held character defenses, the therapist must be continually alert to the possibility of patients' adverse reactions or regressions at critical stages where resistance comes into play.

We will demonstrate that Voice Therapy meets the criteria required of a psychotherapeutic system in that the methodology is derived from a comprehensive, internally consistent theory of neurosis. It is important to emphasize that our overall treatment strategy is based on the author's 30-year study of the problem of resistance to change or progress in psychotherapy. Indeed, the techniques have their roots in an ongoing investigation of resistance and transference reactions, adverse responses to feedback, and regression based on the fear and guilt engendered by breaking dependency bonds. The rationale underlying the practice of Voice Therapy is connected to a systematic theoretical approach: it involves the process of identifying and challenging destructive bonds or imaginary connections and moving toward individuation and personal freedom.

To illustrate, since the voice functions to maintain the fantasy bond or core defense, it is logical first to expose and understand the role of the negative thought patterns; then to gain access to and release the underlying affect; and, lastly, to counteract the destructive effect of these thoughts on the patient's behavior through the application of appropriate corrective suggestions. Indeed, the major thrust of the therapeutic endeavor is to help the patient to identify his own unique point of view and gradually to act against the voice and its prohibitions. Identification of voice attacks implies behavior changes that contradict the patient's self-limiting posture and motivate him to take chances that are at first frightening and guilt-provoking. Therefore, since Voice Therapy is closely related to challenging basic defenses, the therapist practicing Voice Therapy will encounter more resistance at certain stages in the therapeutic process than he might encounter in other therapies.

EVALUATION OF PROCEDURES

In judging the merits of any psychotherapeutic method, attention needs to be paid to a number of parameters,[1] including: (1) The ease with which patients are able to learn the techniques and utilize them effectively in sessions; (2) the degree of congruence between the communications of patients during the session and their symptomatology, internal conflicts, and problems in living (Mowrer, 1953); (3) the results obtained—the degree of therapeutic movement during the sessions and durability of positive change measured after termination of therapy;[2] and (4) the relative absence of confounding variables that would bias an independent observer's analysis of the clinical material made available in the sessions (this factor helps determine the research potential of the method). Bearing in mind these criteria, we will discuss relevant issues concerned with the evaluation of Voice Therapy. We will attend to the negative as well as the positive features of this approach.

Positive Aspects

Effective use of technique. The procedures of Voice Therapy, as outlined in the previous chapter, are relatively straightforward and easily learned. Patients generally require only brief instructions or explanations. Most subjects can comprehend and comply with the therapist's instructions and are able to separate alien, self-critical, or attacking thoughts from thoughts of rational self-interest. The ease with which patients learn and use the methods should not be construed to mean that Voice Therapy procedures can be applied without careful attention to patient selection, timing, and sensitivity. To the contrary, the application of these techniques must be carried out with care and knowledge of the ego strength of each patient. The therapist must match the methods employed to the individual patient's needs. Voice Therapy should be practiced only by well-trained, competent clinical psychologists, psychiatrists, or other members of the mental health profession.

Practical aspects and effectiveness. The methods of Voice Therapy, used in conjunction with corrective suggestions, constitute a widespread exposure and challenge to neurotic activity in everyday life situations. Although broadly based, the approach is oriented to practical issues and down-to-earth aspects of patients' lives. The techniques quickly pinpoint self-destructive patterns of thought that connect directly to the patient's core defenses and maladaptive responses. It has been demonstrated that there is a positive correlation between the *recognition* of the contents of the voice and positive *changes* in behavior as reported by patients. This effect or causal relationship was noted even in cases where suggestions for corrective experiences had not yet been introduced into the treatment plan.

In addition, corrective suggestions designed to counteract voice attacks relate closely to behavioral change in problem areas. When approached in a gradual, step-by-step fashion, the resulting expansion in the patient's functioning capabilities is enduring. In that sense, the patient progressively accommodates to the anxiety associated with breaking bonds and routines that are self-destructive and maintains the new habit patterns. The methods can be applied to many divergent aspects of therapeutic endeavor, including personality disorders, conflicts within the marital dyad, interactions in dysfunctional family systems, child abuse prevention, parenting practices, and vocational and management counseling.

Minimal transference reactions. One of the major advantages of Voice Therapy over many traditional psychotherapies lies in the patient's rapid achievement of his own insight. The patient's flow of communication during the process of uncovering hidden thoughts and unconscious material is generally uninterrupted by interpretations from the therapist. Patients and subjects draw their own conclusions from verbalizing the voice and relate the material to problems in their current lives. They also formulate their own ideas about the origins of their distorted perceptions and attitudes.

Considerable information can be gathered from and about patients without the intrusion of the therapist's interpretations or theoretical bias. The lack of interpretation on the part of the therapist reduces transference reactions, establishes a feeling of equality between both parties, and places the burden of responsibility on the patient to work through the material he has uncovered.

Research capability. Because the therapeutic process is not interfered with by interpretation, there are fewer confounding variables to contend with in studying destructive thought patterns and their relationship to destructive behavior. Thus, the approach has the potential of becoming a valuable methodological research tool. Researchers are able to objectify and analyze the discrete words and phrases of the voice process more accurately than if the data were biased by input from the therapist. One proposed area of research involves the area of suicide prediction and prevention. Factor analysis of hostile, self-accusatory thoughts obtained from *non*suicidal individuals and from patients who have made serious suicide attempts might yield important predictive data.

Other aspects. In utilizing the methods of Voice Therapy, especially the abreactive method, patients not only identify their hostile, self-destructive thoughts; in addition, they are able to release the affect associated with these cognitions. As noted in the previous chapter, powerful feelings of anger, sadness, and pain are connected with an individual's self-attacks. The expression of these emotions frequently has considerable positive impact on the patient's overall mood. In our clinical experience, we observed that some patients were limited in their progress until they had undergone some form of catharsis or release of feelings as part of the procedure of Voice Therapy.

Most of our patients and subjects experienced an unusual self-awareness and reported important insights whenever they allowed themselves to give full expression to their suppressed feelings and thoughts while verbalizing the voice. They made connections to childhood trauma and to specific occasions where they recalled parental hostility being directed toward them.

It is important to emphasize that the feeling release component is a prominent part of our procedure. Our psychotherapy groups, individual sessions, and videotaped interviews demonstrate the importance accorded this aspect of our method.

In summary, Voice Therapy is a comprehensive psychotherapy approach because it deals not only with cognitive aspects of the personality but can be utilized to elicit powerful affective components and repressed material. It is a dynamic method concerned with the analysis of defenses, resistance, and the etiology of neurosis. Voice Therapy integrates aspects of several diverse theoretical approaches, including psychoanalytical, cognitive-behavioral, abreactive, and existential psychotherapies. It is practically oriented in directly challenging repetitive patterns of compulsive and self-defeating behaviors, allowing certain patients to go beyond results they achieved in other therapies. Lastly, Voice Therapy techniques lend themselves to continued application after the patient's successful termination of therapy. The method of identifying thoughts that go against one's best interests is *unusually* adaptive as an ongoing form of self-investigation that patients can utilize for continuous change and personal development.

Resistance in Voice Therapy

> Scientific psychoanalysis gives the individual only a new kind of excuse for his willing and a release from the responsibility of consciousness. The task of a constructive therapy on the contrary is to lead the individual who already suffers from the loss of his illusions and begins to destroy even natural science, beyond these justification tendencies to the voluntary acceptance of himself and his own responsibility.
>
> Otto Rank (1936/1972, p. 45)

Resistance occurs in all forms of therapy and is indicative of an underlying fear and aversion to change. Although most patients are dissatisfied with their present-day lives and desire to feel better, they are heavily invested in a defended life-style that precludes "the better life." Movement toward fulfillment, independence, freedom, and happiness is threatening and arouses considerable guilt.

Resistance may take many forms. For example, patients may come late for appointments, act out self-nourishing or self-destructive behaviors outside the session, manifest hostility toward their therapist, or become delinquent in paying for their sessions. Nevertheless, resistance as manifested by patients in Voice Therapy centers around maintaining and protecting the fantasy bond or core defense. Preserving a fantasy of connection with one's parents and symbolically parenting oneself offers an illusion of protection and security and a sense of pseudo-independence. Once invested in fantasy gratification, a person is less willing to take a chance again on real gratification in the interpersonal environment. In other words, the primary defense centers around the fantasy that an individual can nurture himself, thereby avoiding the risk involved in real wanting and possible frustration in relation to others.

The core defense is preserved by certain key components. While these defensive maneuvers overlap each other and are not discrete entities, they may be delineated for purpose of clarification as follows: (1) the idealization of parents and family; (2) the preservation of a corresponding negative self-image (i.e., a basic conception of oneself as "bad"); (3) the displacement of negative parental traits onto others; (4) the retreat from and subsequent loss of feeling; (5) the development of an inward, self-protective posture; (6) the withholding of positive emotional responses and adaptive behaviors; (7) the acting out of self-nourishing habits and routines; and (8) the preference for responses and communications that support a fantasy bond with one's marital partner, family, or other institutions.

Each aspect of the patient's resistance can be examined and understood in terms of how it functions to protect the fantasy bond or core defense. Generally, it can be determined that a one-to-one relationship exists between the types of voice attacks identified by the patient, the behaviors he elects to change, and the particular aspect of the defensive process being challenged. Resistance can be expected to occur at those points where core defenses are challenged by Voice Therapy procedures. The therapist who understands the theoretical basis of Voice Therapy can be alert for signs of resistance and negativity as the patient's progress encroaches on specific defenses.

Secondary defenses consisting of negative attitudes and hypotheses about the self and the interpersonal environment justify and support the primary defense. For example, an analysis of the statements that patients use against themselves reveals that misconceptions of the self are among the most common forms of voice attacks (Firestone, 1985). These negative assumptions about the self are an integral part of the patient's negative self-concept and act to separate him from other people by emphasizing the differences between the patient and others. These two factors, a negative self-image and a sense of alienation from other people, are basic dimensions of a defended posture and life-style.

Patients are resistant to changing negative, hostile perceptions of themselves, idealized views of their parents, and cynical, distrustful views of others, causing them to relive maladaptive, self-defeating patterns of the past. At the same time, they tend to avoid positive experiences with potential for *real* gratification from the interpersonal environment. Every aspect of this secondary line of defense functions to protect the core defense—the fantasy that they and only they can feed and sustain themselves.

When therapists view resistance in terms of protecting the primary defense or fantasy bond from intrusion, they are better able to predict the points at which the patient's anxiety will be aroused. Negative reactions can be anticipated whenever there is any change in the patient's cognitive behavior or affective state that threatens either the self-nourishing process or object dependency.

Keeping this relationship in mind, let us examine the kinds of resistance typically encountered in Voice Therapy. Important areas of resistance may be catalogued as follows:

1. Resistance to utilizing specific Voice Therapy procedures.
2. Resistance to changing one's self-concept.
3. Resistance to formulating personal goals and corrective suggestions.
4. Resistance and regression after answering back to voice attacks.

1. *Resistance to specific procedures.*

Patients' resistance to learning to separate out voice attacks

and self-critical thoughts from a general perception of themselves as feeling and acting in their own interest is directly related to their fear of recognizing a lack of integrity or division
within the personality. People are very reluctant to recognize the
presence of an alien, hostile, or destructive point of view toward
themselves and experience the accompanying sense of fragmentation. For this reason, they may become resistant to learning or
following Voice Therapy procedures that separate out discordant elements of the personality.

Patients exhibit differential forms of resistance to the employment of Voice Therapy techniques. In the analytic method,
patients or subjects may be reluctant to verbalize what they are
telling themselves about the negative events in their lives or their
basic problems. They may refuse to state their self-attacks in the
second person as outside attacks or voices. In the abreactive
method, they may refuse to participate in the dramatization
process or hold back important feelings.

In regard to the technique of answering back to destructive
voices, patients may be unwilling, or in some cases practically
unable to speak up for themselves and their own point of view.
They may tend to agree with their voices and self-attacks even
when unjustified from the standpoint of objective analysis. It is
important to note that not all of the attacks on oneself are necessarily false. However, even when there is basic truth in the al-
legations, it doesn't account for the associated hostility toward
self.

Sometimes patients irresponsibly use Voice Therapy procedures to rationalize negative feelings and attitudes toward self
and others. They attempt to distance themselves from or disown
responsibility for the negative viewpoint, saying, in effect,
"That's just my voice." They continue to act out behavior based
on the voice while refusing to give it away or separate it out. For
example, some individuals tend to use prohibitions of the voice
as rationalizations for undesirable behavior even *after* they have
identified the specific thoughts influencing their actions. Others
refuse to apply the insights gained in the sessions to the major
issues in their lives that are symptomatic of their inner conflicts
and struggles. Their resistance or refusal to apply their new
knowledge of self masks a need to maintain a childish, provok-

236 · VOICE THERAPY

ing mode of interaction with significant others, a posture repetitive of the bond with their families.

Other individuals mistake the outside point of view for their own and to a great extent identify with the attacker. When voices are pervasive and a person submits to the external point of view, there is a basic loss of vitality and feeling for oneself and others. In instances where there is a desperate need for identification with one's parent as a security measure, patients will find it difficult to recognize the connection between their self-attacks and parental abuses. They protect the parent at their own expense and are blocked in their capacity to form insights.

Human beings strive for a sense of internal unity and harmony and react with anxiety when they become aware of and verbalize self-attacks. During critical phases in therapy, patients may refuse to identify the angry, attacking side of themselves. For example, a college student who suffered from severe anxiety attacks noticed that when he became even slightly nervous in the classroom setting, he "heard" a voice that sarcastically baited him with the following attacks:

> See, now you're getting anxious, aren't you? You're going to do something to call attention to yourself; you're going to start shaking any minute now. See, you're falling apart, aren't you?

The young man became increasingly depressed and anxious as he experienced the part of himself that hated him and was sadistically tormenting him. It scared him and caused him much distress until he came to better understand the voice process.

Resistance is frequently encountered when patients begin to realize that they are not operating from their own point of view and that more often than not they are behaving in a manner similar to one of their parents. They are disturbed to discover that, in not actively pursuing their goals and priorities, they are acting against themselves. At these times, they are, in a sense, more than "51 percent" on the side of the introjected parent and implicitly believe their hostile, self-accusatory thoughts. In these instances, they frequently take on the character and style of the parental figure, even when they resented the particular traits in the parent. They are no longer oriented toward their own goals and interests but are acting upon the prescriptions of the voice.

Their behavior is controlled, in effect, by another person, a significant figure from their past who may have felt either overt or covert hostility toward them.

2. *Resistance to changing one's self-concept.*

There is fundamental resistance in Voice Therapy to separating out voices and self-attacks that challenge the basic self-concept. One would imagine that people would be happy to see through and modify negative views of themselves that make them feel bad. Surprisingly, this is most often *not* the case because to accept changes in one's identity implies a disruption of the fantasy bond with one's family. It may interfere with the idealization of the family necessary for successful self-parenting and therefore threaten one's sense of security; for example, "If I was not bad, inadequate, or unlovable, then they must have been at fault." In this sense, positive changes in our self-concept are linked to the exposure of parental weaknesses, and this exposure threatens our sense of security within the family constellation.

Also, altering one's basic self-concept to a more positive outlook implies changes in behavior and in the style of relating to the important people in one's current life. Valuing oneself and increasing one's sense of personal worth will have an impact on such divergent aspects of living as asking the boss for a raise, refusing to accept personal abuse or submission to another, leaving an unsatisfying relationship, or other symbolic acts asserting one's point of view and independence. Because there may be considerable anxiety in asserting one's belief in oneself, many people prefer to hold on to and preserve a static, albeit negative, view of themselves.

3. *Resistance to formulating personal goals and corrective suggestions.*

As noted earlier, corrective suggestions fall into two major categories, those related to limiting or discontinuing self-destructive habit patterns and those that encourage the individual to take positive chances and adapt to the new circumstances. Resistance may be encountered in every aspect of this process. Most people are reluctant to formulate definitive goals and choose specific actions appropriate to working toward them. People rarely live in an adult, rational mode, that is, separate and self-directed, and they often feel guilty about competing directly for satisfactions in life. There is a tendency to accuse oneself of selfishness, superiority, or even unfairness to others. Strong voices are aroused when individuals take bold steps to pursue their own lives in a manner that is free, nonconforming, or independent.

Although corrective suggestions are generally initiated by patients and develop out of their own motivation to alter self-defeating behaviors, the situation still lends itself to the arousal of strong feelings of resistance. Intrapsychically, corrective suggestions for behavioral change represent a separation from parental introjects. Interpersonally, patients usually institute specific changes in order to break habit patterns that have been modeled after undesirable behaviors displayed by their parents. The subsequent differentiation from parental figures and symbolic separation from the family bond frequently bring the patient to a crucial point in his therapy.

Otto Rank understood that this symbolic separation/individuation process was related to the patient's resistance and that it was an expression of the patient's "counter-will." In *Will Therapy,* Rank (1936/1972) writes of the patient's perception of separation:

> The "being separated" is apprehended as compulsory and is responded to with counter-will, which can manifest itself not only as resistance, or protest, but also in the form of love fixation and gratitude. (p. 81)

Although initially collaborating on the suggestion as an equal partner with the therapist, a patient may subsequently reverse his point of view concerning the desire to change. At this time, patients tend to distort the situation and deal with it in a paranoid manner. For example, they may believe that the therapist is telling them how to run their lives or accuse the therapist of making decisions for them. They project their desire to change onto the therapist and perceive the therapist as having a stake in their progress.

Subsequent negative transference reactions may include childish, dependent ploys for help or, on the other hand, attempts to provoke anger and rejection from the therapist. Resistance functions to disrupt the patient's active and equal participation in the therapy process and therefore acts to establish a bond with the therapist.

Fierman (1965) described this reaction in writing about Hellmuth Kaiser's explanation of the universal psychopathology: "the attempt to create in real life by behavior and communication the illusion of fusion" (p. 208-209). Kaiser (1965) emphasized that "every neurotic disturbance might center around the patient's effort to obviate the *inner experience* [italics added] of being an individual" (p. 133). He then enumerated the conditions under which a patient might experience a heightened sense of separateness and individuality:

> Whenever the patient comes close to having it driven home to him that it is *he himself* who is going to make a decision; or that the conviction in his mind is really his, originated by his own thinking; or that it is he, and he alone, who is wanting something, a piece of delusional ideology rolls like a fog over the mental scenery. (p. 133–134)

Unfortunately, during the cooperative planning of corrective experiences, many patients tend to respond to the "inner experience" of being a separate decision-making individual by attempting to form a bond or connection with the therapist with renewed efforts to extract parental or caretaking responses. Others maintain their independent point of view, take responsibility for their actions, and progress to new levels.

4. *Regression and resistance after answering back to voice attacks.*

Regressions in Voice Therapy are not fundamentally different from those in other therapies and arise from two principal but divergent sources: (a) unusual positive developments, acknowledgment, and personal achievement; or (b) negative events, i.e., guilt reactions, rejection, or frustration in relation to goal-directed activity. The latter are not difficult to understand, as setbacks or negative experiences in life cause pain and anger, and one's failures are often turned against oneself in the form of increased voice attacks.

Regression based on positive events is more complex and

difficult to understand. Personal successes and progress in therapy initially generate positive emotional responses. These positive feelings generally last until a person becomes self-conscious about them. The change in one's identity, the newfound sense of independence and strength, the unusual feeling of joy and happiness, and the unique adventurous interest in life all act to increase one's sense of vulnerability. The new sense of excitement may precipitate a state of anxiety, as the individual now finds himself in a high-risk situation. He now has something to lose and is set up for any experience that contradicts the new reality. This predisposes a person to overreact emotionally to small indications that challenge one's new identity and system of beliefs. These dramatic reactions precipitate regressive behavior and a return to one's traditional view of oneself and others.

Another interesting, albeit painful, source of regression is the guilt reaction caused by the breaking of bonds and moving away from destructive relationships and ties. Many patients in Voice Therapy regress when they have contact with original family members, particularly if members of their family either actually manipulate them to activate their guilt feelings or indirectly foster guilt in the patient because of the negative quality of the family members' lives. Also, contact with family members tends to reinforce parental introjects and voice attacks even when the interaction may be uneventful or even positive on the surface. Becoming aware of this situation causes a conflict for patients who have no desire to hurt their families yet would tend to avoid them because they recognize that they feel bad after contact. Social pressures to conform and prescriptions against choosing a unique or original life-style also militate against constructive change and personal development.

The problem of disrupting strong dependency ties and destructive relationships arises in every therapy and may well be a key factor underlying therapeutic failure. In some sense, individuals are always in a state of flux, moving either towards defensive security measures (bonds or connections with parents or parental substitutes); or, on the other hand, moving toward independence, self-assertion, and freedom. As noted earlier, moving away from family connections and toward increased individuation necessarily arouses strong feelings of guilt and anxiety, which in turn have a significant impact on the patient's resistance to continued progress in the therapeutic endeavor.

Resistance is often encountered following sessions where patients directly challenge the voice. In attempting to counteract the effect of the voices on their lives, behavior, and emotional states, patients may elect to answer the voice dramatically with strong anger. Even when the voice is disputed or contradicted analytically with an absence of emotional expression, resistance may be manifested.

In general, we have found that it is more productive for patients matter-of-factly to identify and struggle with behaviors they wish to change and, in this manner, to challenge indirectly the prohibitions of the voice. We have observed that assuming an angry, attacking posture in relation to parental attitudes and prohibitions (the voice) was less effective than initiating behavior change and was frequently counterproductive. In fact, we would caution therapists against using this method with many patients. "Yelling back" even at *symbolic* parental figures unleashes feelings of hatred for which one may feel tremendous guilt. Voicing angry, hostile feelings toward parents in sessions tends to cut a person off from imagined or symbolic sources of security, and regressive trends may follow.

To illustrate, one subject angrily refuted her voice charging her with inadequacy as a mother, loudly affirming her own view: "I'm a good mother! I like children. I really enjoy their company. I'm not like *you!*" Later, she found herself becoming distant and alienated from her children. In another case, a man who firmly avowed his self-appraisal: "I like challenges! I'm not afraid of living with uncertainty the way you were. I feel like I'm an adventurous person!" subsequently experienced increased fear and uncertainty in his new relationships and job situation.

A woman who had grown up believing she lacked the intelligence necessary for completing a college education angrily answered her voice: "I'm *not* stupid! I'm not the way *you* saw me. I really am intelligent." She dropped out of school some months later, complaining the courses were too difficult for her.

During the early phases of his therapy, a male patient gave up his excessive use of alcohol and began to emerge from a severe depression. In a Voice Therapy session where he dramatically expressed strong feelings of self-hatred and self-accusatory thoughts, he vividly recalled the beatings he had received at the hands of his alcoholic father. In an impassioned counterattack directed symbolically against his father, he raged: "You *bastard*! You *never* cared about me! *I* care about my kids. I'm not a drunken bum like *you*! I'm through with drinking once and for all." Some weeks later, however, the patient became resistant and assumed his father's point of view about therapy, claiming that the sessions were a waste of time and money. A short time after terminating his therapy sessions, he resumed his drinking pattern.

We have observed that many other patients, after responding angrily to voice attacks and differentiating themselves from their parents, e.g., "I'm not like you, you bastard," or "I'm different," reverted to habit patterns that strongly resembled their parents' characteristics.

In anticipating these regressive trends, therapists need to be very sensitive to their patients' strengths and weaknesses and carefully monitor corrective experiences and the process of answering the voice. They must be aware that many patients, in answering back with fury, tend to exceed their own tolerance levels and will subsequently fall back. The premature breaking with the voice and separating from parental introjects can be analogous to the premature separation from one's family, i.e., leaving home too soon. The person inevitably returns, feeling more dependent and afraid than before. Similarly, in the case of challenging the voice too directly, there will be increased submission or subordination to the voice.

In general, the most effective procedure for the therapist to follow in relation to the problem of answering the voice would be a gradual, step-by-step collaborative planning of corrective actions that go against the voice, rather than direct verbal confrontation. The patient cannot dramatically obliterate the part of himself that is antithetical to his interests. Instead, the therapist would help the patient move slowly and consistently toward his personal goals, keeping in mind at all times the patient's level of tolerance.

Although in our application of Voice Therapy, we have not

experienced severe regressive reactions, suicidal behavior, or psychotic episodes, our methods have been applied with care and respect both for patient selection and alertness to the dynamics involved. It has been our concern that moving too quickly toward behavioral suggestions or expressing too much aggression in answering back can lead to serious problems.

The Problem of Anger in Psychotherapy

In general, the problem of voicing aggression toward parents and parental introjects is a serious issue in any therapeutic endeavor. When patients become aware of the damage they sustained in their early development, they experience a good deal of pain and sadness. These memories and insights give rise to primitive feelings of anger and outrage. Feeling their murderous rage is symbolically equivalent to actually killing, or expressing death wishes towards the parents themselves. Therefore, patients often experience intense guilt reactions and anxiety when they mobilize these emotions. To compound matters, the symbolic destruction of parental figures leaves the patient fearful of object loss.

The combination of the two emotions, guilt and fear of losing the object, can precipitate regressive trends in any therapy. Intense negative transference reactions in psychoanalysis usually indicate the presence of strong death wishes toward parental figures. Often there will be a serious breakdown in the therapeutic alliance at this stage. Similar problems may be encountered in Primal Therapy or Feeling Release Therapy where patients progress steadily until they uncover intense rage reactions about the abuses they suffered. Because of their guilt and fear, they often turn the anger against themselves, taking on the parental point of view, and generally regress to a more childlike mode of interaction. In many cases, the patients never fully work through their aggression, and the therapeutic process from then on may lack the energy manifested in earlier sessions. In conclusion, much attention must be paid to the possibility of negative trends in psychotherapy directly following the patient's expressions of intense negative affect toward either parents or parent symbols.

this   is all ver
Sood

COMPARISON WITH COGNITIVE-BEHAVIORAL THERAPIES

As noted earlier, Voice Therapy is similar in certain respects to Aaron Beck's Cognitive Therapy and Albert Ellis's Rational-Emotive Therapy; however, there are a number of basic differences. Beck and Ellis postulate faulty cognitive processes that contribute to, or are primarily responsible for, the development of emotional disorders. Their phenomenological reports appear to coincide with certain aspects of the voice process. For example, in his recent book, *Cognitive Therapy of Depression,* Beck (1979) refers to automatic thoughts, dysfunctional schemas that provide the basis for "molding data into cognitions," (p. 12) and depressogenic assumptions as causative agents in depressive states. Ellis (1979) exposes the patient's "irrational beliefs," and actively confronts his "grandiose, perfectionistic *shoulds, oughts,* and *musts*" (p. 226) through three therapeutic methods: "cognitive, emotive, and behavioristic" (p. 203).

The major differences between Cognitive Therapy, Rational-Emotive Therapy, and Voice Therapy can be found in (1) the importance that each system places on investigating the etiology of the patient's illness; (2) the theory of personality upon which the therapeutic methodology is based; (3) the techniques utilized to identify and correct dysfunctional thinking; and (4) the view of emotion or affect.

(1) Cognitive Therapy is a brief, short-term, or time-limited treatment procedure. Beck's focus is almost exclusively on the here-and-now and is not concerned with an investigation of the patient's past history or the sources of his problems.[3] As Beck (1976) states:

> It is not necessary to get at ultimate causes of his [the patient's] misinterpretations of reality—either in terms of their historical antecedents or present "unconscious" roots. The therapist focuses more on *how* the patient misinterprets reality rather than on *why.* (p. 319)

Albert Ellis (1979), in a chapter on Rational-Emotive Therapy in *Current Psychotherapies,* states that:

> Unlike most modern systems of psychotherapy, RET empha-

sizes the biological aspects of human personality. . . . [People] have exceptionally powerful innate tendencies to think irrationally and to harm themselves. (p. 194–195)

Ellis lists a number of primary tendencies to be self-defeating that he believes all human beings possess and concludes as follows:

> Humans are born with an exceptionally strong tendency to want and to insist that everything happens for the best in their life and to roundly condemn (1) themselves, (2) others, and (3) the world when they do not immediately get what they want. (p. 195–196)

It is apparent that our perspective is at variance with Cognitive Therapy's approach to the etiology of neurotic disorders in that we are concerned with the dynamic origins of the voice. In spite of the fact that our methods are not historical, our patients make important connections between their current problems, destructive thinking processes, and early family experiences. We are concerned with bringing to the surface destructive aspects of thinking that were previously unconscious, releasing the associated affect and helping to synthesize the experience in relation to appropriate changes in behavior.

We strongly disagree with Ellis's primarily biological viewpoint that human beings have powerful innate tendencies to think irrationally; instead we believe disordered thinking is a function of deficient child-rearing practices. We feel that the tendency to "condemn self, others, and the world" and the development of an essentially suspicious or victimized orientation toward life are largely caused by suppression of angry reactions due to real frustration in the family. The child learns to justify his aggression because he cannot accept his "irrational" anger. We hypothesize that the distorted or paranoid view, i.e., that the world is *supposed* to be "fair" or "satisfying," reflects the need to give a rational or righteous basis to one's aggression. We feel that the source of the destructive voice is not in the child's inherent irrationality, but derives from the abuses of childhood and the child's subsequent anguish.

(2) Cognitive-behavioral therapies reject many of the basic tenets of psychoanalysis as applied to personality development and neurosis. Beck's theoretical approach to normal and patho-

logical personality development can be found primarily in his works, *Cognitive Therapy and the Emotional Disorders* (1976) and *Cognitive Therapy of Depression* (1979). His major thesis is that the special meaning which a patient assigns to a particular event determines his emotional response. While Beck does *not* base his model on assumptions that involve defensive structures, repression, or other unconscious processes, he does concede that the "depression-prone person may become *sensitized* [italics added] by certain unfavorable types of life situations, such as the loss of a parent or chronic rejection by his peers" (1976, p. 107). He notes that:

> A set of dysfunctional "cognitive structures" (schemas) formed at an earlier time becomes activated when the depression is precipitated (whether by psychological stress, biochemical imbalance, hypothalamic stimulation, or some other agent). (1979, p. 20)[4]

According to Ellis (1979), RET is related to a number of other theoretical approaches, both analytical and behavioral:

> Although RET practitioners are much closer to modern neo-analytic schools, such as those of Karen Horney, Erich Fromm, Wilhelm Stekel, Harry Stack Sullivan, and Franz Alexander, than to the Freudian school, they employ considerably more persuasion, philosophical analysis, activity homework assignments, and other directive techniques than practitioners of these schools generally use. (p. 188)
>
> RET has much in common with conditioning-learning therapy or behavior modification. (p. 189)

Voice Therapy theory and procedure is more deeply rooted in the psychoanalytic approach than in a cognitive-behavioral model. Our theoretical focus is on understanding the psychodynamics of the patient's functional disturbance in the present, and our methods are based on an underlying theory of personality that emphasizes a primary defensive process. As described earlier, we postulate a "fantasy bond" or core defense that serves a self-parenting function. Preserving this bond or illusion of connection causes a person repeatedly to seek gratification in a fantasy process while rejecting gratification in the real world. We conceive of self-destructive or neurotic tendencies as the perpetuation of defenses that originally had survival value but later predispose maladaptive responses and increase personal misery. The "voice" reflects the end process of incorporating parental rejecting attitudes into oneself, and as such it refers to an alien viewpoint embedded in the personality that acts as an integrated, negative force in the direction of self-hatred and self-attacks.

(3) Cognitive therapists, by skillful questioning, attempt to help patients identify their "automatic thoughts," uncover clusters of false assumptions underlying dysfunctional thinking, and then challenge these beliefs through "cognitive restructuring." Patients keep daily records of dysfunctional thoughts, the precipitating event or situation, the accompanying negative emotion, and the rational response to the negative thought. Automatic thoughts are stated and/ or written down by the patient.

Although Beck (1979) rejects "noncollaborative" therapeutic techniques, believing that "changing the patient's misinterpretations and dysfunctional behavior should be a collaborative enterprise between the patient and the therapist" (p. 57), cognitive therapists spend considerable time pointing out to patients the irrational and arbitrary quality of their thoughts.

RET therapists directly refute and attempt to argue the patient out of his false beliefs using logic, humor, questioning, negative imagery of the "worst situation," and other "strong and direct confrontational methods." As Ellis (1975) states: "[We] do not hesitate to show clients that they lie to themselves or that some of their ideas amount to arrant nonsense" (p. 209).

Ellis believes that only with the greatest effort through reeducation in therapy can people learn how to think and behave rationally. Rational-Emotive Therapy attributes little importance to major environmental factors that may have contributed to the patient's disordered thinking. By deemphasizing what *we* consider to be an important element in the genesis of emotional illnesses, Ellis may very well be neglecting a vital ingredient of effective psychotherapy, for unless patients uncover the source of the voice and ventilate the repressed feelings connected with it, they will be unable to perceive their parents more objectively and will tend to maintain a negative view of themselves.

Both Ellis and Beck attempt to point out the illogic in the patient's thinking process, whereas we neither refute the patient's logic nor focus on it. Patients in Voice Therapy make symbolic or direct memory connections to the sources of their disordered thinking. It is important to emphasize that Voice Therapy is primarily not an educational, analytical approach, nor do we directly persuade our patients to think or behave rationally. Our goal is to help them discover *what* they are telling themselves about important or central situations in life and to assist them in moving away from negative parental attitudes and prohibitions. We attempt to support our patients in their search for personal freedom and help to remove the barriers to further individuation.

(4) Although Cognitive Therapy and RET acknowledge the importance of emotions associated with cognitive processes, nevertheless, their focus is primarily on correcting the patient's disordered thinking. Both therapies, at times, employ special exercises in an attempt to elicit emotional responses in patients. As Beck (1979) states:

> We have found that the spontaneous expression of emotions and intensification of emotions through techniques such as "sensory awareness" and "flooding" are important tools—*as long as they are woven into the program of cognitive modification* [italics added]. (p. 36)

In recent years, Ellis (1975) has devoted more attention to the emotional aspects of RET. He uses "emotive exercises or techniques . . . as part and parcel of long-range cognitive and training processes: to help people to make major philosophic reconstructions" (p. 210).

As noted earlier, when we first encouraged patients to verbalize their self-attacks as a voice, strong emotional responses were elicited. We were not aware at this time that very powerful emotions of sadness and rage were attached to the process. In addition, we were profoundly affected by the intensity of the negative affect toward self that we witnessed. Although my colleagues and I had been involved in a wide range of therapy approaches, we had not observed this degree or intensity of emotion outside of Primal or Feeling Release Therapy. We were surprised at the depth and scope of clinical material brought out through Voice Therapy procedures.

Other reviewers have noted the limitations of cognitive therapy. Although cognitive theorists have expressed some concern for affective components, Patterson (1980), states:

> The problem with the newer cognitive therapies (Meichenbaum and Beck, for example), is . . . the neglect, if not the exclusion, of affective elements, which results in an attempt to develop a purely cognitive therapy, as some behaviorists attempt without success to develop a purely behavioristic therapy[5]. (p. 667)

Patterson has also noted that:

> The fallacy of cognitive therapy is that learning requires direct teaching or instruction. . . . [However, Patterson affirms that] the client is the expert on the subject matter—himself—although the therapist may think he or she knows more. In this respect the client is superior to the therapist. The client educates the therapist about himself or herself—the client is the teacher. (p. 667)

The present author substantially agrees with Patterson's commentary. Voice Therapy cannot be considered a "cognitive therapy" in the sense that it is *not* a didactic, instructional procedure. The major thrust of our therapeutic endeavor is not simply the identification of the voice process but includes a serious focus on the accompanying affect. Voice Therapy reflects an attitude of empathy and a strong orientation toward feeling. Our methods attempt to access the patients' inner lives and sense of self, helping to free them from the constraining influences of destructive self-parenting. Voice Therapy techniques and presentations have been described by observers as creating a sensitive and moving atmosphere in our treatment that enhances each patient's feeling of compassion for himself.

CONCLUSION

In summary, Voice Therapy is a broadly based therapy technique with an emphasis on both cognitive and affective components. It is derived from a systematic theory of neurosis, based on the conceptualization of the fantasy bond as a core defense that underlies an individual's fundamental resistance to change or progress. The rationale underlying Voice Therapy is that of exposing the patient's negative thoughts and the accompanying affect; forming insight into their sources in parental abuses; and gradually modifying behavior toward one's stated goals in juxtaposition to the dictates of the voice. This process involves breaking away from fusion or fantasies of connection with parental figures and moving toward self-sufficiency and autonomy.

Because the methods are relatively simple, easily applied, and often immediately understood by the subject or patient, Voice Therapy could be potentially dangerous in the hands of an inadequately trained or personally immature therapist. The techniques are contraindicated if utilized by untrained practitioners because, as noted earlier, serious regressions can occur after answering back to the voice or when prematurely disrupting defenses. Movement toward individuation in a direction away from dependency bonds must be undertaken with care and diligence, and a deep understanding of personality dynamics.

Ideally, a voice therapist would tend to be nonintrusive, never predetermining and setting goals for his patients, or imposing his values and biases on their development. Instead he would attempt to gain greater access to the patient's point of view. The patient would be encouraged to take a strong role in separating the alien view toward self from his own point of view.

Further, the therapist would not set himself apart, would not assume a parental, caretaking function, and would avoid, as much as possible, establishing a doctor/patient bond. Instead he would be open to investigating voices within himself and would be aware of his own self-limiting behavior patterns and thoughts. In this respect, Voice Therapy tends to be a "great equalizer"; that is, the therapist is a real person in the therapeutic relationship, *not* a "superior" human being applying a predetermined technique.

Voice Therapy lends itself well to group and family interaction. We have observed that when one person expresses self-attacks that reflect core issues in his life, strong feelings are often aroused in the other participants. This is particularly evident when the abreactive technique is being utilized. The universality of the types of negative thoughts and feelings that people exhibit is remarkable in any psychotherapy group; however, in Voice Therapy groups, the voices expressed are so similar in content, so restrictive, and frequently sound so much alike, that one person verbalizing his voice invariably strikes a familiar chord in every other individual. Participants tend to experience deep feelings of empathy for the person going through this process, as well as compassion for themselves.

Finally, Voice Therapy procedures could be of significant value even to those psychotherapists wedded to other theoretical systems. It is possible to use the techniques as an adjunct to other approaches. Even when Voice Therapy techniques are not the treatment of choice, the theory and methodology have value in understanding the core of resistance to any form of psychotherapeutic movement or constructive behavioral change.

NOTES

[1]The parameters listed do not exhaust the many dimensions along which methodologies may be evaluated or measured. Other measures may be found in: Ford and Urban (1963), Patterson (1980), and Beck (1976).

[2]Rogers and Dymond (1954), *Psychotherapy and Personality Change*; Rogers (1957), "The Necessary and Sufficient Conditions of Therapeutic Personality Change"; and Walker, Rablen, and Rogers (1960), "Development of a Scale to Measure Process Changes in Psychotherapy."

[3]Bowlby (1980) writing in *Loss: Sadness and Depression,* states:

> Although, like many clinicians, Beck assumes that experiences of childhood play some part in the development of these schemas [cognitive], he pursues the matter no further, remarking with justice that research in this field is fraught with difficulty. (p. 250)

[4]A discussion of the formation of depressogenic schemas may be found in Beck's (1972) *Depression: Causes and Treatment.*

[5]It is important to note that this statement of Patterson's partially contradicts Beck's earlier quote concerning the role of affect in his (Beck's) system.

12

The Dilemma of Psychotherapy

It is all right to say, with Adler, that mental illness is due to "problems in living,"—but we must remember that life itself is the insurmountable problem.

Ernest Becker (1973, p. 270)

Monday, March 31, 1986—6:00 p.m.

A man turns on the evening news and within three minutes is bombarded with:

. . . countless people dying from poisoned wine in Italy;

. . . three deaths from a contaminated supply of common pain relievers in Pennsylvania;

. . . another terrorist attack on an airliner en route to Athens;

. . . a 300-square-mile area threatened by toxic gas escaping from a chemical fire in San Francisco;

. . . a survey showing over 100,000 child abductions in the United States annually.

What price for aliveness and involvement?

What quality of experience is available to a feeling person finely tuned to the realities of life?

Defenses are almost mandatory when one is faced with man's inhumanity to man. Yet cruelty and injustice are an outgrowth of dishonest and defended patterns of thinking and living that preclude man's feeling for himself and his fellow man.

The tragedy of the human condition is that man's awareness and true self-consciousness concerning existential issues contribute to an ultimate irony: Man is both brilliant and aberrant, sensitive and savage, exquisitely caring and painfully indifferent, remarkably creative and incredibly destructive to self and others. The capacity to conceptualize and imagine has negative as well as positive consequences because it predisposes anxiety states that culminate in a defensive form of denial.

Therapeutic progress inevitably leads to a heightened sense of awareness and new levels of vulnerability. Prior to therapy, people's defensive patterns served the function of numbing them to the pain inherent in everyday living. A breakdown of these defenses and the associated misery were most frequently the driving force behind the individual's motivation to seek psychotherapy. As noted earlier, defenses are formed originally in response to emotional deprivation, rejection, and separation trauma and are later strengthened by the growing awareness of death. Positive developments in therapy free individuals to feel more of both the joy and pain of living, inevitably bringing them face to face with death anxiety.

Abandoning habitual defenses causes patients to be more sensitive to reality and increases their exposure to a world that is abrasive and destructive to the undefended person. In addition, the conventions and mores of society are generally opposed to the state of openness and vulnerability brought about by the process of dismantling major defenses.

Moving away from the imagined safety of familiar support systems, individuals experience their aloneness. They feel considerable guilt and fear in separating from dependency bonds. Although more capable of sustaining genuine and close relationships, they find themselves in a high-risk situation. In their personal interactions, they may feel deeply wounded by retaliation from others who are defended and cannot accept their love, generosity, warmth, and acknowledgment. Furthermore, on a societal level, there is a great deal of *unavoidable* suffering and anguish inherent in living an undefended life. One is constantly aware of such external issues as crime, poverty, economic recession, financial setbacks, illness, and the potential threat of a nuclear holocaust.

Finally, all people are confronted with an insurmountable problem in life—the fact that they are trapped in a body that will certainly die. Recovering aspects of their child selves and emotional vitality makes them more poignantly aware of the inevitable loss of self through death. In a sense, individuals must mourn the anticipated loss of their lives in order to retain their capacity for genuine feeling. Sadness is therefore an inescapable part of a feelingful existence.

Who wants to live with this new awareness, this heightened vulnerability to rejection, loss, and death? Therein lies the dilemma, for how can the therapist symbolically influence the patient to embrace life fully in the face of a predictable future with a negative outcome?

The patient's dilemma is evident from the beginning of the therapeutic process. The basic conflict centers on the choice between avoidance or contention with the realities of life. Individuals in crisis enter therapy desperately searching for relief from painful symptoms, failures, phobias, anxiety reactions, or depression. In the majority of cases, motivation to seek help reflects a desire to escape from pain. At the same time, patients want to hold on to basic character defenses and stubbornly refuse to give up self-nourishing habits or dependency bonds that, if maintained, would continually lead to symptom formation. Thus, a person's motives in seeking professional help may seriously conflict with the goals of a conscientious approach to the psychotherapeutic endeavor. In this condition, patient and therapist find themselves at odds.

The effective therapist accesses his patient's inner life and spirit and helps him become a real person rather than simply attempting to erase his pain. Any attempt to support dishonest defenses or misperceptions that temporarily reduce a person's discomfort does a serious injustice to both the patient and the therapist in the long run. To illustrate, in the play *Equus* (Shaffer, 1974), the psychiatrist is acutely aware of the consequences of complying with the demands of the court magistrate to take his adolescent patient's pain and madness away and restore him as a functioning member of society. He cries out in futile protest:

> *All right!* I'll take [his pain] away! He'll be delivered from madness. *What then?* . . . Do you think feelings like his can be simply re-attached, like plasters? . . . My desire might be to make this boy an ardent husband—a caring citizen. . . . My achievement, however, is more likely to make a ghost! . . .
>
> I'll set him on a nice mini-scooter and send him puttering off into the Normal world where animals are treated *properly*: made extinct, or put into servitude, or tethered all their lives in dim light, just to feed it! I'll give him the good Normal world where we're tethered beside them—blinking our nights away in a nonstop drench of cathode-ray over our shrivelling heads! (p. 123–124)

This quote reveals the essential truth that adjustment or even "feeling good" may be very inappropriate to circumstances in life that are intolerable and unacceptable. Indeed, fitting into an abnormal society may represent a form of psychopathology.

In the following pages, we will explore the dimensions of the patient's dilemma and the fundamental issue of choice: whether to reinstate or strengthen defenses, destructive bonds, and deadening habit patterns in a renewed attempt to avoid pain, or to live fully, with appropriate emotions, meaningful activity, and compassion for oneself and others.

DEFINITIONS OF PSYCHOTHERAPEUTIC "CURE"— SOME PERSPECTIVES

Clinicians face a difficult task in evaluating the effects of psychotherapy. Many researchers "argue that traditional assessment methods are too global, imprecise, and rooted in a 'medical model' conceptualization of psychological problems" (Stiles, Shapiro, & Elliott, 1986, p. 170). In addition, psychoanalysts tend to feel that the "subtleties of dynamic change . . . [can]not be captured by symptom scores or personality inventories" (p. 171). Indeed, in terms of actual attempts to measure therapeutic success precisely or scientifically, there is conflicting evidence to support the hypothesis that patients really improve over the course of treatment. Whereas a number of studies indicate a point of view that there is *no* apparent change associated with therapy sessions, many others demonstrate favorable outcomes.[1] The problem is that these measurable changes occur in circumscribed areas referring to specific, operationally defined, discrete aspects of the patient's personality and may fail to register other equally important, but more subtle, developments.

Although there is still considerable disagreement about the issue of evaluation, a vast accumulation of clinical and personal data from both therapists and patients exists, indicating that the psychotherapy experience is valuable and has considerable impact. It is a matter of unusual complexity. For example, in estimating positive change, the extent to which therapy may have prevented further deterioration cannot be scientifically assessed. In some instances, patients may have been significantly helped in the sense that the sessions prevented more serious regression or eventual institutionalization.

The key issue in evaluating outcome in psychotherapy lies in determining how one defines the "healthy, well-adjusted" individual. Psychotherapeutic "cure" is often determined by the diminution of the patient's more obvious symptoms; in general, the terminating patient no longer suffers from devastating anxiety attacks, bizarre thinking disorders, or serious depression. In this sense, the patient is no longer diagnosed as clinically ill, and the remaining disturbances are subclinical.

Most often, we find that "mental health" or "cure" is defined by various clinicians in terms of the patient's increased ability to function and respond appropriately to his interpersonal world. For example, Freud (1930/1961) described the healthy or non-neurotic individual simply as one who is able to derive satisfaction from love and work.[2] Carl Rogers (1951), in his investigations, defined positive change in terms of patients' perceptions of self: "The result of therapy would appear to be a greater congruence between self and ideal" (p. 141). Rogers interpreted these findings as demonstrating that the therapeutic relationship allows the patient to experience "himself as a more *real* person, a more unified person" (p. 142).

Mowrer (1953) emphasizes that a mentally healthy patient

takes a "realistic problem-solving approach," which, in turn, allows his "emotions, now in proper context . . . [to be] both proportionate and appropriate" (p. 148-149). Arthur Janov (1970) describes the "well patient" as a "real adult" who no longer needs the destructive, limiting defenses that, prior to therapy, had kept him alienated from his genuine feelings.

The author's concept of "cure" is similar in many respects to Janov's conclusion. We perceive the healthy, adjusted individual as moving *away* from defenses, support systems, and painkillers toward openness, feeling, and emotional responsiveness, while changing from an inward, self-parenting posture to an active pursuit of gratification in the external world. The patient is now free of the compulsive repetition of familiar, destructive patterns, opening the possibility for continuous change and development.

In conclusion, all definitions of therapeutic "cure" or improvement point toward an integrated, feeling self and a positive adaptation to life that allows the individual more flexibility and exposure to real experience.

However, a nondefensive approach to life obviously has its disadvantages as well as its advantages. The problems involved in retaining an open and vulnerable orientation have been described by a number of clinicians. Wolberg (1954), in writing about the dilemma of psychotherapy, states:

> Society itself imposes insuperable embargoes on certain aspects of functioning. *It supports many neurotic values which necessitate the maintenance of sundry defenses for survival reasons* [italics added]. (p. 554)

Consider also Rank's (quoted by Taft, 1958) and Becker's (1973) cogent descriptions of the paradox faced by the "cured" patient:

> It is not so much a question as to whether we are able to cure a patient, whether we can or not, but whether we should or not. (Rank, p. 139)
> Not everyone is as honest as Freud was when he said that he cured the miseries of the neurotic only to open him up to the normal misery of life. (Becker, p. 271)

On the other hand, people do not necessarily remain successfully defended. As Rollo May (1983) indicates in the following statement, the "adjusted," albeit defended, patient may feel less anxious and be symptom-free; nevertheless, his adaptation to society has its own negative consequences in a loss of freedom.

> The kind of cure that consists of adjustment, becoming able to fit the culture, *can* [italics added] be obtained by technical emphases in therapy. . . . Then the patient accepts a confined world without conflict, for now his world is identical with the culture. And *since anxiety comes only with freedom, the patient naturally gets over his anxiety* [italics added]; he is relieved from his symptoms because he surrenders the possibilities which caused his anxiety. (p. 164–165)

As can be seen from the above statements, the road to mental health is paradoxical in many respects. In the following pages, we will examine the dimensions of a non-defensive life-style that contribute to the dilemma.

PARADOX OF FEELING

> Feelings, in and of themselves, do not hurt. Tensing up against the feeling is what seems to hurt. . . . Sadness doesn't hurt. But if one is deprived of his sadness, if he isn't permitted his misery, *then* he will hurt.
>
> Arthur Janov (1970, p. 99)

> Therapy is concerned with . . . helping the person experience his existence—and any cure of symptoms which will last must be a by-product of that.
>
> Rollo May (1983, p. 164)

A psychologically healthy person has a strong emotional investment in living and will respond with appropriate affect to both good and bad experiences in life. Basing one's emotional reactions on real events and circumstances, rather than a self-protective posture, leaves one open to painful feelings.

Many patients mistakenly believe that improvement in therapy will make them *less* sensitive to hurts and more impervious to painful feelings arising from failure, rejection, or loss. In general, our findings indicate an opposite trend. Emotionally healthy individuals are acutely sensitive to events in their lives that impinge on their sense of well-being or that adversely affect the people closest to them. Indeed, they appear to be *more* susceptible, not less, to emotionally painful situations than prior to therapy. However, more importantly, by fully experiencing their emotional reactions, they are better able to cope with anxiety and stress and are far less susceptible to infantile regression and neurotic symptom formation.

In addition, individuals who are connected to their emotions retain their vitality and excitement. The capacity for feeling contributes to their spontaneity and creativity and adds dimensions to their personality. By contrast, people who do not have access to their inner experience tend to be more rigid, constricted, and superficial.

Those individuals who are inward and cut off from feeling often have melodramatic overreactions to minor personal slights or imagined rejections, yet they may display a curious lack of feeling or affect in response to real adversity. Role-determined emotions and conventional reactions tend to dominate their responses, and at times they appear to be one step removed from directly experiencing the world around them. Their defenses act to suppress feelings; consequently, their reactions are more automatic and cerebral. In an important sense, the defended person has disengaged from himself as a hurting child and now, as an adult, lacks feelings of compassion for himself and others.

In contrast, emotionally healthy individuals are more open to their emotions and can tolerate irrational, angry, competitive, or other "unacceptable feelings." Therefore, they are not compelled to act out these feelings on friends and family members. This manifestation of mental health has broad psychological implications. For example, in cases of both emotional and physical child abuse, we found that the *inability* to accept feelings of anger, hostility, and resentment caused many parents to extend these feelings to their offspring. Later, when the parents were able to recognize and accept destructive feelings in themselves toward their children, tension was reduced and damaging responses were minimized.

In relation to physical pain, it appears that patients who have progressed in therapy suffer far less from psychosomatic illness; e.g., migraine headaches, asthma, or chronic neurasthenia. On the other hand, many improved patients report a heightened sensitivity to physical pain and generally feel more appropriate concern about their physical health and well-being.

A prevailing view of emotional suffering has been that it is unacceptable and that people who are in psychological pain are sick or abnormal. To the contrary, only by experiencing the painful emotions that arise in life can people feel joy or experience genuine happiness. Furthermore, when painful feelings are accepted or allowed full expression, there is a corresponding reduction in compulsive reliving and attempts to manipulate or control others in the interpersonal environment.

Many individuals are reluctant to experience or express deep feelings of sadness. Anticipating these feelings appears to arouse primal fears and considerable tension, whereas the actual experience of sadness frequently brings relief. After expressing emotional pain or deep feelings of sadness, people usually feel more unified or integrated and report a stronger sense of identity. For example, in therapy groups with young adolescents, we observed that when the youngsters expressed previously suppressed feelings of sadness, their outlook on their problems shifted considerably. Prior to these group discussions, many of the youngsters had been involved in acting out negative, hostile behaviors. It appeared that they engaged in these actions in an attempt to avoid underlying feelings of sadness that they perceived as being embarrassing or unacceptable.

Similarly, in our work with patients in Feeling Release Therapy and Voice Therapy, we discovered that as people became less defended and more open to expressing deeply repressed feelings, they manifested important changes in their overall approach to life. They developed a depth of compassion and a basic trust in others that had a powerful effect on their relationships. The toxic, intrusive behaviors that they had previously acted out in their closest personal interactions diminished to a remarkable degree. Consequently, they began to have a positive influence on their mates, friends, and families, rather than continuing to have a deleterious effect.

GUILT AND FEAR REACTIONS ARISING FROM BREAKING BONDS

> It is always the inability to stand the aloneness of one's individual self that leads to the drive to enter into a symbiotic relationship with someone else.
>
> Erich Fromm (1941/1965, p. 180)

Movement toward emotional health and independence creates both guilt and fear. Guilt reactions associated with increased individuation and the disruption of the fantasy bond with one's family often have their basis in the family's interpretation of separation. For example, Joseph Richman (1986) cites what he believes to be an important factor contributing to suicide attempts in adolescents. His studies stress the fact that the suicidal patient's family frequently perceives the adolescent's moves toward independence, particularly the establishment of peer relationships outside the family circle, as being extremely threatening to family cohesiveness or even family survival. Writing about the "myth of exclusiveness" symptomatic of these disturbed families, Richman states: "The formation of outside friendships and relationships is labeled as disloyalty" (p. 32).

Richman defines the relationships that exist between these family members as "symbiotic bonds" wherein "the development of uniqueness or individuality in a key member opens up the threat of separation and must therefore be opposed or 'corrected'" (p. 19).

The guilt reactions documented by Richman are typical for individuals striving to separate from destructive bonds with parents and parental substitutes. Parents and mates who are immature and dependent are capable of manipulating the guilt feelings of improving patients, causing considerable damage and often precipitating serious setbacks.

Parents and other family members are intimidating and controlling of one another by acts of direct intimidation and hostility, by judgmental and condemning attitudes that support the voice, and by "falling apart" or other self-destructive actions. Indeed, anything that reinforces one's inner sense of "badness" can be damaging. Threats of being excluded, imprisoned, or sent to reform school for "being bad" are terrifying to young people, who take these warnings quite seriously. These threats are representative of an early form of parental control and manipulation.

Internally, a patient's progress or improvement initially leads to intensified voice attacks about the new developments. When people refuse to submit or alter their behavior based on these attacks and, in a sense, do not "obey" the introjected parent, they can eventually adapt successfully to their new circumstances. Voice attacks tend to decrease over a period of time, in a manner analogous to parents' gradual accommodation to the independence of their offspring as they get older. It is almost as though the "voice," when ignored, like the parents themselves, gets tired of nagging and cautioning and is finally quieted. Paradoxically, people are afraid of losing the constant companionship of their destructive voices. Just as self-assertion and movement toward independence from the family bond disrupt a vital support system, separation from introjected parental voices severs an important symbolic tie.

Living without imaginary bonds or connections, with the relative absence of voice attacks, leaves one in a state of uncertainty and ambiguity. James McCarthy (1980), in *Death Anxiety,* describes Erich Fromm's interpretation of man's basic existential dilemma in terms of his choice between health and mental illness.

> Fromm elegantly dichotomized the two simple possibilities of adult emotional response into autonomy and health versus regression and despondency. (p. 97)
>
> In Fromm's view, an adult who remains overly attached to his parents avoids the anxiety inherent in the awareness of living as a distinct, separate entity. (p. 96)

To some extent, all people cling to internal and external security mechanisms because they are frightened of their aloneness. The experience of being separate and alone can be terrifying when it is related to primal feelings of helplessness, dependency, and repressed infantile feelings. On the other hand, the feeling of freedom inherent in being a separate adult person can be very exhilarating. It can be compared to sailing on uncharted seas, where one always faces the unexpected—without guidelines, without established regimens, without connection to land or harbor, and *with* the burden of responsibility for one's survival. One needs courage for the voyage, but one's reward is an adventurous life.

Unfortunately, most people refuse the challenge of living in a new and unfamiliar world rather than the world they were trained to live in. In a sense, they commit micro-suicide on a daily basis, progressively giving up their lives by numbing themselves to feeling and misperceiving reality. As noted earlier, we conceptualize mental illness as a subclass of suicide rather than the reverse, i.e., because defenses and defensive living necessarily constrict one's life space and freedom of choice and, at the same time, culminate in neurotic symptom formation. Too guilty and fearful to consider alternatives, defended individuals continue to live within the narrow confines of a way of life for which they were programmed, and, as such, they relinquish the only life they know.

PROBLEMS IN PERSONAL RELATIONSHIPS

We are threatened with suffering from three directions: from our own body, which is doomed to decay and dissolution and which cannot even do without pain and anxiety as warning signals; from the external world, which may rage against us with overwhelming and merciless forces of destruction; and finally *from our relations to other men* [italics added].

Sigmund Freud (1930/1961, p. 77)

CIVILIZATION AND ITS DISCONTENTS ANCHOR BOOKS 1958, P. 17

Perversely, a sensitive, compassionate human being evokes negative as well as positive reactions in other people. Many people lash out with hostility when they are loved and befriended. Feeling cared for and valued causes them emotional pain if they did not feel loved and secure as children. People are unable to defend themselves selectively against hurt and rejection, a fact that causes them to react negatively to any experience that has the potential for arousing unpleasant feelings of sadness. When threatened or anxious about making basic changes in their self-concept, they cling to their identity within the nuclear family.

In protecting themselves, they unintentionally cause damage to the individuals closest to them. In this sense, people cannot be innocently defended. To defend against anxiety, pain, and sadness—emotions that are inherent in personal relationships—they must push away or punish other individuals who care for them. For example, the man who perceives himself as cold or unattractive will be suspicious of a woman who shows an interest in him; a woman who has an image of herself as unlovable will punish the man who offers her love. Generally speaking, punitive responses will be set into motion whenever a defended person is treated with unusual consideration, respect, or affection. Therefore, a person who has developed increased empathy and understanding as a result of therapy will often be retaliated against whenever he is the most giving and understanding.

A number of writers are sensitive to this issue and have described the paradox in significant works. Notably, Carson McCullers (1940/1953), in *The Heart Is a Lonely Hunter,* depicted the philosophy that the *beloved* always resents and hates the lover. This phenomenon is so common that almost every person at some time has had the experience of being rejected following intervals of special closeness.

A patient related an incident from his adolescent years that bears on this subject:

> He was the leader of a group of teenage boys in his New York City neighborhood and had befriended another youngster, Ben, who was crippled by polio and walked with a noticeable limp. My patient had been the one responsible for the disabled youngster's assimilation into the group. Through his influence, the other boys had gradually grown to like the new member of their gang. However, one day the youths were bored and began taunting Ben about his limp.
>
> While leaving the subway station, Ben grabbed my patient from behind and began to choke him. The incident left a deep emotional scar. Ben had attacked the one person who befriended him, despite the fact that he had taken no part in the abuse.

This story points out an important truth—namely, that we are prejudiced against those who tempt us to lower our barriers and expose us once again to pain and rejection. Basically, most people have considerable anger, albeit unconscious, toward a person whom they feel is responsible for "luring" them into a less defended position.

There are many other painful issues that psychologically healthy individuals face in everyday interactions. Their strength and self-confidence frequently arouse dependency feelings in others who turn to them for support and leadership. Increased responsibility and emotional load put more pressure on the improved individual at the same time that he is moving away from his own dependency relationships. In addition, passive, dependent individuals tend to be paranoid toward a strong person, and these negative reactions are confusing and demoralizing. Self-assurance and a positive outlook are often misinterpreted as vanity or greeted with jealousy and suspicion. If a person develops leadership potential and becomes powerful and effective in his field of endeavor, his motives are often misunderstood or interpreted as exploitive. People who have a neurotic, victimized orientation to life mistakenly perceive assertiveness as meanness.

In general, these distrustful attitudes are supported by a distorted interpretation of the Judeo-Christian ethic that condemns actions based on self-interest. Basically, the social order reinforces the "voice" process and, later, self-limiting, self-destructive individuals create a form of social pressure, thereby completing the cycle. In this sense, society represents a pooling of the defense systems of its members, leading to a kind of Orwellian perspective wherein love is feared, hated, or distrusted; selflessness and self-denial are admired; honest striving is condemned; and strength is suspect.

Moreover, our society is permeated with mixed messages concerning these issues. Competitiveness and entrepreneurship are highly valued and encouraged, while at the same time, success and power are given negative connotations or condemned. Examples of negative power, passive-aggressive manipulations, and rejection of honest competition prevail. A humanitarian concern with the rights of the "underdog" has led to an unfortunate and incorrect assumption: that those who are successful achieved their advantages at the expense or disadvantage of others. The reason that this view persists is that many people have never developed psychologically beyond the conception of themselves as victims (which they often *were* as children) and are geared for failure rather than success. Thus, the tyranny of the helpless and powerless can become a form of blackmail to the individual who is pursuing his needs.

The person who is alive to his experience may unconsciously hold back his enthusiasm, sensing that his vitality might threaten a person who is more self-denying. Worse, he may even lose his sense of excitement altogether in the presence of others who are limiting themselves and are not pursuing their goals or priorities. For example, a person delighted with the purchase of a new car would not rush over to show it to a friend who just lost his job. A woman in a happy love relationship feels awkward describing her life to a friend who is a wallflower and has no dates. In our clinical experience, we have observed that people are very susceptible to negative social pressure from unhappy or self-sacrificing family members. In particular, they find it extremely difficult to surpass the parent of the same sex, personally or vocationally, without experiencing considerable guilt.

Emotionally healthy people are acutely aware of duplicity and dishonesty in others. Their sensitivity can be likened to that of a musician who reacts painfully when a wrong note grates on his nerves. Their open style of communication may threaten or disturb inward, defended people who are uncomfortable with directness and who are afraid to hear the truth. An honest person is susceptible to blackmail and manipulation by mates or family members, who may break down emotionally or become self-attacking when confronted. Attempts to communicate also bring out angry, punitive reactions in people who are defensive.

Close scrutiny will reveal that most marriages and family constellations are characterized by intimidating, controlling, self-hating, or self-denying behavior on the part of one member or another. Irrational or self-destructive behavior is intimidating for two reasons: first, because of the fear of actual object loss, loss of the bond, or breakup of the relationship; and second, because of the guilt inherent in feeling that one is somehow being held accountable for another person's unhappiness or self-destruction. In addition, the "social martyrdom" practiced by many individuals produces a sense of guilt in close friends, associates, and family members. Similarly, the tyranny of illness and weakness exerted by disturbed individuals clearly has manipulative effects. Consider, for example, the man whose doctor orders him to reduce his caloric intake because of a dangerous heart condition, yet who continues to overeat and gain weight. Obviously, his wife is alarmed and deeply concerned. Many people unconsciously use self-destructive behaviors as threats to gain leverage over others and strengthen dependency ties. These destructive manipulations and a variety of other adverse personal reactions impinge on the world of the "cured" individual with a potential for causing considerable distress.

INCREASED DEATH ANXIETY

> Man cuts out for himself a manageable world. . . . He uses all kinds of techniques, which we call the "character defenses": he learns not to expose himself, not to stand out; he learns to embed himself in other-power, both of concrete persons and of things and cultural commands; the result is that he comes to exist in the imagined infallibility of the world around him.
>
> Ernest Becker (1973, p. 23)

Most people have very little awareness of how much they are afraid, or even terrified of, freely pursuing their goals, achieving personal power, and finding satisfaction in loving interactions. Prior to therapy, the patient may have underestimated the pain and anxiety involved in establishing a new identity and long-lasting relationships that are free from a bond. The essential dilemma of "cure" may be stated as follows: the patient who progresses in therapy faces an increased awareness of death and intensified feelings of death anxiety. As he reaches out to life, there is a greater realization of a finite existence.

Existential thinkers have divergent views as to the extent that death anxiety manifests itself in neurotic, as compared with "self-actualizing," individuals. In *Existential Psychotherapy,* Yalom (1980) summarizes one school of thought when he states: "I believe that one particularly useful equation for the clinician is: *death anxiety is inversely proportional to life satisfaction*" (p. 207). However, Yalom also points to the paradox raised by this proposition:

Of course, there is a circularity about this equation since it is *because* of an excessive death anxiety that the individual lives a constricted life—a life dedicated more to safety, survival, and relief from pain than to growth and fulfillment. Searles poses the same dilemma: "The patient cannot face death unless he is a whole person, yet he can become a truly whole person only by facing death." (p. 208)

Norman O. Brown (1959), in *Life Against Death,* suggests a return to unrepressed living and the primary pleasure of the body as an antidote to excessive death anxiety stressing that:

> The hard truth which psychoanalysis must insist upon is that the acceptance of death . . . cannot be accomplished by the discipline of philosophy or the seduction of art, but only by the abolition of repression. (p. 108–109)

In his book *Death Anxiety: The Loss of the Self,* James B. McCarthy (1980) cites three components of the fear of death as delineated by the philosopher, Jacques Choron: "the fear of dying, the fear of what happens after death, and the fear of ceasing to be" (p. 10).

The author (1985) believes that man's existential anxiety centers on his dread of cessation of consciousness and loss of self:

> The thought of losing one's life, losing all consciousness, losing all ego through death is so intolerable that the process of giving up offers relief from the anguish. (p. 256)

According to our view, man is presented with an essential paradox: if he gives up his customary defenses and fully lives his life, he is immediately struck with the magnitude of the potential loss he faces through death; if, on the other hand, he shrinks from life and fails to develop his unique potentialities, he is plagued with ontological guilt and regret for a life not really lived.

The fantasy bond is a basic survival mechanism because it is connected in an individual's mind with immortality. There are a myriad of conventional defenses against death anxiety that are utilized in one's efforts to deny and transcend death. An individual may imagine oneness with God and a guarantee of life after death or invent theories of reincarnation. He may search for immortality through creative works or an ongoing business corporation, through his children, or through dedication to a cause that lives on after him. However, each attempt to gain control over death ultimately ends in despair because no project or belief can guarantee an individual the survival of his corporeal body, his physical being as he knows it. The discontinuity of his personality, identity, body, consciousness, and awareness is a truth that he cannot really escape. On some level, he recognizes that living on through his children or through a cause is not a genuine living on as he knows or cares about it.

When a fantasy bond is threatened, we are extremely defensive and angry at those people who disagree or dissent. Indeed, we mobilize action against these "enemies" in a manner similar to medieval crusaders who attempted to impose their fanatic religious beliefs on "heretics" in bloody holy wars—i.e., in order to preserve their conception of eternity. People will defend to the death belief systems that they know to be wrong on some inner level of incongruence.

Book burning, control of political thought, propaganda, rewriting history are barbaric responses to this type of paranoia. Altering or denying the truth of experience disturbs an individual's basic sense of reality and is a primary causative factor in mental illness. In a sense, *all* defenses represent a dishonest choice of magical safety over real and appropriate insecurity.

No death is acceptable to a fully alive, feeling person who has invested meaning and affect in his life experience—a car accident or a plane crash, an extended illness, a slow and painful deterioration, senility, or a quiet death in one's sleep. As Simone de Beauvoir (1966/1976) wrote concerning her mother's death:

> The knowledge that because of her age my mother's life must soon come to an end did not lessen the horrible surprise. . . . There is no such thing as a natural death: nothing that happens to a man is ever natural, since his presence calls the world into question. All men must die: but for every man his death is an accident and, even if he knows it and consents to it, an unjustifiable violation. (p. 526)

Accommodation to Death Anxiety

Living with the poignant awareness that we share an unavoidable fate with all human beings appears to be too agonizing for many of us to endure. Consequently, we slowly commit suicide, causing anguish to those who care about us.

The voice plays a central role in the process of progressive self-denial, predicting and rehearsing negative outcomes; advising the individual to reject positive experiences over which he has no control; and guiding him toward negative consequences which are more under his control. Just as people tend to protect themselves against potential rejection in personal relationships by withdrawing interest and affect, they are able to gain an illusory sense of control over death by withholding their emotional involvement in life itself.

Thus, the apparently universal tendency toward self-destruction is not due to a death instinct as formulated by Freud, Klein, and Menninger, but represents instead a powerful defense against death anxiety. The voice's predictions and injunctions to avoid excitement and spontaneity support people's desperate efforts to accommodate to this fear by persuading them to give up meaningful activities and close associations with others. Ironically, in deadening themselves in advance, people barely notice the transition from living to dying.

Despite a person's strong tendency to adopt a life-style that would ease the dread surrounding death, we feel it is possible to adopt a positive philosophical outlook. Margaret Mead (1956/1960) eloquently depicted the dimensions of this choice in *The Age of Anxiety*:

> Acceptance of the inevitability of death, which, when faced can give dignity to life . . . ennobles the whole face rather than furrowing the forehead with the little anxious wrinkles of worry. *Worry in an empty context means that men die daily little deaths* [italics added]. (p. 177)

The author's sentiments are similar, as we feel that one's awareness of a finite existence makes life and living all the more precious. Our position suggests that we embrace life fully and cherish every aspect of real experience, however temporal.

CONCLUSION

> The distinguishing characteristic of selfhood . . . is not rationality but the critical awareness of man's divided nature.
>
> Christopher Lasch (1984, p. 258)

The dilemma faced by patients who have progressed and developed in psychotherapy is essentially no different from that faced by every human being. The alternatives are clear: without challenging destructive aspects of ourselves as represented by the voice, we will gradually submit to an alien, inimical point of view and shut down on our authentic self and unique outlook; on the other hand, disrupting powerful, self-protective defenses intensifies our awareness of life's tragic aspects and threatens at times to overwhelm us with feelings of helplessness and dread.

The patient's fear of change is related to each dimension described earlier: an increased potential for feeling and experiencing both happiness and distress; the problematic nature of one's closest relationships; the circumstances of a troubled world; and lastly, the fear of losing through death everything one has gained through expanding boundaries. Juxtaposed against this fear is the patient's knowledge that only by relinquishing defenses and bonds can one avoid inflicting incidental damage on other individuals, especially one's children. In addition to expanding opportunities for personal gratification, remaining vulnerable and undefended becomes an ethical or moral choice, given the alternatives.

Ideally, an effective psychotherapy would enable the patient to discover an implicit moral approach toward himself and other human beings. In recognizing and gradually giving up the authority of the voice as an anti-feeling, anti-life, regulatory mechanism, a person feels far less victimized or blaming and far more compassionate. One becomes, in the best sense of the word, an explorer, an investigator, as it were, uncritically accepting and examining one's most irrational thoughts and feelings, while at the same time viewing others and the world with a very real curiosity and concern. As Thomas Malone (1981) said:

> The task of psychotherapy is to make the ordinary a full experience . . . to uncover, or reactivate . . . the experiential dimensions of the ordinary experience. (p. 91)

We must conclude that there is no hidden significance to life that may be discovered; rather, it is only each individual's investment of himself, his feelings, his creativity, his interests, and his personal choice of people and activities, that is special. Indeed, we imbue experience with meaning through our own spirit rather than the opposite, and our priorities express our true identity. The therapeutic venture, through counteracting the dictates of the voice and disrupting fantasies of connection to internal images and external objects, offers the opportunity to fulfill our human potentiality, thereby giving life its unique meaning. The dilemma of psychotherapy has an important positive aspect in that the awareness of death itself may serve to enhance life's value for each of us.

NOTES

[1]The reader can find summaries of recent outcome studies in the Special Issue (February 1986) of *American Psychologist* and in the companion Special Issue (February 1986), "Psychotherapy Research," *Journal of Consulting and Clinical Psychology*. Especially pertinent is the Lambert, Hatch, Kingston, & Edwards (1986) study, "Zung, Beck, and Hamilton Rating Scales as Measures of Treatment Outcome: A Meta-Analytic Comparison."

[2]Freud (1930/1961) discussed the "purpose of human life" in terms of the pleasure or satisfaction man is able to derive from his work in *Civilization and Its Discontents*.

No other technique for the conduct of life attaches the individual so firmly to reality as laying emphasis on work; for his work at least gives him a secure place in a portion of reality, in the human community . . . whether narcissistic, aggressive or even erotic, on to professional work and on to the human relations connected with it lends it a value by no means second to what it enjoys as something indispensable to the preservation and justification of existence in society. (p. 80)

References

CHAPTER 1
Arieti, S. (1955). *Interpretation of schizophrenia*. New York: Robert Brunner.

CHAPTER 2
Firestone, R.W. (1984). A concept of the primary fantasy bond: A developmental perspective. *Psychotherapy, 21*(2), 218–225.
Freud, S. (1957). On narcissism: An introduction. In J. Strachey (Ed. and trans.), *The standard edition of the complete psychological works of Sigmund Freud* (Vol. 14, pp. 67–102). London: Hogarth Press. (Originally published, 1914.)
Goldbrunner, J. (1964). *Individuation: A study of the depth psychology of Carl Gustav Jung* (S. Godman, trans.). Notre Dame, Indiana: University of Notre Dame Press.
Hesse, H. (1929). *Steppenwolf* (B. Creighton, trans.). New York: Holt, Rinehart and Winston. (Originally published, 1927.)

CHAPTER 3
Freud, S. (1959). Inhibitions, symptoms and anxiety. In J. Strachey (Ed. and trans.), *The standard edition of the complete psychological works of Sigmund Freud* (Vol. 20, pp. 87–156). London: Hogarth Press. (Originally published, 1926.)

Harvey, J.C. (1984). The impostor phenomenon: A useful concept in clinical practice. Paper presented at 92nd Annual Convention of the American Psychological Association, Toronto, Canada.

Ikuru, E. (1985, April). The voice inside me. *Saturday Night*, pp. 30–39.

Maslow, A.H. (1954). *Motivation and personality*. New York: Harper & Brothers.

Murray, H.A., et al. (1938). *Explorations in personality*. New York: Oxford University Press.

CHAPTER 4

Bettelheim, B. (1979). Individual and mass behavior in extreme situations. In *Surviving and other essays* (pp. 48–83). New York: Alfred A. Knopf. (Originally published, 1943.)

Breskin, D. (1984, November 8). Dear mom and dad. *Rolling Stone*, pp. 26–79.

Freud, S. (1955). Group psychology and the analysis of the ego. In J. Strachey (Ed. and trans.), *The standard edition of the complete psychological works of Sigmund Freud* (Vol. 18, pp. 67–143). London: Hogarth Press. (Originally published, 1921.)

Guntrip, H. (1969). *Schizoid phenomena, object-relations and the self*. New York: International Universities Press.

Laing, R.D. (1965). *The divided self: An existential study in sanity and madness*. Middlesex, England: Penguin Books. (Originally published, 1960.)

Novey, S. (1955). The role of the superego and ego-ideal in character formation. *International Journal of Psycho-analysis, 36*, 254–259.

Nunberg, H., & Federn, E. (Eds.) (1967). *Minutes of the Vienna Psychoanalytic Society, Volume II: 1908–1910* (M. Nunberg, trans.). New York: International Universities Press.

Rank, O. (1972). *Will therapy and truth and reality* (J. Taft, trans.). New York: Alfred A. Knopf. (Originally published, 1936.)

Rapaport, D. (1951). Toward a theory of thinking. In D. Rapaport (trans.), *Organization and pathology of thought*. New York and London: Columbia University Press.

Shneidman, E.S. (1985). *Definition of suicide*. New York: John Wiley & Sons.

Westen, D. (1986). The superego: A revised developmental model. *Journal of the American Academy of Psychoanalysis, 14*(2), 181–202.

CHAPTER 5

Bateson, G., Jackson, D.D., Haley, J., & Weakland, J.H. (1956). Toward a theory of schizophrenia. *Behavioral Science, 1*(4), 251–264.

Bettelheim, B. (1979). Individual and mass behavior in extreme situations. In *Surviving and other essays* (pp. 48–83). New York: Alfred A. Knopf. (Originally published, 1943.)

Blumberg, M. L. (1980). The abusing mother—criminal, psychopath or victim of circumstances. *American Journal of Psychotherapy, 34*(3), 351–362.

Bowlby, J. (1965). *Child care and the growth of love* (2nd ed.). Middlesex, England: Penguin Books.

Bowlby, J. (1973). *Attachment and loss, Vol. II, Separation: Anxiety and anger.* New York: Basic Books.

Firestone, R.W. (1985). *The fantasy bond: Structure of psychological defenses.* New York: Human Sciences Press.

Gerbner, G., Ross, C.J., & Zigler, E. (Eds.) (1980). *Child abuse: An agenda for action.* New York: Oxford University Press.

Gil, D.G. (1970). *Violence against children.* Cambridge, Massachusetts: Harvard University Press.

Helfer, R.E. (1974). *A self-instructional program on child abuse and neglect.* Committee on Infant and Preschool Child, American Academy of Pediatrics, Chicago, Ill., and National Center for Prevention and Treatment of Child Abuse and Neglect, Denver, Colo. (p. 2–4).

Janov, A. (1970). *The primal scream.* New York: G.P. Putnam's Sons.

Justice, B., & Justice, R. (undated). *The abusing family.* New York: Human Sciences Press.

Kempe, C.H. (1971). Paediatric implications of the battered baby syndrome. *Archives of Disease in Childhood, 46,* 28–37.

Kempe, C.H., Silverman, F.N., Steele, B.F., Droegemueller, W., and Silver, H.K. (1962). The battered-child syndrome. *Journal of the American Medical Association, 181*(1), 17–24.

Korbin, J.E. (Ed.). (1981). *Child abuse and neglect: Cross-cultural perspectives.* Berkeley: University of California Press.

Laing, R.D. (1972). *The politics of the family and other essays.* New York: Vintage Books. (Originally published, 1969.)

Miller, A. (1981). *Prisoners of childhood: The drama of the gifted child and the search for the true self* (R. Ward, trans.). New York: Basic Books. (Originally published, 1979.)

Miller, A. (1984). *For your own good: Hidden cruelty in child-rearing and the roots of violence* (2nd ed.) (H. Hannum & H. Hannum, trans.). New York: Farrar, Straus and Giroux. (Originally published, 1980.)

Miller, A. (1984). *Thou shalt not be aware: Society's betrayal of the child* (H. Hannum & H. Hannum, trans.). New York: Farrar, Straus and Giroux. (Originally published, 1981.)

O'Brien, D.H., Schneider, A.R., & Traviesas, H. (1980). Portraying abuse: Network censors' round table, *60 Minutes*: "Mommy, Why Me?" In G. Gerbner, C.J. Ross, & E. Zigler (Eds.), *Child abuse: An agenda for action.* New York: Oxford University Press.

Parr, G. (Producer and director) (1986). *The inner voice in child abuse* [Video]. Los Angeles: Glendon Association.

Rheingold, J.C. (1967). *The mother, anxiety, and death: The catastrophic death complex.* Boston: Little, Brown & Co.

Wilson, J.Q., & Herrnstein, R.J. (1985). *Crime and human nature.* New York: Simon & Schuster.

CHAPTER 6

Berne, E. (1961). *Transactional analysis in psychotherapy.* New York: Grove Press.

Clance, P.R., & Imes, S.A. (1978). The impostor phenomenon in high achieving women: Dynamics and therapeutic intervention. *Psychotherapy, 15*(3), 241–247.

Fairbairn, W.R.D. (1952). A revised psychopathology of the psychoses and psychoneuroses. In *Psychoanalytic studies of the personality* (pp. 28–58). London: Tavistock Publications. (Originally published, 1941.)

Firestone, R.W. (1957). *A concept of the schizophrenic process.* Unpublished doctoral dissertation, University of Denver.

Firestone, R.W. (1984). A concept of the primary fantasy bond: A developmental perspective. *Psychotherapy, 21*(2), 218–225.

Firestone, R.W. (1985). *The fantasy bond: Structure of psychological defenses.* New York: Human Sciences Press.

Green, H. (1967). *I never promised you a rose garden.* London: Pan Books Ltd. (Originally published, 1964.)

Guntrip, H. (1969). *Schizoid phenomena, object-relations and the self.* New York: International Universities Press.

Janov, A. (1970). *The primal scream.* New York: G.P. Putnam's Sons.

Kaiser, H. (1965). The problem of responsibility in psychotherapy. In L.B. Fierman (Ed.), *Effective psychotherapy: The contribution of Hellmuth Kaiser* (pp. 1–13). New York: The Free Press. (Originally published, 1955.)

Laing, R.D. (1965). *The divided self: An existential study in sanity and madness.* Middlesex, England: Penguin Books. (Originally published, 1960.)

Laing, R.D. (1971). *Self and others* (2nd ed.). Middlesex, England: Penguin Books. (Originally published, 1961.)

Tansey, M.H., & Burke, W.F. (1985). Projective identification and the empathic process. *Contemporary Psychoanalysis, 21*(1), 42–69.

Willi, J. (1984). *Couples in collusion: The unconscious dimension in partner relationships* (W. Inayat-Khan & M. Tchorek, trans.). Claremont, California: Hunter House. (Originally published, 1975.)

Winnicott, D. W. (1958). *Collected papers: Through paediatrics to psycho-analysis.* London: Tavistock Publications.

CHAPTER 7

Autobiography of a schizophrenic girl (1970) (G. Rubin-Rabson, trans.). New York: New American Library. (Originally published, 1951.)

Becker, E. (1964). *The revolution in psychiatry: The new understanding of man.* New York: The Free Press.

Becker, E. (1973). *The denial of death.* New York: The Free Press.

Bowlby, J. (1973). *Attachment and loss, Vol. II, Separation: Anxiety and anger.* New York: Basic Books.

Firestone, R.W. (1985). *The fantasy bond: Structure of psychological defenses.* New York: Human Sciences Press.

Freud, S. (1957). Thoughts for the times on war and death. In J. Strachey (Ed. and trans.), *The standard edition of the complete psychological works of Sigmund Freud* (Vol. 14, pp. 273–302). London: Hogarth Press. (Originally published, 1915.)

Freud, S. (1961). The ego and the id. In J. Strachey (Ed. and trans.), *The standard edition of the complete psychological works of Sigmund Freud* (Vol. 19, pp. 3–66). London: Hogarth Press. (Originally published, 1923.)

Fromm, E. (1947). *Man for himself.* Greenwich, Connecticut: Fawcett Publications.

Guntrip, H. (1961). *Personality structure and human interaction.* New York: International Universities Press.

Kafka, F. (1969). *The trial* (W. Muir & E. Muir, trans.). New York: Vintage Books. (Originally published, 1937.)

Kaplan, L.J. (1984). *Adolescence: The farewell to childhood.* New York: Simon & Schuster.

Klein, M. (1964). The importance of symbol-formation in the development of the ego. In *Contributions to psycho-analysis 1921–1945* (pp. 236-250). New York: McGraw-Hill. (Originally published, 1930.)

Laing, R.D. (1971). *Self and others* (2nd ed.). Middlesex, England: Penguin Books. (Originally published, 1961.)

Lifton, R.J., & Olson, E. (1976). The nuclear age. In E. S. Shneidman (Ed.), *Death: Current perspectives* (pp. 99–109). Palo Alto: Mayfield Publishing Co. (Originally published, 1974.)

Lifton, R.J., & Olson, E. (1976). The human meaning of total disaster: The Buffalo Creek experience. *Psychiatry, 39,* 1–18.

Maslow, A. H. (1968). *Toward a psychology of being.* New York: Van Nostrand Reinhold.

May, R. (1958). Contributions of existential psychotherapy. In R. May, E. Angel, & H. F. Ellenberger (Eds.), *Existence: A new dimension in psychiatry and psychology* (pp. 37–91). New York: Basic Books.

McCarthy, J.B. (1980). *Death anxiety: The loss of the self.* New York: Gardner Press.

Rank, O. (1972). *Will therapy and truth and reality* (J. Taft, trans.). New York: Alfred A. Knopf. (Originally published, 1936.)

Reik, T. (1941). *Masochism in modern man* (M.H. Beigel & G.M. Kurth, trans.). New York: Farrar, Straus & Co.

Rubin, T.I. (1975). *Compassion and self-hate: An alternative to despair*. New York: David McKay Co.

Sechehaye, M.A. (1951). *Symbolic realization* (B. Wursten & H. Wursten, trans.). New York: International Universities Press.

Styron, W. (1979). *Sophie's choice*. New York: Random House.

Tillich, P. (1952). *The courage to be*. New Haven: Yale University Press.

Yalom, I.D. (1980). *Existential psychotherapy*. New York: Basic Books.

CHAPTER 8

Achté, K.A. (1980). The psychopathology of indirect self-destruction. In N.L. Farberow (Ed.), *The many faces of suicide: Indirect self-destructive behavior*. New York: McGraw-Hill.

Center for the Study of Anorexia and Bulimia (1982). *The eating disorder bulimia*. New York: Institute for Contemporary Psychotherapy.

Center for the Study of Anorexia and Bulimia (1982). *Anorexia nervosa*. New York: Institute for Contemporary Psychotherapy.

Durkheim, E. (1951). *Suicide: A study in sociology* (J.A. Spaulding & G. Simpson, trans.). New York: The Free Press. (Originally published, 1897.)

Farberow, N.L. (1980). Introduction. In N.L. Farberow (Ed.), *The many faces of suicide: Indirect self-destructive behavior*. New York: McGraw-Hill.

Gove, W.R., & Hughes, M. (1980). Reexamining the ecological fallacy: A study in which aggregate data are critical in investigating the pathological effects of living alone. *Social Forces, 58*(4), 1157–1177.

Kaplan, L.J. (1984). *Adolescence: The farewell to childhood*. New York: Simon & Schuster.

Menninger, K. (1938). *Man against himself*. New York: Harcourt, Brace & World.

Nelson, F.L., & Farberow, N.L. (1982). The development of an indirect self-destructive behaviour scale for use with chronically ill medical patients. *International Journal of Social Psychiatry, 28*(1), 5–14.

Nietzsche, F. (1966). *Beyond good and evil* (W. Kaufmann, trans.). New York: Vintage Books. (Originally published, 1886.)

Parr, G. (Producer and director) (1985). *Micro-suicide: A case study* [Video]. Los Angeles: Glendon Association.

Paykel, E.S. (1974). Recent life-events and clinical depression. In E.K.E. Gunderson and R.H. Rahe (Eds.), *Life stress and illness* (pp. 134–164). Springfield, Illinois: Charles C. Thomas.

Seiden, R.H. (1966). Campus tragedy: A study of student suicide. *Journal of Abnormal Psychology, 71*(6), 389–399.

Seiden, R.H. (1984a). Death in the West—A regional analysis of the youthful suicide rate. *Western Journal of Medicine, 140*(6), 969–973.

Seiden, R.H. (1984b). The youthful suicide epidemic. *Public Affairs Report, 25*(1).

Shneidman, E. S. (1966). Orientations toward death: A vital aspect of the study of lives. *International Journal of Psychiatry, 2*(2), 167–200.

Sours, J. (1980). *Starving to death in a sea of objects.* New York: Jason Aronson.

CHAPTER 9

Arieti, S., & Bemporad, J.R. (1980). The psychological organization of depression. *American Journal of Psychiatry, 137*(11), 1360–1365.

Bach, G.R., & Torbet, L. (1983). *The inner enemy: How to fight fair with yourself.* New York: William Morrow.

Beck, A.T. (1976). *Cognitive therapy and the emotional disorders.* New York: New American Library.

Beck, A.T., Rush, A., Shaw, B.F., & Emery, G. (1979). *Cognitive therapy of depression.* New York: Guilford Press.

Beres, D. (1966). Superego and depression. In R.M. Loewenstein, L.M. Newman, M. Schur, & A.J. Solnit (Eds.), *Psychoanalysis—A general psychology* (pp. 479–498). New York: International Universities Press.

Bowlby, J. (1980). *Attachment and loss, Vol. III, Loss: Sadness and depression.* New York: Basic Books.

Butler, P.E. (1981). *Talking to yourself.* New York: Stein and Day.

Clance, P.R., & Imes, S.A. (1978). The impostor phenomenon in high achieving women: Dynamics and therapeutic intervention. *Psychotherapy, 15*(3), 241–247.

Ellis, A., & Harper, R.A. (1975). *A new guide to rational living.* No. Hollywood, California: Wilshire Book Co. (Originally published, 1961.)

Farberow, N.L. (Ed.) (1980). *The many faces of suicide: Indirect self-destructive behavior.* New York: McGraw-Hill.

Firestone, R.W. (1984). A concept of the primary fantasy bond: A developmental perspective. *Psychotherapy, 21*(2), 218–225.

Freud, S. (1957). Mourning and melancholia. In J. Strachey (Ed. and trans.), *The standard edition of the complete psychological works of Sigmund Freud* (Vol. 14, pp. 239–260). London: Hogarth Press. (Originally published, 1923)

Greene, B. (1985). *Good morning, merry sunshine.* New York: Penguin Books. (Originally published, 1984.)

Grunberger, B. (1979). Suicide of melancholics. In *Narcissism: Psy-*

choanalytic essays (J.S. Diamanti, trans.) (pp. 241–264). New York: International Universities Press. (Originally published, 1968.)

Hartmann, H., & Loewenstein, R.M. (1962). Notes on the superego. In R.S. Eissler, A. Freud, H. Hartmann, & M. Kris (Managing Eds.), *Psychoanalytic study of the child, Vol. 17* (pp. 42–81). New Haven: Yale University Press.

Harvey, J.C. (1984). The impostor phenomenon: A useful concept in clinical practice. Paper presented at 92nd Annual Convention of the American Psychological Association, Toronto, Canada.

Hubert, D., & Addis, B. (Producers) (undated). *Suicides* [Film]. Los Angeles: Neuropsychiatric Institute, UCLA Health Science Service.

Janouch, G. (1971). *Conversations with Kafka*. New York: New Directions.

Kaufman, G. (1985). *Shame: The power of caring* (rev. ed.). Cambridge, Massachusetts: Schenkman Publishing Co.

Kaufman, G., & Raphael, L. (1984). Relating to the self: Changing inner dialogue. *Psychological Reports, 54*, 239–250.

Klein, M. (1964). A contribution to the psychogenesis of manic-depressive states. In *Contributions to psycho-analysis, 1921–1945* (pp. 282–310). New York: McGraw-Hill. (Originally published, 1935.)

Klein, M. (1964). Mourning and its relation to manic-depressive states. In *Contributions to psycho-analysis, 1921–1945* (pp. 311–338). New York: McGraw-Hill. (Originally published, 1940.)

Kuhn, T.S. (1962). *The structure of scientific revolutions*. Chicago: University of Chicago Press.

Litman, R.E. (1967). Sigmund Freud on suicide. In E.S. Shneidman (Ed.), *Essays in self-destruction* (pp. 324–344). New York: Jason Aronson.

Mahler, M.S. (1979). On sadness and grief in infancy and childhood: Loss and restoration of the symbiotic love object. In *The selected papers of Margaret S. Mahler, M. D., Vol. 1, Infantile psychosis and early contributions* (pp. 261–279). New York: Jason Aronson. (Originally published, 1961.)

Menninger, K. (1938). *Man against himself*. New York: Harcourt, Brace & World.

Munter, P.K. (1966). Depression and suicide in college students. In L. McNeer (Ed.), *Proceedings of Conference on Depression and Suicide in Adolescents and Young Adults*. Fairlee, Vermont.

Parr, G. (Producer and director) (1985). *The inner voice in suicide* [Video]. Los Angeles: Glendon Association.

Raimy, V. (1975). *Misunderstandings of the self: Cognitive psychotherapy and the misconception hypothesis*. San Francisco: Jossey-Bass.

Rochlin, G. (1959). The loss complex. *Journal of the American Psychoanalytic Association, 7,* 299–316.

Rosenbaum, M., & Richman, J. (1970). Suicide: The role of hostility and death wishes from the family and significant others. *American Journal of Psychiatry, 126,* 1652–1655.

Seiden, R.H. (1966). Campus tragedy: A study of student suicide. *Journal of Abnormal Psychology, 71*(6), 389–399.

Seiden, R.H. (1971). The problem of suicide on college campuses. *Journal of School Health, 41*(5), 243–248.

Seiden, R.H. (1984a). Death in the West—A regional analysis of the youthful suicide rate. *Western Journal of Medicine, 140*(6), 969–973.

Seiden, R.H. (1984b). The youthful suicide epidemic. *Public Affairs Report, 25*(1).

Shneidman, E.S. (1966). Orientations toward death: A vital aspect of the study of lives. *International Journal of Psychiatry, 2*(2), 167–200.

Shneidman, E.S. (1985). *Definition of suicide.* New York: John Wiley & Sons.

Stricker, G. (1983). Some issues in the psychodynamic treatment of the depressed patient. *Professional Psychology: Research and Practice, 14*(2), 209–217.

CHAPTER 10

Alexander, F. (1932). *The medical value of psychoanalysis.* New York: Norton.

Arlow, J.A. (1979). Psychoanalysis. In R.J. Corsini & contributors, *Current psychotherapies* (2nd ed.) (pp. 1–43). Itasca, Illinois: F.E. Peacock Publishers.

Parr, G. (Producer and director) (1984). *Voice therapy with Dr. Robert Firestone* [Video]. Los Angeles: Glendon Association.

Parr, G. (Producer and director) (1985). *Closeness without bonds: A study of destructive ties in couple relationships* [Video]. Los Angeles: Glendon Association.

CHAPTER 11

Beck, A.T. (1972). *Depression: Causes and treatment.* Philadelphia: University of Pennsylvania Press.

Beck, A.T. (1976). *Cognitive therapy and the emotional disorders.* New York: New American Library.

Beck, A.T., Rush, A., Shaw, B.F., & Emery, G. (1979). *Cognitive therapy of depression.* New York: Guilford Press.

Bowlby, J. (1980). *Attachment and loss, Vol. III, Loss: Sadness and depression.* New York: Basic Books.

Ellis, A., & Harper, R.A. (1975). *A new guide to rational living.* No. Hollywood, California: Wilshire Book Co.

Ellis, A. (1979). Rational-emotive therapy. In R.J. Corsini and contributors, *Current psychotherapies* (2nd ed.) (pp. 185–229). Itasca, Illinois: F. E. Peacock Publishers.

Fierman, L.B. (Ed.) (1965). *Effective psychotherapy: The contribution of Hellmuth Kaiser.* New York: Free Press.

Firestone, R.W. (1985). *The fantasy bond: Structure of psychological defenses.* New York: Human Sciences Press.

Ford, D.H., & Urban, H.B. (1963). *Systems of psychotherapy: A comparative study.* New York: John Wiley and Sons.

Kaiser, H. (1965). The universal symptom of the psychoneuroses. In L.B. Fierman (Ed.), *Effective psychotherapy: The contribution of Hellmuth Kaiser* (pp. 14–171). New York: Free Press.

Masterson, J.F. (1985). *The real self: A developmental, self, and object relations approach.* New York: Brunner/Mazel.

Mowrer, O.H. (1953). *Psychotherapy: Theory and research.* New York: Ronald Press.

Patterson, C.H. (1980). *Theories of counseling and psychotherapy* (3rd ed.). New York: Harper & Row.

Rank, O. (1972). *Will therapy and truth and reality* (J. Taft, trans.). New York: Alfred A. Knopf. (Originally published, 1936.)

Rogers, C.R. (1957). The necessary and sufficient conditions of therapeutic personality change. *Journal of Consulting Psychology, 21*(2), 95–103.

Rogers, C.R., & Dymond, R. (Eds.) (1954). *Psychotherapy and personality change.* Chicago: University of Chicago Press.

Walker, A.M., Rablen, R.A., & Rogers, C.R. (1960). Development of a scale to measure process changes in psychotherapy. *Journal of Clinical Psychology, 16,* 79–85.

CHAPTER 12

Becker, E. (1973). *The denial of death.* New York: Free Press.

Brown, N.O. (1959). *Life against death: The psycho-analytical meaning of history.* Middletown, Connecticut: Wesleyan University Press.

DeBeauvoir, S. (1976). Epilogue to *A very easy death.* In E.S. Shneidman (Ed.) *Death: Current perspectives* (pp. 523–526). Palo Alto: Mayfield Publishing. (Originally published, 1966.)

Firestone, R.W. (1985). *The fantasy bond: Structure of psychological defenses.* New York: Human Sciences Press.

Freud, S. (1961). Civilization and its discontents. In J. Strachey (Ed. and trans.), *The standard edition of the complete psychological works of Sigmund Freud* (Vol. 21, pp. 59–145). (Originally published, 1930.)

Fromm, E. (1965). *Escape from freedom*. New York: Avon Books. (Originally published, 1941.)

Janov, A. (1970). *The primal scream*. New York: G.P. Putnam's Sons.

Lambert, M.J., Hatch, D.R., Kingston, M.D., & Edwards, B.C. (1986). Zung, Beck, and Hamilton rating scales as measures of treatment outcome: A meta-analytic comparison. *Journal of Consulting and Clinical Psychology, 54*(1), 54–59.

Lasch, C. (1984). *The minimal self: Psychic survival in troubled times*. New York: W.W. Norton.

Malone, T.P. (1981). Psychopathology as non-experience. *Voices, 17*(2), 83–91.

May, R. (1983). *The discovery of being*. New York: W.W. Norton.

McCarthy, J.B. (1980). *Death anxiety: The loss of the self*. New York: Gardner Press.

McCullers, C. (1953). *The heart is a lonely hunter*. New York: Bantam Books. (Originally published, 1940.)

Mead, M. (1960). One vote for this age of anxiety. In C.A. Glasrud (Ed.), *The age of anxiety*. Boston: Houghton Mifflin Co.

Mowrer, O.H. (1953.) *Psychotherapy: Theory and research*. New York: Ronald Press Co.

Richman, J. (1986). *Family therapy for suicidal people*. New York: Springer Publishing Co.

Rogers, C.R. (1951). *Client-centered therapy: Its current practice, implications, and theory*. Boston: Houghton Mifflin.

Shaffer, P. (1974). *Equus*. New York: Avon Books.

Stiles, W.B., Shapiro, D.A., & Elliott, R. (1986). "Are all psychotherapies equivalent?". *American Psychologist, 41*(2), 165–180.

Taft, J. (1958). *Otto Rank*. New York: Julian Press.

Wolberg, L.R. (1954). *The technique of psychotherapy*. New York: Grune & Stratton.

Yalom, I. D. (1980). *Existential psychotherapy*. New York: Basic Books.

Index

Ego and the Id, The (Freud), 134
Ego states
  internal, 113
  and modes of experience,
    113–129
  and parental introjects, 75–76
Ellis Albert, 184, 185, 244–248
Equus (Shaffer), 255
Existential Psychotherapy
  (Yalom), 267

Failure, 40, 153, 254
Fairbairn, W. R. D., 106
Family, 18, 174, 230
  bonds, 19, 23, 71, 106, 137,
    238, 263; *see also* Fantasy
    bond
  and guilt, 147–149
  influence of, 19
  and negative conception of
    self, 23, 69
  and regression in therapy, 240
  therapy, 222–226, 250
Fantasy bond, 18, 19, 23, 71, 77,
    81*n*, 128, 141, 233, 234,
    246
  addictive nature of, 109–110
  core defense in, 108, 109, 111,
    117
  and corrective suggestions, 210
  and death anxiety, 268–269
  guilt at breaking, 261
  manifestations of, 108
  in marital relationships, 224
  as micro-suicide, 168
  self-destructiveness in, 167
  and withholding behavior, 168,
    224
Fantasy gratification, 110, 111,
    152, 153, 233, 247
Farberow, Norman, 159, 186

Feeling release therapy, 23, 207,
    243, 260
  and childhood trauma, 87–90,
    103, 110, 117
Freud, Sigmund, 31, 71, 128, 256,
    257, 263, 270, 272*n*
  on depression, 183–184
  on guilt, 134–135, 142
  on suicide, 77
Fromm, Erich, 149, 261, 262

Goldbrunner, J., 33
Green, Hannah, 113
Greene, Bob, 176
Grunberger, Bela, 198
Guilt, 18, 36, 53, 133–156, 211,
    232
  in child abuse, 85
  and death anxiety, 153–156
  and difference from family,
    147–149
  existential, 135–136, 149–151,
    153, 156, 266
  and expression of emotions,
    61–62
  forms of, 134–136
  neurotic, 134–135, 145, 156
  in schizophrenia, 151
  and self-hatred, 143–145
  and separation, 137–143
  and success, 42–43
  in therapy, 240, 243, 261
Guntrip, H., 75–76, 108–109

Hallucinations, 50–51
Harvey, J. C., 70
Heart Is a Lonely Hunter, The
  (McCullers), 264
Herrnstein, R. J., 95
Hesse, Herman, 51
Homicide, and paranoia, 52